FROM

Washington

TO

Roosevelt.

A. Collection of

ESSAYS ON THE AMERICAN REVOLUTION; WITH
OTHER HISTORICAL STUDIES,
AND PERSONAL IMPRESSIONS OF AMERICA.

BY

VERY REV. JAMES O'BOYLE,

B.A., P.P., V.F., BALLYMONEY, IRELAND.

Publishers :

NEW YORK, CINCINNATI, CHICAGO.

BENZIGER BROTHERS

PRINTERS TO THE | PUBLISHERS OF
HOLY APOSTOLIC SEE | BENZIGER'S MAGAZINE

1911.

GEORGE WASHINGTON.

PREFACE.

ONE beautiful Sunday evening in July, 1904, I wended my way after midday towards the Monument of General Grant, erected at the extremity of New York City, on Manhattan Island. As I sat alone on the steps leading up to the plateau upon which stands the proud pedestal of the conquering hero of the Civil War, looking with greedy eyes at the beautiful seas and cliffs and sky that everywhere met my gaze, I was accosted by a fine, manly type of American manhood. " I guess you are an Irish priest?" he said. I answered, "Yes; you, I presume, are from the Old Country also?" "Well, no," he said; "my forefathers came out here about a hundred and fifty years back. They came from some part of County Antrim. I am not of your way of thinking in creed. By-the-way," he added, "is not that a lovely panorama to behold? You are standing and looking on historic ground. Away out across those rippling waters are the Jersey Heights. You can see Forts Washington and Lea in the distance, which were captured by the English after the retreat of Washington's forces from Brooklyn. When New York was captured by the English in 1776, it was across those lovely waters that the General, in the dead of night, carried over his soldiers in small boats to the Jerseys ; and it was over the country you see that he and his famished soldiers, in the frost of winter, were hunted, shoeless and hungry, tracking the ground with bloodstains as they ran towards Trenton. Higher up you can see the lovely Hudson, lordly in its flow. This river was the great dividing line over which the English never crossed in the war. It preserved the New England States intact for American liberty. It was above its source, in 1777, Burgoyne lost his army. Along its waters, at West Point, Washington kept his stores, in the fortress which Benedict Arnold in vain betrayed." I stood in wonderment at the knowledge thus imparted to me in good Yankee style, and I told my new-found friend I was a stranger to his country's history. I stood like a stranger in a strange land, gazing on the beauties of nature around me. All I saw in the scene before me was a similarity to the view from Howth Hill over the charming waters of Dublin Bay. The beautiful panorama I was gazing on recalled no revered historic memories to my mind. However, I thanked my good guide for his information, and vowed within myself that when I returned to Ireland I would become a student of his nation's history. The volume I now present to my readers is, in part, the outcome of that excursion into American history. In giving these essays to the public, I am actuated by the desire of instructing and, I hope, pleasing the ever-increasing body of readers interested in the democratic institutions of the New World. I have delved in my leisure hours into many heavy tomes, chronicles of the great events of past generations in American history, and have chiefly made a study of that portion of it bearing on the struggle for American Independence. My endeavour in this portion of my book has been to give lively pictures of the scenes and battles of the Revolution, making the central figure of all the immortal Washington.

It was my desire to bring out a life of the hero of the war in a separate volume, but I have deferred that ambition for the present, in the belief that this first expression of my views on the subject will better catch the public eye in the more popular form of essays and sketches. At some not far distant date I hope to return to my theme, and give a popular life of Washington and his times.

Anyone who has travelled over the States, as I have done, must wish for knowledge about this mighty Republic of the West ; any Irishman who knows a little of the part taken by our forefathers in gaining liberty and a free home and country for emigrants from every land, must desire to know more of the events and characters that have made America to-day the true land of liberty and freedom, fraternity and independence for all.

This mighty nation has proved the great mustard tree for emigrants from every nation. All who are willing to help to build up its greatness and become citizens are protected by its wonderful Constitution and just laws. So attractive and assimilative are its institutions that in but a few weeks after landing on its free soil it becomes natural to the emigrant to be enthusiastic in its praises, anxious to learn its history, and obey its laws.

I trust my little effort will help to make better known the greatness and renown of unrivalled, democratic America.

J. O'BOYLE.

CONTENTS.

Scenes and Characters of the Revolution.

Miscellaneous Essays, and Some Personal Impressions of Present-Day America.

Scenes and Characters of the Revolution.

THE essays here grouped together, and forming the first part of our collection of American sketches, were written at various times. They are all, however, concerned with the War of Independence and the birth of the Republic, and, though not in exact order of time, they give, I think, a fairly clear and logical account of those momentous events. At no time, within the memory of the present generation, were the political institutions of our transatlantic friends of more vital interest and importance than now. Not even, perhaps, were they so intimately the concern of the world at large at that exciting epoch when the Declaration of Independence was being forged in the furnace of Civil War ; for then, although "revolution" was in the air, and the great political cataclysm in France was about to shake the world to its foundations, the incident of America's enfranchisement from the Mother Country was regarded as but in the nature of a landslide, stupendous in its way, no doubt, but not foreign to the natural order of things. Events have happened since which give it a different aspect ; and to-day, when the fall of a throne is an episode worthy only of a few days' gossip in the newspapers, and when the English House of Lords itself—that gigantic figurehead of feudalism—having seemingly outlived its usefulness, is being threatened with extinction, we turn to America, where popular government has been on its trial a hundred years, for light and guidance on the perplexing questions that confront us, in common with the other peoples of the earth. The studies of the Revolution War do not pretend to be exhaustive history, but they do, I modestly believe, reflect with some verisimilitude the life of the early settlers in America, and the atmosphere of political thought out of which the great idea of democratic government was born.—J. O'B.

WASHINGTON.

In these drab days of monotonous commercial life, and
"peaceful revolutions," so remote from anything that might
stir the blood, or fire the heart with enthusiasm, it is well-nigh
a matter of impossibility to realise all that was meant—all
the effulgence and potent charm conveyed to the mind of
eighteenth century America by the magic name of Washington.
One can easily believe how, in pagan times, the perfect hero
whose shining deeds shed such a lustre on his name,
would, in the passing of years lose in the memory of men
his merely human characteristics, and come to be regarded
as a god. How great was the spell exercised by the name of
Washington we may gather, in some faint way, from the
accounts we have of the profound emotion that agitated mankind at the epic moment when the immortal spirit, the eternal
ground and basis of all that was conveyed by the name, was
called away from earth, and a mourning country was plunged
into the darkness of an utter forlornness at its departure.

On that dark morning in December, 1799, when the soul
of the great commander fled from the busy scenes of earth to
seek its Maker and its God, the curtain fell on a human life
brimful of the most brilliant and inspiring scenes that ever
attended the lot of mortal here below, a life of noble and unsel-
fish effort, crowned with complete success, and recorded, as
on a monument of brass, for the eternal nerving and encouragement of his own countrymen, and weak man all the
world over; and, simultaneously, it may be said, before the
astonished eyes of humanity there stepped forth, on the stage
of the universe, the child of his mind, that young American
nation, the great protagonist of free, democratic institutions,

B

which has since enacted a part in the world's history full of stimulus and enlightened example to all peoples yearning to be free, and full of lessons for all governments desirous of the welfare of humanity—lessons which it will be our object to point, and illustrate, in the following pages as to a time, perplexed on constitutional issues, looking out on a dark and uncertain future, and in our view, in sore need of just that kind of democratic light and leading which American history provides. We begin our excursion into American annals, therefore, standing at the bier of Washington—not, it is true, a strictly logical, or chronological point of departure, but a scene which set throbbing the great heart of America, and which found the minds of Americans filled with the ideals of liberty, equality, and fraternity, in a purity which, perhaps, they have never known since, and consequently, therefore, a fitting period at which to begin a survey of the stupendous democratic developments which America has provided for the encouragement and enlightenment of the rest of the world.

The message announcing the death of Washington was delivered to Congress on the 18th December, 1799, by Mr. Marshall, Lord Chief Justice. The members were struck dumb with grief. Anguish of soul was visible in the eyes of all. The news, at first, was so unexpected that they would fain have hoped it unfounded ; but it was confirmed on the 19th. Marshall addressed Congress in these stirring words:— " If, sir, it had even not been usual openly to testify respect for the memory of those whom Heaven had selected as its instruments for dispensing good to men, yet, such has been the uncommon work, and such the extraordinary incidents, which have marked the life of him whose loss we all deplore, that the whole American nation, impelled by the same feelings, would call with one voice for a public manifestation of that sorrow which is deep and universal. More than any other individual, and as much as to any one individual was possible, has he contributed to found this, our wide-spreading empire, and to give to the western world its independence and freedom.

Having effected the great object for which he was placed at the head of our armies, we have seen him converting the sword into the ploughshare and voluntarily sinking the soldier into the citizen. When the debility of our Federal system had become manifest, and the bonds which connected the parts of this vast continent were dissolving, we have seen him, the chief of those patriots who formed for us a constitution, which by preserving the Union will, I trust, substantiate and perpetuate those blessings which Revolution had promised to bestow. In obedience to the voice of a great people, calling on him to preside over them, we have seen him once more quit the retirement he loved ; and, with calm and wise determination, pursue the true interests of the nation, and contribute to the establishment of that system of policy which will, I trust, yet preserve our peace, our honour, and our independence. Having been twice unanimously chosen the Chief Magistrate of a free people, we see him, at a time when his re-election with the universal suffrage could not have been doubted, affording to the world a rare instance of moderation by withdrawing from his high station to the peaceful walks of a private life. However public confidence may change, and the public affections fluctuate with respect to others, yet with respect to him they have, in war and peace, in public and private life, been as steady as his own firm mind and as constant as his own exalted virtues." ⌐ /

It is impossible at this distance to realise the effect upon the nation of the intelligence that Washington was no more. For the first time the entire nation, governors and governed, had brought home to them how much he had been to them. On every side his name and fame and achievements in liberty's cause were proclaimed aloud from pulpit and platform, North and South, East and West, over the Union. The intensity of the nation's sorrow proclaimed, with golden tongue, the fact that he had been the hero, the Saviour, the " Father of his people." They mourned as children for a well-loved father. The manner of his death is recorded

4

with pathetic simplicity in the following letter sent by the secretary who attended him to the President :—

Mount Vernon,
December 15th, 1799.

Sir,—It is with inexpressible grief I have to announce the death of the great and good General Washington. He died last evening between ten and eleven o'clock, after a short illness of about twenty hours. His disorder was an inflammatory sore throat, which proceeded from a cold of which he made but little complaint on Friday. On Saturday morning, about 3 o'clock, he became worse. Dr. Craik attended him in the morning, and Dr. Dick of Alexandria and Dr. Brown of Port Tobacco, were soon after called in. Every medical assistance was offered, but without the desired effect. His last scene corresponded with the whole tenor of his life. Not a groan, nor a complaint, escaped him. In extreme distress, with perfect resignation, and with full possession of his faculties, he closed his well-spent life.

Your obedient servant,

Tobias Lear.

The chorus of appreciation uttered on this mighty occasion by senators and sages, judges and generals, public boards and State assemblies, would fill a volume. The Senate expressed itself in these glowing terms :—" Washington yet lives—on earth in his spotless example ; his spirit is in heaven. Let his countrymen consecrate the memory of the heroic general, the patriotic statesman, and the virtuous sage. Let them teach their children never to forget that the fruit of his labours, and his example, are their inheritance." John Adams, in reply to the Senate, spoke thus:—" For himself he had lived enough, to life and to glory ; for his fellow citizens, if their prayer could have been answered. he would have been immortal. His example is now complete, and it will teach wisdom and virtue to magistrates, citizens and men, not only in the present age but in future generations, as long as our history shall be read." In Europe, the news was received with feelings of profound regret. Even the British Fleet, lying at anchor in the English Channel, under command of Lord Bridport, lowered their flags to half-mast; and Buonaparte, as first Consul of France, gave public expression of his own and the nation's sorrow, He also issued an order to the army to wear mourning, and he commanded an oration to be delivered before the civil and military authorities, at which he attended.

The funeral was attended by representatives from all the States, and funeral orations were pronounced in town and village. The bells throughout the Union sounded their mournful dirges ; the coloured habit of everyday life was cast aside for the crape and sable of mourning. The veterans joined with the younger volunteers, to vie in showing how they idolized the dead general. His bones were laid to rest in the old vault, which is situated on the hill side, almost immediately in front of his residence at Mount Vernon, appropriate orations and parting salutes being given over his closed grave.

In attempting to appreciate the character of Washington as a soldier and statesman, to glean from his life the wealth of example it contained for the leaders and rulers of future ages, and to garner in the mind and heart the harvest of glowing ideals it reflected applicable to the lives of all men, however common their clay, it will be well, at the outset, to recall the memorable sayings regarding him of his great contemporaries. Lord Brougham, the great English statesman, spoke of him thus :—" It will be the duty of the historian and sage of all nations to let no occasion pass of commemorating this illustrious man; and until time shall be no more will a test of the progress which our race has made, in wisdom and virtue, be derived from the veneration paid to the immortal name of Washington." Lord Byron immortalized him in verse. Who does not recall the inspiring stanza ?—

"Where may the wearied sight repose,
    When gazing on the great,

Where neither guilty glory glows,
Nor despicable state ?
Yes, one, the first, the last, the best,
The Cincinnatus of the West,
Whom envy dare not hate,
Bequeathed the name of Washington."

Goldsmith, too, might well have had Washington in mind
when he wrote :—

" As some tall cliff that lifts its awful form
Swells from the vale and midway leaves the storm,
Though round its breast the falling clouds are spread,
Eternal sunshine settles on his head."

Frederick the Great, of Prussia, honoured him by
sending him his portrait with the following inscription written
upon it :—" From the Oldest General in Europe to the Greatest
General in the World." His own countryman and namesake,
Washington Irving, says :—" The character of Washington
may want some of those poetic elements which dazzle and
delight the multitude, but it possessed fewer inequalities,
and a rarer union of virtues, than perhaps ever fell to the
lot of one man. Prudence, firmness, capacity, moderation,
an overruling judgment, an unmovable justice ; courage that
never failed ; patience that never wearied ; truth that dis-
armed all artifice, and magnanimity without alloy."

Washington was not the idol of a day ; he is the hero of
ages. It is some consolation when one considers the prevalence
of the violent ambition and criminal thirst for power of which
his contemporary Napoleon was the most striking example,
to find a character whom it is honourable to admire and virtuous
to imitate. A conqueror in the cause of his country, a legis-
lator for its security, a magistrate for its happiness. His
glories were never sullied by excess. He was full of virtue and
exempt from vice. Washington was truly a favourite of God
and man. Whatever he attempted succeeded. His name
is greatest among the roll of great men that shine immortal

in American annals, and in the history of the world's noblest
characters he will ever be held in the first rank. As the years
roll on his name and fame increase. Cities, towns, counties,
and societies of every kind in the United States, inscribe his
name on their titles, and men of every party honour and revere
his memory. His birthday is celebrated with joy, and, now that
his life has been scrutinized by succeeding ages, it has been
found stainless. His principles were unimpeachable, and the
integrity of his character as well as his personal virtue give to
his name unsurpassed lustre. To be attacked by enemies is
the common lot of the great, but no enemy or rival ever assailed,
in life or death, George Washington, with any other result than
to place in bolder relief his unquestioned greatness.

Washington was of a commanding appearance, a soldier
by training, and a gentleman by nature. He stood six feet
in height, and when on his famous white charger, he was a
most remarkable personality, inspiring respect and confidence
in his soldiers. He was endowed with a healthy constitution,
and the outdoor exercise which he enjoyed as a surveyor
and soldier, from youth upwards, enabled him to cheerfully
undergo the fatigue and hardship of the Revolution without
difficulty, never repining, and always confident of final
success. He faced danger wherever he met it, in camp or on
the field of battle, with a resolution and courage unsurpassed
in the annals of war. His was a mind, pure, noble, and
patriotic. Every thought, word and desire of his life as
Commander-in-Chief was devoted to the liberation of his
country. He always arrived at sound and safe conclusions,
studied the causes and circumstances, and weighed every
detail before he decided on action. Prudence and due
deliberation were with him virtues which he never laid aside.
As a General he ran no unnecessary risks, never hastened an
event or looked to chance to assist him. His motto was "look
before you leap" as "prevention is better than cure." His judg-
ments of men and things, his plans and devices, were invariably
arrived at after sifting and weighing all the antecedents and

concurrent circumstances, after taking council with his officers after scrutinizing the reports of his scouts, the recommendations of his friends, and the opinions and resolutions of Congress and the State Assemblies. When his judgment, so maturely formed, differed from the supreme Council of the Confederation, he submitted, after remonstrance, to the superior tribunal, even though by so acting he was invariably acting wrongly, and against his better judgment. He was humane towards his army, and never unnecessarily cruel to his enemy. He was just and exact in h:s dealings, and always obeyed the laws of the civil authorities even in the most trying crises through which he had to pass. He dealt firmly with traitors, and all insubordination wherever reported in the ranks. He was reserved and discreet, a better listener than talker, and this reserve tended to increase his personal influence. It is recorded of him that never once during the war was he known to smile. By nature he was of a modest and humble disposition, and only that circumstances drew him forth from retirement, it was his ardent desire to live and die a private citizen on his own farm.

In religion Washington was a practical Christian, but he never made a parade of his beliefs. We know, however, from the records of his life that he often in the depth of the forest, away from his camp and out of view of his soldiers, in the most trying scenes of the campaign, communed with God in prayer for aid and guidance. He was not a fanatic, or a bigot, in religious matters, a fact which is well testified in the Articles of the Constitution over the deliberations of the framers of which he presided.

That great document leaves all forms of belief free before the law, and opens all offices of State to every American citizen. We are told that when Franklin, the octogenarian sage, rose up in the 1787 Convention at Philadelphia, and proposed that the Deity should be invoked to give guidance and light to the deliberations of the delegates, Washington's eye beamed, and his countenance shone with delight at the proposition. To him, mainly, is to be attributed the practice common over the States to-day of beginning all public functions by prayer. If we look for a further proof of the reliance that Washington placed in God, we have only to search the records of his public and private letters, and allocutions. We cannot better conclude this sketch of his good qualities and characteristics than by giving a pen picture of him by Thomas Jefferson, one who laboured by his side during the war, and who studied him as his first Secretary of State after the year 1789.

" His mind was great and powerful, without being of the first order ; his penetration strong though not so acute as that of Newton, Bacon, or Locke ; and as far as he saw, no judgment was ever sounder. It was slow in operation, being little aided by invention, or imagination, but sure in conclusion. Hence the common remark of his officers of the advantage he derived from councils of war. No general ever planned his battles more judiciously, but if deranged during action—if any member of his plan was dislocated by sudden circumstance —he was slow in readjustment. The consequence was that he often failed in the field and rarely against an enemy in station, as at Boston and York.

He was incapable of fear, meeting personal dangers with the calmest unconcern. Perhaps the strongest feature of his character was prudence, never acting until every circumstance was maturely weighed, refraining if he was in doubt, but, when once decided, going through with his purpose whatever obstacle opposed. His integrity was the most pure, his justice the most inflexible, I have ever known, no motives of interest or consanguinity of friendship or hatred being able to bias his decisions. He was, indeed, in every sense of the word, a wise, a good, and a great man.

His temper was naturally irritable and high toned, but reflection and resolution had obtained a firm and habitual ascendancy over it. If ever, however, it broke its bonds, he was most tremendous in his wrath. In his expenses he was

honourable and exact, liberal in contributions to whatever
promised utility, but frowning and unyielding on all visionary
projects and all unworthy calls on his charity. His heart
was not warm in its affections, but he exactly calculated every
man's value, and gave him a solid esteem in proportion to it.
His person was fine, his stature exactly what one would wish,
his deportment easy, erect and noble, the best horseman of
his age, and the most graceful that could be seen on horseback.
Although, in the circle of his friends, where he might be un-
reserved with safety, he took a full share in conversation, his
colloquial talents were not above mediocrity, possessing neither
copiousness of ideas, nor fluency of words. In public, when
called on for a sudden opinion, he was unready, short and
embarrassed, yet he wrote readily, rather diffusely and in a
correct style. This he acquired by conversation with the
world; for his education was reading, writing and arithmetic,
to which he added surveying at a later date. His time was
employed in action. His correspondence became necessarily
extensive, owing to his varied and busy life.

On the whole his character was perfect, in nothing bad,
in few points indifferent, and, it may be said, that never did
nature and fortune combine more perfectly to make a man great
and to place him in the same constellation with the worthy few
who have merited from man an everlasting remembrance. For
his was the singular destiny and merit of leading the armies of
his country successfully through an arduous war for the
establishment of its independence; of conducting its councils
through the birth of a government, new in its forms and principles, until it had settled down into a quiet and orderly
train; and of successfully obeying the laws through the whole
of his career, civil and military, of which the history of the
world furnished no other example."

NAPOLEON AND WASHINGTON.

HISTORY assigns to these two heroes the highest niche of fame. They stand pre-eminent amongst the renowned generals of both ancient and modern times. Hannibal and Caesar, Cyrus and Alexander, shall live in history as long as history records the rise and fall and growth of Greece and Rome, Egypt and Persia ; Washington and Napoleon, the modern bearers of the mantle of these great men, shall live in history and stand out as colossal monuments of their times, till time shall be no more. Their fame and achievements are more enduring than the Pyramids. They approach nearer to the conception we have of the giant cliffs around our rugged headlands, planted by the God of nature. Centuries of sea and storm only bring out in bolder relief their ruggedness and grandeur. Time and storm, ebb and flow, and the swelling of the endless billows, merely clear away the unevenness of the shore, and smooth the roughness of the boulders and rocks at their bases, whilst the grandeur and sublimity of these works of nature stand forth imperishable proof against all destructive agencies. So it would seem to be with the world's greatest men. Their lofty greatness increases with time. Memory forgets the minor notables who made them great, and, as the years pass on history ceases to record the very existence of the lesser satellites that clustered around them. Few, to-day, are familiar with the names and exploits of Ney, Murat, Duroc, Kebler, Dessaix, Massena, or Augereau, and soon, too, the world outside the United States will cease to enquire who were Greene and Lincoln, Gates and Knox, Hamilton and Putnam. Although those men and many causes and circumstances combined to make the history of their time and country, future generations shall only know of the imperishable figures of the two immortals, Napoleon and Washington. Each shall remain in history the symbol of his epoch, and landmark of a crisis in the history of the world.

Napoleon and Washington are central figures representing great ideals, colossal objects that command the close scrutiny of the historical student. The scenes on which they battled and made history may be localized ; the effects of the Revolutions they were instrumental in carrying to completion will live for ever, and have their influence on the nations down the centuries. In some sense they may be called sons of destiny, doomed to become great by force of circumstances. Emerson, speaking of Napoleon, says, " Nature must have the greater share in every success. Such a man was wanted, and such a man was born—a man of stone and iron, capable of sitting on horseback sixteen hours, of going many days together without rest or food, except by snatches, and with the speed and spring of a tiger in action ; a man not embarrassed by any scruple, instant, selfish, prudent, and of a perception which did not suffer itself to be baulked by any pretence of others, or by any superstition, or any heat or haste of his own. ' My hand of iron,' he said to himself, ' is not at the extremity of my arm, it is immediately connected with my head.' He called himself, the child of destiny. ' I could not replace myself,' he said, ' I am the creature of circumstances.' He never opposed nature, he always marched with the opinions of great masses. He led the democracy of France to almost sixty victories, yet circumstances made him monarch, and he became a dictator."

Inevitably we are forced to recognise in the history of the times that brought forth these two great men, the all-wise providence of the Ruler of the universe. The populace in France and America were ripe for revolt and many causes contributed to make revolt possible. Whilst circumstances were moving the minds of the masses, leaders goading them on to revolt, and bad laws being enacted and enforced by tyrannical methods and unsympathetic agents, their future generals were being trained and prepared for the mission before them. Neither was distinguished by any brilliancy at school ; both were famed for thoroughness and great application in every thing they essayed. Neither had talents for languages or literature; both seemed to have a passion for the life of a soldier. These qualifications of themselves would not seem to supply sufficient foundations for the building of heroes to last for all time. No, it needed the times in which they lived to make them great ; two great men were wanted by the age and they arose, like the Apostolic College, from out the obscurity. The island of Corsica produced the European, and the Virginian plantations presented Washington to his beloved countrymen in the hour of their trial. In the Corsican general we see at first but a little uncouth soldier, in height about five feet four inches, unknown to fame and unknown to the soldiers who were destined to march with him to many victories. Unexpectedly we find him a bold, an ambitious and fearless man, slipping out unasked and taking command. In the Virginian we see a beautiful character, soldier-like in every movement, a gentleman from head to foot, a retiring, reserved and unassuming personality, who stepped forth into the arena of publicity, when called by his country, but who would have preferred to end his days in peace at home. How different are the two heroes of these two mighty Revolutions and how the difference becomes more marked, as they loom larger and larger in the public gaze.

Napoleon thus writes of himself : " I must dazzle and astonish. If I were to give liberty to the press my power would not last three days." His chief aim was to make a great name. A great reputation is a great noise, the more there is of it the further off it is heard. Laws, institutions, movements, nations all fall, but the noise continues, and resounds in after ages. He again says, " There are two levers for moving men, interest and fear. Love is a silly infatuation depend upon it. I love nobody ; I do not even love my brothers—perhaps Joseph a little. I may have many pretending, but no true friends. Leave sentiment to women, but men should be firm and resolute." How different are the ideals as history presents them to us, of the American general and statesman ! Yet the circumstances which brought each forth required different types of leaders. When Washington had risen to the pinnacle of prominence and fame the " little general " was a boy at school studying the arts and science of war ; America had gained her independence, and had carved for herself a permanent constitution out of the divergent elements the thirteen States composing the original Union.

Washington came forth at the call of his countrymen to battle for liberty. It was duty and conscience that called him, hence honour and virtue and chivalry were his guiding stars in the conduct of affairs in his public as well as private capacity.

We cannot find any similarity in the motives which drew forth Napoleon from comparative obscurity and raised him to fame. No doubt the moving, seething masses of democracy in France were bursting with discontent, and looking out for guidance and leaders. Demagogues had inflamed them. The Bourbons were out of touch with the nation. Voltaire and Rousseau, by their infidel and revolutionary writing, had undermined Christian ideals, and sown the seeds of Revolution and anarchy. The nobility were proud and unbending ; the French Court very corrupt ; the clergy, because of monarchial leanings, were suspected by the lower strata—the rabble that cheered the goddess of Reason, in the person of a naked female, carried in public procession through the streets of Paris. Robespierre, Marat and Danton, young, godless men, had no difficulty in reaping the first fruits of the Revolution. These bad men were only links in the chain that called forth the genius and talents of Napoleon. How unlike in origin the rise of these two men ; nay, how unlike the results achieved by each. The victories of the one dazzle and bewilder by their suddenness and brilliancy, but the results are not permanent. The great Washington built up his name and fame and nation by slow and sure stages. The Father of his Country would seem to have been called forth by the common Father of us all, whilst Napoleon would rather seem to have been evoked by Satan, and used by him to decimate and devastate Europe.

How noble does not Washington appear, an ideal hero, set up for emulation in the ages that come after him ! The code of conduct that he mapped out for his life's guidance when a boy; the moral precepts learned from his mother in youth, were firmly embedded in his mind, and were the guiding principles of his action in army and Senate during the thirty years he devoted to his country and countrymen. Truth, justice, honour, prudence and diligence were the lessons he learned in youth and practised in every circumstance of his career that called them forth. Washington, by his successes, in consonance with these high ideals, and not in spite of breaches of the law of God, falsified the old Italian maxim, " If you would succeed, you must not be too good ? " He listened to no monitors like Fontane, who in 1804 thus advised Napoleon, " Sir, the desire of perfection is the worst desire that ever affected the human mind." Truth, and candour, and straightforwardness, were natural to Washington's character. How stands it with Napoleon in respect of these virtues ? It is said of him that he regarded truth and falsehood as alike good, provided they were serviceable as means to gain his end. As a soldier, Napoleon was amongst the greatest of all time ; as a man, he is one of the most perplexing characters to be found in history. You need not expect to find him when inexpedient telling the truth, keeping a promise, trusting a friend, behaving generously to an enemy, honouring a woman, caring for the poor and down-trodden, or doing anything noble. He worshipped no God but ambition. As regards creeds and religions, it is said he made pretence of preaching several in turn, and if it suited his object, he was prepared to propagate any opinion. He played on the vanity and loyalty of the French populace like a skilled musician on the strings of a harp.

When he entered Italy he promised the army the fertile country around as a reward for valour. His historic phrase is most characteristic, that "each private soldier had a marshal's baton in his knapsack." He cajoled the masses by terrorising the nobility, and he boasted to the " new order " that he had the " old order " under his heel. This insincerity in the interests of democracy was proved by the fact that he made himself King as well as his two brothers, and his brother-in-law, and by the creation of new titles for his friends and followers. The leader of democracy became the first of autocrats.

We may sum up our comparison of these two great men by saying that " ever and always an intense ambition and craving for fame and glory were the highest patriotism and ruling ideals of Napoleon; whilst love of liberty, and love of country, and hate of tyranny was the motive power behind Washington, spurring him on to do and dare and live and die for his country. The following noble words from an address of Washington's to Adet, the French Ambassador in 1796, when presenting the new Flag of France to the people of America, show forth the high idea he had of liberty :—" Sir, born in a land of liberty, having early learned its value, having engaged in a perilous conflict to defend it, having, in a word, devoted the best years of my life to secure its permanent establishment in my country, my anxious recollections, my sympathetic feelings, and my best wishes are irresistibly excited whensoever in any country I see an oppressed nation unfurl the banners of freedom."

EVENTS BEFORE THE REVOLUTION.

THE history of the American Revolution has been frequently written, but it is mostly contained in heavy tomes which only the most courageous of general readers ever attempt to negotiate. To help the historical orientation of the reader in following these little sketches of scenes and character, we propose to give a short account of the events which immediately led up to the War of Independence.

The thirteen States which, in times immediately following the charter of their independence, were known as the United States of America, were at first separate colonies, with little union among themselves, further than their recognition of British Sovereignty over them. Each State had its own Governor, its own Council, and its own Assembly. In most of the States the Governor and his Council of advisers were either chosen directly by the crown, or by the proprietory landlords. Only in two of the States were the Governors and Council, as well as the Assembly, elected by popular suffrage, to wit, in Connecticut and Rhode Island. In all the States the representatives of the Assembly of Burgesses were the free choice of the people. It may be incidentally mentioned that the two States above-mentioned, which had a complete democratic form of government, without any crown interference or privileged class representation, were the first to rebel against English interference in their internal government, and were the first to appeal to arms against aggressive enactments directed against the Republican form of Government, which they enjoyed by charter for generations. The Assembly in each State, as in the case of our House of Commons, alone possessed the right to levy taxes and raise funds for State purposes. From time to time there was much friction in those less republician States, between the Assembly of the people and the Governor and their Council. Often, indeed, the tension approached to the verge of open rupture. Franklin, the sage, scientist, and statesman, as early as 1754, saw the necessity that existed for some bond of union among the colonies. He proposed a Congress or Grand Council of six nations, similar to the National Congress of Philadelphia, established prior to the war. This Council was to meet at Albany, and formulate a Union that should empower the Congress to levy taxes on the six united nations for mutual defence, to raise and maintain armies for self-defence, the Council to have supreme authority in Colonial affairs as distinct from imperial matters.

The scheme failed, because of the opposition of the Parliament of England, and on account of its non-acceptance by the States concerned. The King feared such a Council, because such a Union would show the Colonies their power in Union, and England did not wish to make her Colonies too powerful. The Colonies themselves, jealous of their individual rights to tax themselves, did not wish to concede the right to a foreign body, such as they considered the Council to be. We may note here that the jealousy of every State to be considered as a separate and independent entity, was the cause of so much delay, after the war, in drawing up a constitution that would be acceptable to all the States, and it was this same jealousy aroused again over the question of Slavery, that led to the Civil War over a hundred years later.

The advantage of such a union as Benjamin Franklin proposed would have been most beneficial, both to England and the Colonies, during the inter-colonial wars which began about this time. It would have ensured united efforts on the part of the different States, in repelling Indians and French aggressors, and would have materially aided in protecting the frontiers from unjust encroachments against the property of the backwood settlers. It often happened, during those years of strife, that the onus of repelling the enemy fell alike heavily on the Crown, and some of the Colonies more exposed to invasion, and there was no controlling power in existence to tax or compel sister colonies to co-operate and bear their share of the battle for colonial rights.

There was, however, a spirit of union growing and increasing in the Colonies, as they advanced in experience and consciousness of their rights and powers. This union, nevertheless, was not built on a desire to be freed from England, the Motherland; it assumed rather the form of a union to encourage passive resistance to English domination in colonial and domestic affairs. It aimed at checking the encroachments of the English garrison, the Governors and other Councils and their followers, in the different States. It was a union arising from the growing spirit of resistance to the seizure of all profits arising from government and trade and commerce, by the English Loyalist party in the States, and the English merchants. But, above and beyond all, it was due to the determination of the Colonists to resist all control claimed by the English Parliament, to levy direct taxes on the Colonies. The Colonists held that " taxation without representation was tyranny," and that since the distance by sea from America to London rendered representation impossible, no English Assembly had any right to levy taxes on them in natural justice, with or without their consent, no more than they would have a right to enter their homes and take away their private property. It was Virginia that first announced the doctrine in Congress, which afterwards became universal among the States, and which might be called the foundation of that union, which proved so disastrous to England, " that an attack upon one Colony was an attack upon all."

The spirit of discontent among the States had been growing stronger, year by year, for over a hundred years, and it culminated into loud protestations when, in 1765, the Stamp Act was passed by the Granville administration, which legislated under the more or less personal rule of George III.

So fierce and so resolute was the opposition to this Act among the Colonies that it was repealed in 1766. The Stamp Act imposed a direct tax, varying from six cents to 30 dollars on all paper issued in the Colonies for newspapers, almanacs, pamphlets, advertisements, and all legal documents. The people ignored the law. They married and transacted business without this paper, in some places it was burned, and in most places it was stowed away in stores to rot. Pitt, Burke, and Barre, two of whom were Irishmen, and among the most eloquent members of Parliament of the day opposed the Stamp Act and denied the right of the House of Commons to impose it. Pitt, in a memorable speech on the repeal of the Stamp Act, said, " Sir, I rejoice that America has resisted. Three millions of people, so dead to all feelings of liberty, as voluntarily to submit to be slaves, would have been fit instruments to make slaves of us all."

England, and all mother countries in those days, claimed the right to tax indirectly her colonies, as a recompense for protecting them. This pretended right was exercised by the method of trade monopolies and privileges, restricting the Colonies from trading with other nations, and compelling them to buy from and sell to England at her own prices. These arbitrary restrictions exercised by the English for many years prior to the bold attempt made in '65 to directly tax the Colonies were, as the Navigation Laws revealed, almost unbearable to a free and progressive people.

The internal form of Government in the States was framed on democratic lines. It trained the people in many ways. It taught the people's representatives to stand up for their rights, and safeguard them against the encroachments of the Governors and their officials. It taught them that they had a country of their own worth living for, and living in, a country which their fathers had won by the sword and defended for years, in the Indian and Colonial Wars, at the cost of their lives. No doubt, England aided them, by her armies, but she taxed them for the upkeep of her forces, and she penalized them most tyrannically, by her trading restrictions. She sent over her greedy governors and their friends to rule them and they taxed themselves to pay her officials. The Colonists were beginning to see the selfish motive, in all that England had been doing for them. They came to the conclusion that England fought the other nationalities and the Indians in past years more in the interest of her trade and commerce, than for the mere protection of life and Colonial property. England at the time of the Stamp Act, was in sore straits for revenue to defray expenses and pay her debts, piled up to a hundred million by her German, French, and Spanish Wars. During her Colonial Wars, which ended, happily for her, in the treaty of Fontainebleau which made her mistress of North America, she saw the great possibilities of America, as a country that could well afford to aid the Motherland in her financial difficulties. These Colonial Wars taught also a lesson to the Colonials. They taught them that on their native plains and in their own valleys and on their own rugged mountains the Colonists as soldiers were equal, and in many cases superior, to the trained veterans by whose side they fought. These wars, moreover, gave the colonists a wide experience of their native colonial territory put by them in later years to good account. And they benefited further in a consciousness of power and pride of country, which made them more friendly with each other, and consequently more cohesive iu combination. The glowing reports which the soldiers going home to England brought of the loyalty of the Americans to the old country, and of the rich new land flowing with milk and honey, able to bear the burdens of the over-taxed Exchequer of George, and, as they thought, willing to submit to any arbitrary laws passed for their acceptance, caused the Parliament to essay direct taxation. How little did they gauge the true spirit of the men, who fled from England in past generations, to found homes in the Western wilderness, rather than submit to regal tyranny in church or state. America, at this juncture, when her liberty was threatened, organized her sons and daughters in societies known as the " Sons and Daughters of Liberty." They not alone refused to use the stamped paper but refused to buy or use any goods manufactured in England, which mode of boycott had Washington's entire support and sympathy. Hence, we see, as a result of these societies for spinning and weaving, all the Colonials without exception wore home-made clothing, and they even refused to kill or eat sheep lest they should not have sufficient wool for home use.

The States that came most prominently to the front, in refusing to recognise the right to tax the Colonies, were Massachusetts and Virginia. Patrick Henry, a son of Virginia, in a memorable speech at Congress, in Williamsborough, at which Washington was present, said : " The General Assembly of the Colony had the sole right and power of laying taxes on the Colony." " Cæsar," he said, " had his Brutus ; Charles I. had his Cromwell ; and George III."—at this the Loyalists in the Assembly shouted wildly " Treason "—proceeded Henry, " may profit by their example. If this be treason make the most of it."

Lord Macaulay, in his essay on " The Earl of Chatham," thus speaks of the Stamp Act :—" When Pitt was absent from Parliament, Grenville proposed a measure, destined to produce a great revolution, the effect of which will long be remembered by the whole human race ; we speak of the Act for imposing stamp duties on the North American Colonies. The plan was eminently characteristic of the author. Every feature of the parent was found in the child. A timid statesman would have shrunk from a step of which Walpole, at a time when the Colonies were far less powerful, had said : ' He who shall propose it will be a much bolder man than I.' But the nature of Grenville was insensible to fear. A statesman of large views would have felt that, to lay taxes on New England and New York, was a course opposed, not indeed to the letter of the statute book, or to any decision contained in the Term Reports, but to the principles of good government, and to the spirit of the constitution. A statesman of large views would also have felt, that ten times the estimated produce of the American stamps would have been dearly purchased by even a transient quarrel with the Colonies. But Grenville knew of no spirit of the constitution distinct from the letter of the law, and of no national interests except those which are expressed by pounds, shillings, and pence. That his policy might give birth to deep discontents in all the provinces ; that France might seize the opportunity of revenge ; that the Empire might be dismembered ; that the debt—that debt, with the amount of which he perpetually reproached Pitt—might, in consequence of his own policy, be doubled—these were possibilities that never occurred to that small, sharp mind. The Stamp Act will be remembered as long as the globe lasts, but at the time it attracted little attention in England." The language used by Grenville when Pitt applauded the Americans for resistance, and when he maintained, in a defiant tone, that it was contrary to the Constitution to tax the Colonies directly, was such, says Macaulay, " as Stafford might have employed in the reign of Charles I. They were traitors, and those who excused them were little better. Frigates, mortars, bayonets, sabres, were the proper remedies for such distemper."

When the Stamp Act was repealed there was great re-joicing in England. Merchants from all the British ports were waiting around the lobbies of Parliament up till midnight, to learn the decision. As soon as it was known that the Act was annulled by a sweeping majority, wild " hurrahs " were raised for Pitt, and Burke, and Barre; and the appearance of Grenville and his party in opposition, was the occasion for fierce groans and hisses. The people felt that civil war was averted. Grenville and George III., alike tyrannical and obstinate, supported, as they were, by their sycophants and rotten boroughs, were obdurate. The late minister said, " If the tax were still to be laid on, I would lay it on. For the evils which it may produce, my accuser (Pitt) is answerable. His profession made it necessary. His declarations against the constitutional powers of the King, Lords and Commons, have made it doubly necessary. I do not envy him the huzza. I glory in the hiss. If it were to be done again I would do it." Whilst the King and his tools in Parliament had many adherents for the tax, most of the lords and the clergy were in favour of the Grenville policy. The Colonists had also some of the most brilliant Whigs in the Commons defending them, and it is evident that the many petitions sent from America to Westminster, were tempered with the expression of a spirit of loyalty if not of submissiveness, that did not truly represent the Assemblies from which they emerged, but was inserted simply that the written documents might not hamper the friends of liberty in the Commons.

How analogous, in many respects, the constitutional question in America was at this epoch to that now agitating the British Isles is vividly brought home to us by the great speech of Pitt on " taxation without representation," and modern English politicians might read this and other pronouncements of that critical epoch of history with much advantage to themselves, and much consequent clarification of the issues before the people of to-day.

It might be said truly that the Americans took the following as their text in the organisation of that resistance which they carried to a successful issue in the War for Independence : " Taxation is no part of the governing or legislative powers of a State, and taxes are a voluntary gift and a grant of the Commons alone. The concurrence of the Peers and of the Crown is necessary only as a form of law. This House represents the Commons of England (not fully at that time or for many years later, we may be allowed to amend ; cities like Liverpool, Manchester and Birmingham had no representatives, and rotten boroughs like Old Sarum, without any inhabitants still retained their members). When, in this House, we give and grant, we give and grant what is our own, but can we give and grant the property of the Commons of America. It is an absurdity in terms."

Franklin was one of the delegates sent over from America to present a petition against the Stamp Act. He obtained a hearing at the bar of the House, and when questioned in person would the American people submit to this Act, he emphatically answered—" No! never, unless compelled by force."

The Act was repealed, not because Franklin spoke against it, and petitioned on behalf of America, not because Pitt and others were opposed to it, but because England's commerce with the Colonies was ruined. She was now carrying on only one-third of her normal trade with America (about thirty millions annually). The falling off was remarkable. Americans were having recourse to smuggling, as well as adopting the non-importation policy.

In America, rejoicing at the repeal of the Act was of short duration. The leaders of thought were educating the people in the school of liberty, by speech, and through the press. The trusted leaders of the people were many, and were men of great abilities. You had lawyers like John Adams, Otes, and Jefferson, and Henry; journalists like Samuel Adams and Franklin; merchants like Hancock; soldiers like Washington; doctors like Warren, Benjamin Rusk; and farmers like Putnam and Allan, tried and trusted men, prepared to risk all in defence of liberty. England had nothing in her Western possessions to place in opposition to those giants, but paid officials, venal governors, some salaried Churchmen, and large land owners. A spirit of distrust of the Motherland was fast growing in the Colonies. Some men went so far as to believe that the unjust levying of taxes on the Colonies by Westminster, was a deep laid scheme of the Cabinet to goad them on to rebellion, so that England might with some show of reason crush them by force, annex, and plunder them.

King George, chagrined at the repeal of the Stamp Act, urged his minions in the Cabinet to devise a new scheme of taxation, less objectionable. Accordingly, they agreed to keep a standing army in America, ostensibly to protect the Colonists, but, in reality, to terrorize them, and to aid the loyal governors and their hangers-on to Anglicise the Colonials, subdue their liberty-loving propensities, and trample on public opinion, public speech, and all attempts at organization in self-defence.

About 15,000 soldiers were billeted in their chief cities, and, to aid in their support, an indirect tax was levied on glass, iron, lead, paper, paint, and tea. A Board of Inland Revenue was instituted to carry out the Act. These revenue officers had almost absolute powers to search and harass the people, and to render smuggling or secret trade impossible. Again petitions were forwarded to England. The burgesses over the province rebelled, and again England was compelled to submit. She, however, in order to keep up her semblance of authority, retained the tax on tea, a mere nominal tax of three-pence a pound, which left the article cheaper in America than in England. However, the people of America were not to be bought so easily. They resisted even this tax more reso-lutely than any former tax. Men and women alike refused to drink any tea, and they absolutely refused to use any article that came from England, that they could procure or make at home. Affrays between the soldiers and people became quite frequent. In Boston, in 1770, the soldiers fired on the people and four civilians were slain in the streets, the first martyrs for liberty. Public meetings were frequent, and the people were taught their rights, and trained to self-knowledge and reserve. Faneuil Hall was packed by the people in the evenings, and Boston's eloquent sons spoke, and rekindled in the breasts of all a spark that spread like wild-fire over the provinces. By the press, pamphlets, song, and platform, the seed was spread, and the people instructed to unite and resist English taxation and tyranny.

It was about this time (1773) that Samuel Adams, a clever journalist, a forcible speaker and unpurchasable patriot, John Hancock, who was afterwards Chairman in Congress, when the Declaration of Independence was signed, and Warren, three members of the Massachusetts Assembly, formed the Committee of Correspondence for their own State, an organisation which soon spread over the Colonies and proved a powerful weapon in keeping each colony in touch with the others, and aided powerfully in uniting the whole people, making the views and acts of each State known from Maine to Georgia. It was an admirable idea and by its means the best and bravest and wisest heads and hearts among the Colonists communed with each other, the pulse beat of the Colonies was felt throughout the entire nation, ideas were diffused, and the wishes and aspirations of all known to every hamlet and village in the States.

The crisis was now inevitable, and to try the issue the East India merchants, now become desperate, resolved to import large consignments and land their vessels in the large cities of the States. The Committee of Correspondence advised the town merchants not to receive any tea from the importers, and Boston, New York, Philadelphia and Charlestown, to which cities large importations had arrived, pledged themselves not to allow the cargoes to be unloaded.

It was in Boston city that the issue about the tea was knit. Here in the heart of Massachusetts, the home of the Pilgrims, the law was set at defiance before the very eyes of an army of 5,000 soldiers that constituted the garrison there. When the tea had lain in port for nineteen days it was determined in public meeting that before next day should dawn the despised commodity should be destroyed. Soon a sturdy band of resolute men had disguised themselves in Indian dress, marched in silence to the Griffin Wharf, boarded the vessels, and begun to rip and empty the bales into the sea. Noiselessly they came, each unknown to his neighbour, with darkened faces, following the lead of a recognised head who gave them the word of command. Soon their work was over and quickly they dispersed, each to his own home. The crowd looked on without interfering and without riot. They were a resolute band and true to each other. None were arrested. The victory was complete. Not a bale of the hated tea was left in the boats, and more satisfactory still, there was not an angry word nor a drop of blood shed. Had those brave men seen into the future ; could they have read the consequences of that night's work ? Many a brave heart quailed at the black and uncertain future that was to follow this momentous event in the succeeding struggle for Independence. But the die was cast. Vengeance was sure to follow. The Boston people had slapped the English ministry in the face. They must be punished.

After the destruction of the tea the English nation were furious, and their first act was to close the Port of Boston, withdraw the Customs Officers from the city, suppress the civil authority, close the House of Burgesses, quarter troops over the Colonies, and prohibit all public meetings unless for elective purposes. To put these measures into force they obtained the sanction of Parliament. Lord North was in the ascendancy, and he in his place denounced the Americans in strong language. He said that Boston had always been the hotbed of sedition, and the ringleader in resistance to royal authority. It was from Boston that the spirit of insurrection was communicated to the whole continent of America. He hoped that, by timely severity on this city, he would be enabled to crush the spirit of sedition in the bud. General Gage was appointed military dictator, and a fleet of four or five vessels was despatched to Boston to crush the spirit of the people. Pitt, now raised to the Upper House as Lord Chatham, pleaded for leniency for the Bostonians, but in vain. He said, " My lords, it has been my fixed and unalterable opinion—I will carry it to my grave—that this country has no right to tax America." And Rose Fuller exclaimed, " You will commence your ruin from this day. If ever there was a country rushing headlong to ruin it is this." We find, at this critical juncture in the history of the two countries, the eloquent Colonel Barre entering his final protest at the drastic laws enacted against

America. He said to the ministry " You have changed your ground, you are becoming the aggressor, and offering the last of human outrages to the people of America, by submitting them to a military execution—instead of sending them the olive leaf—I mean a repeal of the late laws, fruitless to you and oppressive to them. Ask their aid in a constitutional manner, and they will give it to the utmost of their abilities. Respect their sturdy English virtue, remember that the first step towards making them contribute to your wants is to reconcile them to your Government."

England, while thus preparing to coerce the New England Colonies, made important concessions for the purpose of conciliating the Canadians to the Colonies north of St. Lawrence. She restored to the Catholics the rich lands, allowed the courts of law to administer law on old French principles, withdrew all distinctions on account of religion, and extended the boundaries of Canada as far South as the Ohio River. At this crisis when all the Colonies were threatened, and when the spirit of revolt was general in the States, fifty-three delegates from twelve States met in Philadelphia, in September of 1774, to devise ways and means to assist each other. Georgia was not represented in this National Congress, owing to the action of its loyal governor.

These delegates came from their respective States, carrying with them instructions from the State Assembly, what part they should take in the crisis forced upon their country. The delegates from the Northern States, especially Connecticut, Massachusetts, and Rhode Island, were, from the first, fired with the resolve to free themselves by force from England ; some of them, such as Maryland, New York and Pennsylvania, although determined to resist English interference in their internal government, and although prepared to join with the other States in opposing taxation, were far from desiring to break their connection with the Motherland. Virginia, however, stands apart among the Southern States as a bold champion, prepared to stand or fall with Massachusetts and

Boston in their encounter with England. If a peaceful and honourable settlement were possible, they were for peace, not for peace at any cost. Patrick Henry and Samuel Adams, one a Virginian, and the other from Boston, were the leaders of the crisis—Henry, styled the orator of the Revolution, and Adams, justly named the Father of the Revolution. Henry, in a memorable speech at this time, said in a voice of thunder, that echoed through the old church of St. John's in Richmond, where it was spoken : " We must fight, I repeat it, Sir, we must fight. I know not what course others may take, but, as for me, give me liberty, or give me death." We may quote here, from Thomas Jefferson's Memoirs, Vol. I., an extract which shows the determined attitude of Virginia, to co-operate with Boston in her manly resistance to tyranny. " When the Boston Port Bill, which gave cause for the Congress in Carpenter's Hall, Philadelphia, was announced to us at Williamsburgh, when in Congress, we passed a resolution recommending to our fellow-citizens that that day should be set apart for fasting and prayer to the Supreme Being, imploring Him to avert the calamities then threatening us, and to give us one heart, and one mind, to oppose every invasion of our liberties." In another place we will give the instructions to the seven delegates from Virginia, viz.: Randolph ; Henry Lee ; George Washington ; Patrick Henry ; Richard Bland ; Benjamin Harrison ; and Edmund Pendleton. In most of all the instructions sentiments of loyalty to George are expressed, and he is called upon in the address that was to be forwarded to disband the army at Boston, and cease to claim the right to tax them, as well as annul the Tea Act. This meeting was a memorable Assembly. From each State came the best and wisest of its sons to deliberate on a serious and solemn subject. The question before it was, as Washington said, " Were they tamely to submit to be slaves ? " Their deliberations lasted four months. Peyton Randolph was chairman, and Charles Thompson was secretary. Mr. West says of the Congress : " The most eminent men of the various colonies, men of property and consideration were, as strangers hitherto, brought together for the first time. The meeting was awfully solemn. The liberties of no less than three or four million people were staked on the wisdom of their counsels. No wonder, then, at the long and deep silence, which is said to have followed their meeting, and the anxiety with which the members looked round upon each other, and the reluctance which each felt to open a business so moment-ous."

By a unanimous vote at the commencement of their deliberations, the delegates pronounced the resolutions submitted by representatives from Massachusetts as legal, viz., " that every person who should accept office under the new and illegal form of government, ought to be held in abhorrence, and considered the wicked tool of that despotism, which was preparing to destroy those rights which God, nature, and compact had given to America." Resolutions were then drawn up embodying their rights, pointing out the acts of England to which they objected as illegal, and to which they were determined not to submit. A non-importation resolution was agreed to, and an Association was to be formed called " the American Association " which would bind all the States to cease commerce with England or her Colonies. The divergent views of the delegates were not divulged to the public and the resolutions of the delegation had, in the eyes of the people, the force of law. Of course, a petition was sent to the English King and people, but the frame of mind of England was against listening to any reasoning, unless America should first be castigated.

That we may have a true estimate of the enlightened character of this Congress, the dignity and firmness with which they conducted the deliberations and issued their addresses to the English and American people, we will introduce to the reader again the distinguished statesman, Pitt, who had been a consistent advocate against tyrannical measures at Westminster, from first to last. " When your

Lordships," said he, " have perused the papers transmitted
to us from America, when you consider the dignity, the firmness, and the wisdom with which the Americans have acted,
you cannot but respect their cause. History, my Lords, has
been my favourite study, and, in the celebrated writings of
antiquity, I have often admired the patriotism of Greece and
Rome. But, my lords, I must declare that, in the master
states of the world, I know not the people, nor the senate, whc
in such a complication of difficult circumstances can stand in
preference to the delegates of America, assembled in General
Congress at Philadelphia."

As Boston was the real seat of the origin of the war for
Independence, and, as the active promoters of revolution
were in and around this city, the reader will find interesting
the following pen-sketch of the city by Botta, after it was taken
possession of by the British; after its government was sup-
pressed, and its chief citizens had been compelled to flee to
Salem, and form a Congress independent of British control.
" The garrison was formidable, the fortifications imposing, so
that there was little hope of wresting the city from the hands of
the British. Nor could the inhabitants flatter themselves with
the hope of escaping by sea, as the harbour was blockaded
by a squadron. Shut up thus, in the midst of an isolated
soldiery, the citizens beheld themselves exposed to all outrage
that might be dreaded from military licence. Their city was
become for them a confined prison, and they themselves but
hostages in the hands of the English general. This consideration was sufficient to embarrass all military and civil operations projected by the Americans. Various means were proposed to extricate them from their cruel position, and, if they
displayed no very great prudence, they gave proof at least of
extraordinary determination. Some persons suggested that
the inhabitants should evacuate the city, and proceed to some
more secure place, where they should be supported at the
common expense. But this was considered impracticable, since
it was open to Gage to oppose its being carried out. Some

suggested that the city should be valued, and then burned, and the losses repaid by the State. This scheme was abandoned also as impracticable. Nevertheless, many of the citizens left the city in disguise, by stealth ; they betook themselves to the country districts, either from fear of hostilities, or that they should be dragged into court as opposed to the British authority. Many, however, resolved to brave all danger, and stubbornly remain in their homes at all hazard. The soldiers were impatient at being confined to camp and city life, and were clamouring to be led against the 'rebels.' The people of Massachusetts were indignant at being called cowards by the soldiers, for not coming to action in defence of their city and its inhabitants, and were longing for some opportunity of proving themselves brave and patriotic."

Boston was not cowardly disposed, as its past record proved, but it would have been reckless waste of life for the citizens to throw themselves, unarmed and without their trusted leaders, on a strong garrison of trained soldiers. Their real leader was away many miles from them, rousing up the Colonies on their behalf. Samuel Adams was at Salem. Adams was the true king in Boston. He was a man of middle height, endowed with great courage and perseverance, and possessing a cultured mind of a very high order. He was of unimpeachable character, a powerful speaker, and a fluent and forcible writer. He was far-seeing in his outlook. He was true to the people and their cause, and he loved the democracy from which he sprung. He was a born leader of men. Although poor he could not be purchased for money ; he spurned an offer from Gage, asking him to take office under his new administration. " No," he said, " we are free and want no King." He was the first American who publily advocated independence from England, and when all Boston was promised pardon for the tea disturbances, Hancock and he were to be sent as hostages to England to be tried for treason. He was descended from an old Puritan family, and he was a strict observer of Sabbath rites and religious observances.

D

The friends of the beseiged Bostonians were not idle, nor were the soldiers of General Gage to be long without feeling the mettle of which the " minute men " were made. The Congress of Massachusetts had passed a resolution, that companies should be raised, and that 20,000 militia should be forthcoming at a minute's notice, hence the name " minute men." General Gage informed the Parliament at home that the Americans would be lions, while we were lambs. This was the keynote to Lord North's policy at this time in America. to overawe the Colonies and subdue them by force. Little did Gage know of the true spirit of America. " Among the blind, the one-eyed man is King," and among ignorant men, the man with a little knowledge is irresistible. Hence the counsel of Gage prevailed ; American presumption and resistance must be crushed. Ah ! Little did the English know of the true state of affairs. Had they listened to the deliberations of the leaders of the people in Philadelphia ; had they been witness of the religious resolve of this brave people. after a solemn day's prayer and fasting, to stand at each other's backs, to the end, against tyrannical laws ; had they listened to the clear, shrill voice of that famous orator, calling on his fellow-countrymen to rebel, crying out " give me liberty or give me death," they would have taken a different view of the situation, and American history would not have been as it has been. The friends of Boston and liberty were many in the Senate of the nation, and were everywhere to be met among the people in every state. There was Franklin, than whom America produced no nobler son. A ripe scholar, self-taught, he rose from a poor apprentice in his brother's printing office, to be the first scholar, statesman, philosopher, scientist, and sage of his day ; a man that any nation, as Pitt said, might be proud of, and worthy to be classed among the Boyles and Newtons in the domain of science. There was John Adams, the learned lawyer, and ripe scholar, and first statesman of his time. Jefferson was working in the cause of liberty, as were Rutledge, Lee and Dickenson, alongside with the Father of the Nation, Washington.

THE CAPTURE OF QUEBEC.

THOUGH an event not immediately or directly connected with the War of Independence, the capture of Quebec, following that struggle of heroes which has made the names of Wolfe and Montcalm so memorable in history, finds a place in our gallery of pictures of the Revolution period, as being a striking example of the bold policy of Pitt in his dealings with the Colonies which, by its lustre, throws into more sombre shadow the dark and sinister, tyrannical, and withal stupid, methods of George and his ill-advisers. Johnson, an able and talented young Irishman, nephew to Sir Peter Warren, had been for many years preparing the Indian tribes to co-operate in the Mohawk and St. Lawrence districts, and join in a general attack on Canada. The British arms for some time had been wavering and sometimes retreating before the French and Indian forces. The ministry at home in England bore the brunt of the blame, rather than the Generals, or their soldiers in the Colonies. Newcastle's administration was intermittent in its fervour, dilatory in tactics, and consequently often unsuccessful in its military engagements. The Colonies were growing impatient. They suffered much. They were prepared to suffer more ; they were thoroughly aroused to the dangers that surrounded them. In numbers they far exceeded the Canadians. In skill in arms they may hitherto have been less distinguished, and more unskilled. In valour they were unsurpassed, and, in love of their Colonial possessions, seeing now that their latent patriotism was aroused, they had no equal in any land. A change of Government in England brought about a change of policy. Just as the Colonials loved their native Colonies, so too was Pitt deeply patriotic, loving his country and all that his country cherished with a fond affection. He saw the peril in which the nation stood in regard to her Colonies. He said " I can save them to the Empire," and Pitt did save them. When he sent across the ocean the choicest of his army, in officers and men, he meant to carry out what he said. He departed from the hitherto beaten track in the selection of generals. His policy was to officer his forces, not with men skilled in the open plain class of warfare, men of the old classic mould, who fought and marched by rul . No, he selected the ablest and most daring men, excellent alike in conception and in execution, and hence the brave young Wolfe, the hero of Quebec, was Pitt's own selection. Wolfe had fought with distinction under Marlborough in the Continental Wars. He was a born soldier. At a tender age he served under his father, who was a soldier under England's great general, and on the famed field of Fontenoy young Wolfe proved himself a true hero and born leader of men. Wolfe was not more than thirty-five years of age when he was chosen to proceed to the Western Wars. He was of a noble and gentle disposition, cultured in mind, with splendid literary abilities, feeble in body, with a romantic disposition. He was of the natural disposition from which heroes spring. He was languid in normal inactivity, fearless as a lion when roused to action, regardless of danger and contemning death, capable, moreover, of enthusing the mind of an army to do and dare. He always led, boldly exposing himself to all danger in front of his army. Wherever the fight was fiercest, and the danger greatest, there was found this young commander, who now appeared on the American shores to command a force of 8,000 soldiers, destined to capture the Crown of Canada and the key to supremacy in America. Wolfe was born on the 2nd January, 1727, at Westerham, in Kent. He was second son of a distinguished father, Colonel Wolfe, who served under Marlborough. He entered the army at the age of fourteen years, but, owing to delicate health, was for a time withdrawn from the service. He fought, not alone at Fontenoy, but on the battlefield of La Filot, and was publicly thanked for his bravery by the Duke of Cumberland. His peculiar characteristic was that his full energies were only to be drawn out by great emergencies and when confronted by the seemingly impossible. Quebec, in 1759, as it is to-day, was the Gibraltar of America, and so long as the French could hold so commanding a fortress, frowning down on the majestic St. Lawrence which connects the Atlantic with the great Lakes,which shuts out the United States from Canada, and which in those days, before steam had expedited transit either by sea or land, opened the way to Western and Central North America and the mighty Mississippi. England's great statesman knew the true importance of Quebec and hence, to capture so important a position, he looked about for the most accomplished and courageous of his generals. His choice fell on the immortal Wolfe. The general plan mapped out to bring the campaign to a successful close, was that Johnston was to capture the forts from Niagara to Montreal, that Amherst was to overcome the opposition of the Indians and the French in Central New York, and then that both generals and their armies should unite with Wolfe and Cook and Townsend in a united effort to capture Quebec.

The cautious tactics of Amherst, and the obstacles in the surrounding district delayed, however, the contemplated union, and Wolfe,.weary of waiting on the banks of the St. Lawrence, and in the month of September, fearing the approach of winter, when his operations would be futile, determined to make a bold effort and surprise the garrison on the heights of Quebec.

Quebec was founded by a famous French explorer and general, named Champlain, in the year 1608. It became the headquarters of the French colony in Canada. It was around this fort that the first French Colonials settled, and here, under the direction of the native Indians with whom they soon began to enter into Christianizing and friendly relations, they cultivated the Indian corn. By the instrumentality of their

missionaries, Jesuits and Dominicans, and by acts of kindness
and goodwill, the French soon won over to their side the savage
Indian tribes in these Northern regions. In the inter-colonial
wars, the alliance thus formed, and of many years standing,
between French and Indians was a source of much trouble to
the British Army, as the Indians were relentless towards their
foes.

Quebec, in those days, when Wolfe approached its majestic
cliffs, was not much different from what it is to-day. It
resembled very much a French city with its tile-roofed houses,
with V shaped gables, projecting over the basement, its French
population, its deep religious and Catholic belief and practices.
Its inhabitants were industrious, frugal and tenacious of old
French traditions and customs. There were then, as now,
many Indians and half-castes in the city, and some Scotch and
Irish, but the chief element was the French. The language
then, as now, was French. It was here that the first French
missionaries preached ; here they built their first church, and
opened their first college and schools. The houses then, as
now, were built on the cliffs above, which stood two hundred
feet above the river. The streets were irregular and narrow,
and ran up the ascending ground. Part of the city lay at the
foot of the cliffs. Warehouses, wharfs, and fishermen's and
labouring men's houses lay along the river's banks. This lower
part of the city stood on what was once portion of the bed of
the river, now made firm in foundation by piles and embankments. This part of the river is the harbour of Quebec,
then studded over with boats and canoes, and trading vessels,
of all sizes and patterns. The city is exceedingly eccentric in
form, with steep and winding streets, connected on the slopes
with flights of steps.

The French general in charge of the forces of Quebec was
Montcalm, a brave and famous commander, illustrious for
his literary attainments, and no less renowned for his devotion
to the Catholic Faith. In the month of June, 1759, Wolfe
landed on the Isle of Orleans, a few miles east of Quebec,,

towards the mouth of the St. Lawrence. From the shores of this island he surveyed the scenes around him and the apparently insurmountable task before him. He advanced up the river from its mouth, as far as Levi Point, which stood on the opposite bank of the river, facing the cliffs on which Quebec was built. This position he reached without much difficulty, and here he erected his artillery and commenced bombarding the lower village on the river's edge in front of him. But his operations, although irritating to the enemy, were futile, as far as the city proper was concerned. How was he to scale the cliff and secure the fortifications, so ably governed, and so watchfully guarded by Montcalm? The thought of lying within cannon range of the Crown of Canada during the inclement winter months inactive, and without having achieved the object Pitt assigned him, and to which his ambition aspired, almost broke down his feeble constitution, and for some time he was prostrated by a malignant fever, the result of over anxiety and severe mental exertions.

Not alone is Quebec protected from invasion by the river St. Lawrence and its own stupendous height, but to the North-East the river Charles intercepts the assault of the enemy, whilst the river Montmorency cuts it off from the plains. This river runs into the St. Lawrence, about three miles to the East of the city, falling over the cliffs indented by its rush, and forming a most pleasing picture, and being deservedly considered the most delightful cascade in North America. After attempting various plans of attack, now from Point Levi, now from the Montmorency river—positions from which because of the nature of the surroundings, and the watchfulness of their men, it was found impossible to dislodge the enemy—Wolfe, at last, after due deliberation and consultation with his officers, consented to a plan suggested by Colonel Townsend. This plan was hazardous in the extreme, and, from its nature, doubtful as a means to the end in view, the idea being to sail past the citadel, land below the cliffs about three miles westward up the river, and then scale the heights.

The conception was bold and daring, but the prospects of camping in the open, inactive during a whole winter, seemed to nerve the young leader to essay the apparently impossible task. About this time he wrote to a friend as follows :—" My constitution is entirely ruined, and I have not the consolation of having done anything serviceable to the State, nor have I any prospects of doing anything just now." He considered the part he took in securing Arcadia as nothing as long as Quebec was in the hands of the enemy, and one of his soldiers has told how he wrote for them the few lines that follow indicative of his frame of mind and of what he considered a soldier's duty to be :

> " Why, soldiers, why
> Should we be melancholy, boys ?
> Why soldiers, why,
> Whose duty is to die ? "

It was now September. Winter would soon be upon them. There was not a day to lose. Attacks from Levi Point and Montmorency were futile. He cannot have the desired co-operation of Johnston and Amherst until after winter, and, without their aid, it is clear the English ministry did not intend Wolfe to achieve the wished-for capture of Quebec. Wolfe, however, made up his mind, and, at midnight on the 12th September, he gave orders for all his small rowing boats to prepare to land his forces on the beach above the city. It was truly a weird sight, those boats loaded with armed men, carrying their muskets and swords and spears, ready to do and dare and die. Silently the valiant crews, aided by the gloom of the dusk, and the shade of the cliffs, with muffled oars, glided along the quiet waters. Not a sound was heard louder than that of leaves falling from the trees in Autumn, not a voice was audible, beyond a subdued whisper, not even an unguarded splash from the harmonious oars. All went merry as a marriage bell. It was a romantic expedition, carried out with calm deliberation and caution, in the dusky shadows of a cool night, with no light to guide except the reflection of the twinkling stars in the blue waters.

Whilst the little fleet with its 5,000 men was, as noiselessly as possible, hastening to the point planned for disembarkation, a sentinel on the outposts of Montcalm's camp, hearing a rustling noise cries out *Qui va la ?* One from the flotilla below answers in good French *La France.* He was a Captain well versed in the language, and instructed in the passwords to use if challenged. Again the sentinel cried out *A quel Regiment ?* and the answer came *De la Reine.* It happened that a regiment was expected down the river that night from the opposite end of the fortifications. The sentinel was, therefore, satisfied, and his contented *Passe* rang out on the calm night air.

Whilst this momentous expedition was hastening towards the landing place beyond, Wolfe, their young general, was seemingly indifferent to all danger, and poet and litterateur as he was, had been heard during the passage to repeat in a low voice, some lines from "Grey's Elegy," which poem had just been published.

> " The boast of heraldry, the pomp of power,
>   And all that beauty, all that wealth e'er gave,
>   Await alike the inevitable hour ;
>   The path of glory leads but to the grave."

" Now, gentlemen," he was heard in tremulous voice to say, " I would rather be the author of that poem than take Quebec."

Again, however, the scene was changed. The men had reached the landing place, a cave by the water's edge, the only available point from which, by almost insurmountable pathways and devious ways, the heights above might be reached. Soon the troops were in motion, and began the hazardous and painful ascent to the cliff, two hundred feet above, and at last, after much delay, all were safely landed on the plains above. They were able, after much exertion, to pull up the rocks one piece of artillery. The general arranged his men, and placed himself at their head, ready for action. Their ascent gave the alarm to the French guards, who fired a few ineffectual volleys down the cliffs on the 78th Highlanders, who made a great noise by scrambling among the trees and underwood, and soon the camp in the city was up in arms. It was for French Quebec, alas! too late to sound the alarm : already the British troops stood in battle array, with arms ready. Wolfe, like a lion roused to pounce on his prey, impatiently waiting to lead his forces into action.

When Montcalm learned that Wolfe and his forces were in line for battle on the Plains of Abraham, he rashly, though bravely, determined to lead out his troops from their fortifications and give him battle outside the citadel. He said, as he approached the army of Wolfe, " I see them where they ought not to be : if we must fight I will crush them." Soon battle was joined, the two armies led in person by their respective commanders. The English forces amounted to 5,000 well chosen, tried veterans. The French numbered about 8,000, mainly composed of Canadian Militia. Both generals led in the charge. Montcalm, surrounded by the most valiant and skilled part of his forces, led the centre of his command, whilst Wolfe commanded the right wing of his forces. The attack was fierce and well sustained on both sides. Wolfe, however, allowed the enemy to expend their first volley, and make the first onslaught with the light troops, before he commanded his men to hurl a volley at close range into the ranks of the enemy. This well ordered and well executed command staggered and confused the troops of Montcalm, and Wolfe with undaunted courage, led in the advance charge, and followed up the advantage gained. Soon confusion and rout were visible everywhere in the French ranks. Still the brave French general took up his position in the next embankment, and presented a solid front to his foe, but again Wolfe, by superior generalship forced them to fall back, and carried their trench by storm. In the meantime, in the midst of the wild fury and confusion of the melee, fought at close quarters, in narrow streets and around embankments, both generals were mortally wounded. Wolfe was struck by a cannon shot, but not wishing his brave soldiers to witness him fall accepted the assistance of an aide de camp, and quietly withdrew out of view of his troops. Townsend, second in command, led on the charge, but already the day was fought and the battle won. The French fled in confusion in every direction. Wolfe made anxious inquiry of the lieutenant who knelt by his side, assuaging the pain of his wound, and when he heard a soldier near him cry out, " See, they run," he raised himself on his elbow and asked, " Who run ? " as if he had been roused from slumber. When told it was the routed remnants of Montcalm's army he gave orders for a soldier to proceed to Colonel Birtan and tell him to make haste and lead a regiment down to Charles river to cut off the French retreat by the bridge. When those around brought water to dress his wound he told them it was useless, as his end was near, but when he was assured that the object of the bold stroke he had planned had been gained and that Quebec was captured he said, " God be praised, I will now die in peace." His death was mourned by the whole English nation and a monument to his memory was placed in Westminster Abbey, where his body is laid.

The vanquished general only lived a few days after his rival. He was a brave and chivalrous antagonist. If he failed to hold the fort of Quebec, it was not for want of courage. He laid down his life in front of an army that was unworthy to have so brave a commander. He was heard to say, before expiring, that if he had such soldiers as Wolfe commanded, instead of the untried and untractable Canadians that he led, the result would have been different. When told that his end was at hand he thanked God that he would not live to see Quebec surrendered, and having resigned his command into the hands of the Governor of the city, he spent the night before he expired in prayer and preparation for death. To the governor, he said, resigning his charge. " I commend to your keeping the honour of France. I refuse to interfere any further in temporal affairs. I have business to attend to of greater moment than your ruined garrison and this wicked country. My time is short. I shall pass this night with God and prepare myself for death. I wish you all comfort and to be happily extricated from your present perplexities." He then called for his chaplain, who with the Bishop of the Colony, remained with him through the night. He died early next morning. Thus passed away, in the prime of life, a true soldier of France, and a pious member of the Catholic Church. A monument in later years stands on the Plains of Abraham on opposite sides of which are written the names of Wolfe and Montcalm—two brave and illustrious foes who laid down their lives for country's sake on the very plain where their memory is thus fittingly handed down to future ages.

On 18th September, the Governor of Quebec surrendered the city in the name of France to Townsend, who succeeded Wolfe in command of the English forces. In a short time, the St. Lawrence, from its entrance to the Lake, was in the hands of the English.

Montreal was the last stronghold to yield to the successful army. In a little time the troops were shipped to the West Indies, and there also they gave a further proof of their efficiency by capturing those Colonies and expelling the French armies. In 1762 a Treaty was signed in Paris by which England became master of Canada, and all the territory East of the Mississippi. Spain had granted her the territory West from the Mississippi to the Rocky mountains. During the wars England captured Havanna from the Spaniards, and now in return for receiving back this island, she ceded Florida to England. We see now at the end of these Colonial wars that England and Spain possessed the whole of North America. The French and Dutch, who did so much in exploring and colonizing the continent, had yielded their sovereignty to the superior force of England.

LEXINGTON AND CONCORD.

THE English Parliament, hoping to deprive the New 'England States of almost every vestige of their ancient liberties, passed an Act for "better regulating the government of Massachusetts Bay," by which Act the Royal Governor was empowered to appoint all the civil authorities, and have also the nomination of juries—functions hitherto vested in the people. We can see in this claim a foreshadowing of the odious jury-packing system that was so common in the last century in Ireland. All public meetings, unless for election purposes, were prohibited, and any person indicted for any capital offence, committed in aiding the magistracy, might be sent by the Governor to England for trial. All trade with Boston, "the ringleader," as Lord North said, in every riot, was banned. Massachusetts people stood loyal to their cause. They resolved in Convention that no obedience was due to any of the recent Acts of Parliament; the garrison party became known as "Tories," and the popular party as "Rebels."

Prior to the arrival of Washington in the summer of 1775, and before the Second National Convention at Philadelphia, in May of same year, two engagements with the enemy had been fought around Boston, the battle of Concord and Lexington, and the battle of Bunker's Hill. From the closing of the port of Boston until this time, when open hostilities began, most of the Northern States had been actively engaged in forming companies, and equipping militia for the emergency which, to all, had become evident and imminent. Rhodes Island and Connecticut made the cause of Massachusetts their own. The Committee of Correspondence had done its work effectively in raising public opinion, and focussing the

eyes of all on the plague spot of English tyranny in their
midst. But more than words, more than resolutions, more
than petitions and addresses were urgently needed—men ready
for action in the field, money and ammunition, and union of
forces for resistance were required—and all the States were
preparing to do their duty. But the idea of lying down under
odious laws, and becoming slaves, was not to be dreamt of by
the descendants of those who sailed for Plymouth in the Mayflower in the 17th century. No, the descendants of the Pilgrim
Fathers, and those on whom fell the mantle of Williams the
Reformer, could never, without a blow, become dispossessed
of their charter and their rights. Soon the watchword of
Patrick Henry became the rallying cry of most of the States.
" Liberty or Death ! " and the wished for opportunity
arrived, which was to try the souls and courage of the " rebels,"
as the English courteously called the revolutionaries. On 18th
April, 1775, General Gage had been informed that John Hancock and Samuel Adams, two " rebel " chiefs, were at Concord,
some eighteen miles from Boston, and that here also some
magazines and stores had been consigned by the minute men.
Gage, accordingly, in a most cautious manner, had a detachment of his troops, amounting to 800, under Major Pitcairn,
despatched to Concord in the middle of the night. It was
impossible for the troops to attempt even the most secret move
of a hostile nature, which was not communicated from the
besieged to the friends of liberty outside the ramparts. Soon
messengers were sent to warn the people along the route, and,
like wind, the riders flew from Boston to Lexington and Concord, breaking through the men on guard who had been placed
to intercept communications. Longfellow has rendered
memorable, for all time, the famous ride of Paul Revere, who
succeeded in out-running on his charger the pursuing soldiers
and enabling the leaders to escape. Let us quote the inspiring
lines :—

" You know the rest in the books you have read,
How the British Regulars fired and fled,

How the farmer gave them ball for ball,
From behind each fence and farmyard wall,
Chasing the Red Coats down the lane,
Then crossing the field to escape again ;
Under the tree at the turn of the road,
And only pausing to fire and load.
So through the night rode Paul Revere,
And so through the night went the cry aloud,
To every cottage and village and farm,
A cry of defiance and not of fear."

It was on the square at Lexington, the first blood was shed in defence of liberty, when a volley of bullets were fired on seventy militia men who were drawn up in the open. Major Pitcairn seeing the little band stand firm, when he shouted out roughly " Disperse, you rebels ; throw down your arms and disperse," ordered his men to fire, and some of the sturdy militia men were mortally wounded. Then after discharging three volleys after the minute men who fled, he proceeded triumphantly on his way to Concord, leaving eighteen of the patriots on the green sward. There was little left for the troops to destroy at Concord, as timely notice had reached them. However, we are told, they destroyed two old cannons, scattered sixty barrels of flour, and committed other acts of spoliation on the inhabitants, and at noon began their march back towards Boston.

They were not permitted to march alone. During the morning and day grim-faced sons of liberty of the " Ironside " type, each man carrying a gun, could be seen hurrying towards Concord. The minute men rallied in their thousands in response to the hurried summons which spread near and far, from tower and steeple, and by ringing of church bells. From workshop and farm, old and young, readily hurried to the heights along the route, and secreted themselves behind the massive oaks along the line of march. Although no formally appointed leader was in command the amiable patriot, Dr. Warren, and the fearless Mayor Buttrick led the irregular and constantly increasing forces of the rustic warriors, as they, in hot pursuit, chased the retreating enemy. As many as 300 of that 800 who set out early that morning were disabled from returning to Boston, and had not Lord Percy on their headlong hunt, reinforced them with fresh troops, few, if any, would have escaped to tell their tale of defeat. We are told that so furious was the chase, and so madly did they run, that when assistance came they lay down panting on the grass with their tongues protruding. In this first encounter we can see similar tactics pursued by the patriots to those used against the pompous Braddock during the Colonial war in the Ohio district. This encounter put new life into the patriots. It taught them what their leaders well knew, that the Redcoats were neither invulnerable nor invincible. "The minute men" might be rough rustics with homespun jackets and home-knit caps, but they were sure marksmen, trained in the forest and plain to take down with sure aim the wild duck and deer, turkey and goose, that swept over their plantations.

The forces of the Colonies now began to multiply in and around Cambridge, a position some miles outside of Boston, which they fortified and were entrenched in.

Macay in his history of the United States says of this battle :—" The news of the affair of Lexington—the first blood shed in the defence of liberty upon the American soil, produced an extraordinary excitement, varying of course according to the feelings and convictions of its recipients. By the more ardent partiots, secretly anxious to throw off the allegiance of England, it was welcomed, as the sequel of a deadly quarrel ; and by those who yet hoped for a reconciliation with the parent country it was, for the same reason, regarded with sorrow and alarm."

When news reached England of the defeat of Pitcairn's forces, the Lords and Commons almost unanimously presented the King with an address declaring " That a rebellion actually existed in the province of Massachusetts Bay, and they besought his Majesty to adopt measures to enfore the authority of the supreme legislature, and solemnly assured him that it was their fixed resolve, at the hazard of their lives and property, to stand by him against his rebellious subjects."

All commerce was now by Act of Parliament forbidden with the New England States, and the right of fishing on the banks of Newfoundland was denied to the Colonists. But why further recount the Acts of a British Parliament? It was now, on both sides, war *a outrance*.

BUNKER'S HILL.

WHAT democratic breast does not still feel the thrill of many emotions at the mention of Bunker's Hill? The name recalls a day when for the first time the scales fell from the eyes of British tyranny and the lesson of Concord was enforced by the astounding discovery that the rude Colonial farmer was no mere rebel, no casual guerilla, but a formidable belligerent, and capable of strange new tactics not set down in the rules of war. To us, who have seen history repeating itself again in England's South African wars, there is something almost ludicrous in the similarity of the circumstances at Bunker's Hill and Colenso, and the failure of British generalship in 1900 to benefit by the experience of the previous century.

Around Boston, after the battle of Concord, a heterogenous multitude of men had assembled. They had no legally appointed leader. They had not, until after Congress had been assembled in May at Philadelphia, with Hancock in the chair, been formally recognised, and duly adopted by the representatives of the States, as the Union army, the nucleus of that force that was to be commanded by Washington. Gage had kept very quiet after his first brush with the patriots.

E

Soon, however, his 4,000 soldiers were augmented to 10,000 by the arrival of four vessels of veterans, commanded by the best generals in the English army, amongst these Howe, Burgoyne and Clinton. The American forces were in good position. They formed a semi-circle round Boston, and held some commanding positions to the right, left, and centre of the city, which stands jutting out on the bay facing the East. The Dorchester Heights stand to the South-East, whilst Cambridge is situated more inland, to the West. Charleston peninsula faces towards the North, on which is Bunker and Breed Hills.

The armies were not far removed from each other. It was almost possible, when much merriment existed in the jovial British camps, for the patriot forces to hear the boisterous laughter of the redcoats. Hope and courage were fast taking possession of old Putnam's camp. Men and money and provisions were daily coming in from near and far. Georgia vied with Virginia, and Connecticut was nothing behind Massachusetts in the number of recruits it forwarded to swell the ranks around Boston. It was from Connecticut that Israel Putnam came. He was told, whilst he ploughed his lands, that war was commenced at Boston. The old veteran who, in days gone by, had fought the Indians in many an encounter, no sooner heard the news than he left his plough, took down his old musket from the wall, mounted his horse just loosed from the yoke, bade a hurried farewell to his friends and family, and joined his countrymen in the cause of liberty.

The arrival of Putnam gave courage to the patriots. He had been famed, near and far, for his deeds of valour and his hair-breadth escapes. When he arrived he was hailed along with Colonel Prescott and Dr. Warren, as a trusted leader of the forces.

In June it was arranged by the English generals that they should lead forth their forces from the city, and commence their work of conquering and subjugation. The task to Gage and the other generals seemed one neither difficult nor likely to be prolonged. Were not those men that they espied in the distance through their glasses, untrained farmers, hurriedly assembled, having no generals of fame to lead them—no skill in arms—men without order or discipline, without ammunition or arms. For rifles, behold, we discern rusty fowling pieces charged by powder and fired by flint. They have little lead, no bayonets, no swords, and if they had were they trained in their use ? It was no wonder, then, that on the morning of the famed battle of Bunker's Hill, Gage, as he passed under review from his watchtower with spy glass in hand this undisciplined mass of men, asked of some one near him, " Will the rebels fight ? " The answer came to his ears, " Yes, to the last drop of blood."

The news flew across to the slopes of Cambridge that, on the 18th June, the English would sally forth from Boston, and attack their adversaries before they could realise the onslaught. They had laid their plans so that by a surprise, as they thought, they might slay or capture the rebels at their own choice. Did they find them napping ? No, on the night of the 16th, Putnam and Prescott led down from their entrenchments, in the silent hours of the night, a strong body of their forces, along the neck near the sea, within earshot of the sentinels as they cried out their " all right " across the Charles river on Boston slopes. Steadily they proceed forward along the sea bank. They could see distinctly in the harbour the English ships, but, heedless of these things, they resolutely passed on, carrying with them spades and mattocks, powder, horns and flints, and fifteen balls per man. To procure sufficient lead we are told they had to melt the lead organ pipes of Cambridge Cathedral. Soon they climbed the heights of Breed and Bunker Hills, and the sounds of mattock and spade were heard, as they dug and delved and felled trees to fortify themselves on the Bunker Heights. They cast a redoubt around the summit, and raised a formidable line of fortifications, and they filled up the entrenchment with green mown grass and newly-felled timber. Lo ! In the morning the

English open their eyes in bewilderment to behold a fearless
and a fortified army facing them from the same heights they
had intended to occupy on the following day. Gage now saw
that to remain longer in Boston would be difficult and dangerous ; there was nothing left for him but to storm the fortress
on Bunker's Hill. This he resolved to essay on June 17th. It
was a hot summer's morning and the sun shone down bright
and strong on the cohorts of the ready ranks of the redcoats.
They were light-hearted and gay. They carried with them
provisions for three days, this fine muster of trained and tried
veterans. They presented a bold and manly front as they
crossed the river Charles with muskets and bayonets, and gold-
braided vests, shining with gilt buttons, reflecting their glittering lustre in the noon-day rays of the scorching sun. Soon the
word of command came from the English general to fall into
line, and prepare to rush the entrenchments on the heights
above. Steadily they approach, wading as they march knee
deep in the luxuriant grass that covers the slopes. Nearer
and nearer the American lines they come, carrying baggage,
over 100 pounds weight strapped to their uniform. Each,
besides his musket and supply of balls, carried three days'
provisions. Now, they fire a futile volley towards the Heights
at long range. During the approach, from steeple and belfry,
from roof and cliff, ten thousand eyes are following the scene
below. Hearts in anxious expectation are throbbing in many
a bosom, and prayers are ascending to the God of battle from
many lips as the fearful moment draws nearer with each
lessening of the distance that separates the combatants.
What, think you, were Putnam and Prescott, and Warren
doing and saying during these momentous moments ? They
were passing to and fro along their ranks, encouraging the
men—if the souls of such stirring patriots required encouragement—to do their duty. Their orders were few and terse.
" Keep low, keep cool," and, to quote the words of old Israel
Putnam, " spare your powder until you see the white of their
eyes." The orders were strictly carried out. As soon as,

and no sooner, than the enemy came rushing up almost to the breastworks, a volley from a thousand muskets, well aimed by resolute men, sure of their mark, hurled them back with frightful havoc, pell mell down the slopes. The officers rallied them in their headlong stampede, and again faced them in files towards the Heights, and, again, a well-aimed volley drove them back with diminished ranks. So dreadful was the havoc of this second attack that General Gage, who led them at one time, stood alone in the ranks. It was at this critical juncture that Clinton, on seeing the confusion in the decimated ranks, hurried over to the aid of Gage with a thousand fresh troops. At last the officers in command, who were not among the slain, rallied for a third charge, their troops now reinforced. The order was given to fire, fix bayonets, and storm the redoubts. This third attempt, although followed with renewed slaughter among the redcoats, was successful. The Americans had now fired their last round of ammunition, and as they were not supplied with bayonets, their position in the trenches now scaled by the enemy became untenable. It is true their courage did not fail them, even when they were in a hand-to-hand encounter against the polished steel of skilled swordsmen. With the butt ends of their muskets they faced the foe, but the encounter was hopeless. The order was given to the patriots to retreat, and boldly, steadily, and defiantly, in good order, they recrossed the neck, in view and range of the harbour, to join their comrades around Cambridge.

They were driven back and nominally defeated, but who will deny to those gallant men the honour of a moral victory? The Americans were neither captured nor cut off from their base. Their losses were few compared with the English, although for the time the encounter lasted, great indeed was the slaughter. About four hundred on the American side and about one thousand on the English side fell dead or wounded on the heights of Bunker's Hill. The position gained by Gage was trifling. The fortifications seized were the work of a few hours' toil by the patriot forces in the early hours of a June morning. It was an inspiration to the whole army at Cambridge, the courage displayed by their comrades on Bunker's Hill. No wonder that Washington exclaimed when he heard the news of the battle, " Thank God, the liberties of the country are safe."

Amongst the roll of prominent patriots who fell at this battle, the most prominent was the immortal Dr. Joseph Warren. He was an experienced physician, a ripe scholar, and a leading patriot of unimpeachable honour and integrity. He was an active force from the first against English tyranny, trusted by the people and exercising great influence amongst them ; and he was foremost in the ranks of valour that day on the heights of Bunker's Hill. He was almost the last to make his retreat, when the English stormed the entrenchments, and his daring courage lost him his life. He was, indeed, the first notable martyr to the cause of freedom.

THE
DECLARATION OF INDEPENDENCE.

Samuel Adams of Boston was the first—and he stood alone —who declared for Independence at the commencement of the Revolution. Events had marched at a quick pace towards separation in the course of twelve months. The King had insulted the American delegates, and had refused to read or consider the petitions they bore from their suffering countrymen. The British armies had entered their ports, burned their towns, pillaged their property, slain their people, and branded them as rebels and traitors. Some 30,000 Hessian soldiers, paid as mercenaries at the rate of almost twenty million dollars, had been shipped from Prussian ports to conquer and slay and subdue the Colonials. Writers in every state had been preparing the public mind for separation. Songs and ballads were everywhere sung over the continent, rousing the patriotism of the people, and filling them with vengeance against England. The Watchword of Patrick Henry," Give me liberty or give me death," soon became the war-cry of the nation.

Lord Macaulay in his essay on the Earl of Chatham has the following apt description of the process that led up to Independence :—" Now the quarrel between England and the North American Colonies took a gloomy and terrible aspect. Oppression provoked resistance ; resistance provoked fresh resistance ; resistance was made the pretext for fresh oppression. The warnings of all the greatest statesmen of the age were lost on an imperious court and a deluded nation. Soon the Colonial Senate confronted the British Parliament. Then the Colonial Militia crossed bayonets with the British regiments. At length the Commonwealth was torn asunder. Two millions of Englishmen, who fifteen years ago had been as loyal to their

Prince, and as proud of their country, as the people of Kent or Yorkshire, separated themselves by a solemn act from the empire. For a time it seemed that the insurgents would struggle to small purpose against the financial and military means of the Mother-country. But disasters following one another in rapid succession, rapidly dispelled the delusions of national vanity."

Virginia, which gave so many men of giant intellects and spotless patriotism to American liberty, was the first state to openly resolve by Act of Congress for separation from Britain. She instructed her delegates to Philadelphia, Charles Patterson and John Cahill, prior to their departure to the second National Congress, in these memorable words :—" We instruct you to cause a total separation from Great Britain, as soon as possible, and a constitution to be established, with a full representative by free and frequent elections. As America is the last country of the world which has contended for her liberty, so she may be the most free and happy, taking the advantage of her liberties and strength, and having the experience of all before to profit by. The Supreme Being hath left it in our power to choose what government we please for our civil and religious happiness. Good government and the prosperity of mankind can alone be in the Divine intention. We pray, therefore, that under the superintending Providence of God, the Ruler of the Universe, a government may be established in America, the most free, happy and permanent, that human wisdom can contrive and maintain."

The hope of reconciliation had at last died over the States. The wish for separation soon became universal. It was brought plainly home to the minds of all that England could never be to them the loving Motherland that they doted on in boyhood days. To all thoughtful minds there was but one honourable course open for patriotic Americans, and that was the course implied in the word Independence. The word sounded from end to end of the Colonies, and soon the voices of the delegates could be heard in loud and clamorous tones in

Independence Hall, proclaiming aloud that " we are and will be free and independent." The statesmen in Congress saw clearly that the time was ripe to assert their rights. If they asked the aid of foreign nations in their struggle, they were more likely to obtain it when they had cut, by their own deliberate will and action, their connection with England and asserted their independence as a nation. Circumstances for a long time had irresistibly tended to this result. The royal authority was virtually abolished. Each State had set up a Colonial system of government, and it only now remained for all the States combined to pass a resolution. This resolution was proposed by Richard Henry Lee of Virginia, on the 7th June. The motion, which was seconded by John Adams, was as follows :—" That the United Colonies are, and ought to be, free and independent States, and that their political connection with Great Britian is, and ought to be, dissolved."

This proposition was debated for a long time by all the delegates, and among its opponents were some of America's best patriots, who thought the occasion inopportune as long as England had not finally closed the doors against reconciliation, but eventually it was passed by a majority of seven States to six. After a little time all the States, by their delegates, gave their adhesion to the resolution, and a committee of five was appointed to draw up a Declaration of Independence. These were Thomas Jefferson, John Adams, Benjamin Franklin, Livingston and Sherman. It was Thomas Jefferson, a young Virginian lawyer of remarkable abilities, who drew it up in its present form, with the exception of a word here and there interpolated by Adams and Franklin. The document drawn up by these men is a masterpiece. Into it, as some one has asserted, Jefferson succeeded in pouring the soul of the American Continent. He appeals to the Supreme Ruler for guidance to produce his monumental work, and some enthusiastic admirers of Jefferson and the Declaration have asserted that it was inspired by Divine providence.

Let us cull from Jefferson's notes some extracts which will show how mature was the judgment of the delegates who passed the Act and on what solid and irresistible reasons they based their convictions about the expediency and necessity of unanimously resolving to separate from England John Hancock of Massachusetts was chairman of Convention, and he in exhorting all to be of one mind said: " Let us all hang together," to which the quick-witted sage, Franklin, made answer, " Yes, let us all hang together or we shall all be hanged separately."

At page thirteen, Volume I., of the Memoirs of Thomas Jefferson, we find the following:—" We argued that no gentleman had opposed the policy or right of separation from Britain, or did anyone assert that we should ever renew our connection. They only opposed its being declared at the present time. By a declaration of Independence we should be only declaring a fact which already exists. That, as to the people or Parliament of England we had always been independent of them, their restraints on our trade deriving efficacy from our acquiescence only, and not from any rights they possessed of imposing them ; and that so far our connection had been federal only, and was now dissolved by the commencement of hostilities." " The bonds that bound us to the King are now broken, when, by Act of Parliament, he has declared us out of his protection. In fact he has levied war on us ; how is he then our protector ? It is a certain position in law that allegiance and protection are reciprocal, the one ceasing when the other is withdrawn." " Delegates don't need power from their constituencies for declaring a fact or existing truth." " The people wait for the Congress to lead them ; they are in favour of the measure." " That a declaration of Independence alone can render it consistent with European delicacy, for European powers to treat with us, or even to receive an Ambassador from us." " That it is necessary to lose no time in entering into alliance with continental European nations, as we need urgently to open up trade with other nations, for our people who want clothes and money for paying the war levies."

The debates on the declaration continued for three days, viz., the 2nd, 3rd and 4th July. On the evening of the third day, the declaration was reported by the Committee of the whole house, agreed to by all except Dickenson, and signed the same evening. The question of slavery then, as seventy-five years later, was a ticklish question with some of the delegates and was touched upon lightly ; also, the harsh phrases about England, which the circumstances of the country might have admitted were moderated out of consideration for the more moderate delegates, who did not entirely despair of renewed union with the Motherland. The declaration put an end to all doubt and wavering as to what the aims of the people of America were. It was the deliberate conviction of all thoughtful men that America never could be again dependent on England. The course of public events had worked up public opinion for the great historic event ; the civil, political and military activities of the country had all been aiming for some time previous at the one goal—that of Independence.

It was a courageous resolve of the delegates, an heroic pledge they gave each other, in the name of their separate States :—"We will support the Declaration in war, or in peace; we will back up our work in Convention, and if necessary, we will sacrifice our lives, our fortunes, our honour, in defence of a united America free from English control." We must admire the native energy of those men, surrounded as they were, and pressed on every side by British arms. They came of a brave stock of pioneer planters, who fled to America seeking the freedom to live as they desired. They were unaccustomed to tyranny from any quarter. They were conscious of their power to govern themselves and of their capacity to fight in defence of their rights. The invasion of their country by the Motherland made them turn from their guardian protector and rely on themselves, and they were beginning, at last, to recognise the strength that lay in Union. No sooner was the declaration signed by the delegates than they formed themselves into a Committee to draw up terms of confederation, and define the powers of Congress. The task of drafting a code of laws for all, and at the same time preserving unanimity was no easy one considering the mutual jealousies of the independent States. People brought up as Colonials were, could ill submit to yield any of their independence to a Congress with merely delegated powers. In their jealousies we see the beginning of the fatal troubles about State rights, which led to the secession of States in the middle of last century and to Civil War.

Many weary days were wasted debating details, and many of the States were slow in signing the Articles of Confederation. It was as late as March, 1781, that Maryland ratified the details of Convention. It was two years before the debates ceased on the Articles, and on the 9th of July, 1778, only ten States had given their assent. New Jersey and Delaware, however, followed the ten some months later. In the late conformity of these two States may be traced the influence of the loyalist population, and it is worth remarking that during the war, New Jersey and Delaware were less active in co-operation than the ten which signed at first. The trouble experienced in coming to a common understanding on the terms of Confederation arose over the question of slavery, the relative voting powers of each State, and the levies and taxes. But one article which was of imminent import was early debated and agreed to, owing to the necessity of raising funds to conduct the war. It was as follows :—" All charges of war and all other expenses that shall be incurred for the common defence or general welfare, and allowed by the United States assembled, shall be defrayed out of a common treasury, which shall be supplied by the several Colonies in proportion to the number of inhabitants of every age, sex, and quality, except Indians not paying taxes in each colony, a true account of which shall be, every three years, transmitted to the

The two men who contributed most in Congress to bring about and perfect the memorable Act of the 4th July were John Adams and Thomas Jefferson. " At the end of this great day," says Bancroft, " the mind of John Adams heaved like the ocean after a storm. The question decided was the greatest ever debated in America, and a greater, perhaps, never was nor will be decided among men. When one looks back over the chain of political events, the causes and effects, one is surprised at the suddenness, as well as the greatness, of this resolution. Britain has been filled with folly and America with wisdom." John Adams himself, fully realising the importance of the event and the consequences following, wrote thus, with his heart filled with great resolve :—" It is the will of heaven that the two countries should be severed for ever. It may be the will of heaven that America shall suffer calamities still more wasting and distress yet more dreadful. If this be so, the furnace of affliction produces refinement in States as well as in individuals, but I submit all my hopes and fears to an over-ruling Providence in which, unfashionable as the faith may be, I firmly believe." Thomas Jefferson, after Washington, is the name best remembered in the history of the Revolution and early Republic. He is remembered firstly as the author or writer of the Declaration of Independence ; and secondly as the Father of Republican Democracy. He was a remarkable man. Like Washington, he was over six feet in height, and reared on a Virginian farm, He was born in the year 1743. The son of a well-to-do settler he received a good primary and secondary education, and was trained for law in the College of William and Mary. He had many accomplishments, being at the same time a good horseman, a skilled violinist, and a fluent and agreeable conversationalist. He was a most effective writer, and has left a monument of epistles and essays which were no mean contribution to the literature of his time. He was a most earnest worker in the cause of his country, during the Revolution crisis, both as national delegate to Philadelphia in the Virginian Burgess, and as Governor in the later years of the war of patriotic Virginia.

When the war was concluded he represented his country at the French court, and by his diplomacy aided much in cementing continental alliances, and in developing and opening a mart for trade and commerce for the infant Republic. When Washington became President, he was a leading member of the Cabinet, and after John Adams' term of office he ruled the Republic as President from 1801 till 1809. He was a wise ruler and a statesman of far-seeing vision. He purchased Lusitania from Napoleon, and thereby secured over a million square miles of territory for his country, and gave Americans predominance for all time in North America. He died at a ripe age in his beautiful country home at Monticello, on the 4th July, 1826. During the years of his retirement he interested himself in farming, spent the evening among his books, wrote some of those charming letters and essays which have been preserved in four volumes by the editorial care of his grandson. He was visited in his later days by statesmen and scholars in his backwoods home, and contemporary history has handed down his name from those days as " the sage of Monticello."

THE MASSACRE OF WYOMING.

The eloquent protest of Chatham, with which all readers of this period of history are familiar, against the use of mercenaries and savages in the war, was but a case of " wasting sweetness on the desert air." His oratory fell upon deaf ears: almost three-fourths of the votes of Parliament were given for the continuation of the barbarous practice. The English King and his Cabinet, too proud in the recollection of their past prestige in military achievements, could not bring themselves to look on it as possible that they should suffer defeat in warfare at the hands of the hitherto subservient colonials. No, the rebels of America must be subdued by every means that God and nature supplied. No doubt, as the great statesman had shown, the principle was a base and brutal one for a civilized people to propound, but it has ever been the maxim with John Bull in his foreign and Colonial wars that " might is right." The principle plainly implied " we intend to conquer our enemies by fair means, if possible, but conquer we must by any means, right or wrong." Surely the British people, unless ashamed of their own traditions, should be the last to complain against the formula wrongly attributed to the Jesuit—" the end justifies the means." At any rate the uncontradicted fact of history is that the wild Indians, under the protection of the British army, supplied with English gold and English rum and ammunition, were encouraged to roam uncontrolled, spreading havoc, slaughtering and burning and pillaging the backwoodsmen from Niagara and round the borders of the six nations down to the Ohio and the Virginian borders. General Schulyer, who was superseded at Saratoga by Gates, and who was a man with large tracts of property on the Indian frontier, in the Lake Champlain district, wrote Congress early in '78 that a number of Mohawks and many of the Onondagas, Cayagas and Sesicas tribes were preparing to commence hostilities almost immediately, in pursuance of the concerted plan mapped out for them by Carleton, the Commander-in-Chief, and Governor Hamilton, who had headquarters in district. The General advised the plan which, though approved by Congress, proved abortive—of carrying the war into Indian territory to avert the danger to the inhabitants of the frontier settlements. The consequence of allowing this warning to pass unheeded was seen in some of the most harrowing scenes of cruelty that are recorded in the history of the Revolution. The valleys of Wyoming, Mohawk and Cherry were literally deluged with blood ; the war of extermination was carried out against these isolated districts without pity or remorse. Death, desolation, famine and banishment were the common lot of young and old in these once fertile and happy plantations. The Wyoming valley in Pennsylvania was the prettiest of all the charming valleys on the borderland. Its beauty has been praised in the pages of history, in song and story. Novelists have celebrated it as the American paradise, and have painted in vivid colours the war and desolation that came upon it during the war. The eyes of the civilized world have from time to time been turned to it with a sad interest as artist, poets, or historian has thrown the glamour of art over the tragic story of the slaughter of the innocents that once crimsoned its smiling fields. The poet Campbell has immortalized it in his poem in three cantos, "Gertrude of Wyoming." In the advertisment to an edition of this poem we have the following notice :—" Most of the popular histories of England as well as the American War give an authentic account of the desolation of Wyoming in Pennsylvania which took place in 1778 by an incursion of Indians. The scenery and incidents of the following poem are connected with that event. The testimonies of historians and travellers concur in describing

the infant Colony as one of the happiest spots of human existence, for the hospitable and innocent manners of the inhabitants, the beauty of the country, and the luxuriant fertility of
the soil and climate.   In an evil hour the junction of European
and Indian arms converted this terrestrial paradise into a
frightful waste.   Mr. Isaac Wild informs us that the ruins of
many of the villages perforated with balls and bearing marks
of conflagration were still preserved by the recent inhabitants
when he travelled through America in 1796."

In the poem itself we have the following verses, than
which no more fitting narrative could be given of this typical
Indian massacre :—

Sad was the year by proud oppression driven,
When Transatlantic liberty arose,
Not in the sunshine and the smile of heaven,
But wrapt in whirlwinds and begirt with wars ;
Amidst the strife of fratricidal foes,
Her birth star was the light of burning plains,
Her baptism is the weight of blood that flows
From kindred hearts—the blood of British veins,
And famine tracks her steps and pestilential plains.
  Sweet Wyoming !   The day when thou wert doomed,
  Guiltless, to mourn thy loveliest bowers laid low ;
  When, where of yesterday a garden bloomed
  Death overspread his pall and blackening ashes gloomed.

Delightful Wyoming ! beneath thy skies
The happy shepherd swains had nought to do
But feed their flocks on green declivities,
Or skim, perchance, thy lake with light canoe.
From morn till evening's sweeter pastime grew
With timbrel, when beneath the forests brown
Thy lovely maidens would the dance renew.
  And scarce had Wyoming of war or crime
  Heard, but in Transatlantic story sung,
  For here the exile met from every clime,

F

And spoke in friendship every distant tongue ;
Men from the blood of waning Europe sprung
Were but divided by the running brook.

The Mammoth comes—the foe—the monster Brant,
With all his howling, desolating band,
These eyes have seen their blade and burning pine,
Awake at once, and silence half your land ;
Red is the cup they drank, but not with wine,
Awake and watch to-night, or see no morning shine !
Whoop after whoop with oath the ear assailed,
As if unearthly fiends had burst their bar,
While rapidly the marksman's shot prevailed,
And aye, as if for death, some lonely trumpet wailed.
    Accursed Brant ! He left of all my tribe,
    Nor man, nor child, nor thing of living birth,
    No ! Not the dog that watched my household hearth,
    Escaped that night of blood upon our plains.

Campbell, it should be stated, learned that the references to Brant's cruelty were unjust, and desired that Brant's name should remain in the poem as that of a creature of fiction.

The Wyoming settlement was embosomed in the heart of the Indian territory. It was sixty miles from the nearest plantations on the Delaware ; it was only accessible through pathless wilds. The six nations were their nearest neighbours, being only a few hours' journey distant. When the war broke out in '75 the people for the most part espoused the cause of their country, and out of their number, which did not exceed three thousand, they sent three hundred picked men to fight in the Continental forces under Washington. The defence of their valley fell on a local militia, composed of the older residents and the young. As a protection against assault they built themselves stockades and wooden forts. The only artillery among them was an old four pounder and a minute gun, and their small arms were chiefly old fowling pieces. Some time previous to '78 a number of loyalists from the valley were imprisoned, and the patriots were instrumental in obtaining their imprisonment. When released, instead of returning to their native Wyoming in peace they set off to the Canadian camp and induced Sir John Johnston and Colonel John Butler to come with their " green rangers " and " Brant's Braves " to attack the valley. It came to the knowledge of the inhabitants that an attack was about to be made upon them, and the local militia, under Colonel Dennison were called out ; some sixty Continentals, led by Colonel Zebulon Butler also coming to their aid. The whole available force did not exceed four hundred. When a messenger was sent to Washington for aid from the main army he could not see his way to weaken the forces under him by sending off a regiment to their assistance. To respond to the appeals for aid that came to be general from near and far was beyond his power, nor did he advocate such a policy, thinking that isolated districts should come to each other's aid for mutual protection, offensive and defensive.

The Indians on the borderland converging to the Ohio, and under the Governorship of Hamilton of Detroit, were, as historians of the war allege, incited to outrage their white neighbours. They were encouraged to roam at will, and burn and pillage and even received a bounty for the white men's scalps carried to the British fort. The luxuries of the garrisons were freely distributed among these savages, and they found an easy market among the British for their furs. The wealthy Royalists around were the most deadly foes of these settlers, and they used their savage neighbours to aid in harassing them. When news was carried into Colonel Dennison's camp by a drunken Indian that an attack on them was imminent it was resolved that the women and children should be placed in forts for protection, and that the men in battle array should go forth to meet the foe rather than wait a surprise attack. Colonel Butler did not agree about the advisability of attacking at once, but the militia asked to be led into action. Butler put himself at their head to lead them. The brave Wyoming peasants were impatient to repel the approaching enemy. They feared, if they allowed them to enter their valley, that havoc and desolation would follow to their rich corn fields and to their happy homesteads before aid from outside could reach them. About the beginning of June a force of 1,600, of whom 900 were Indians from the six nations, assembled at Niagara, under the command of Colonel John Butler, and proceeded by the Susquehanna river towards Wyoming. When they reached Fort Wintermoot on the 2nd of July they pitched their camp. It was when the enemy marched so far in their hostile expedition that Colonel Zebulon Butler—a cousin by the way of the British Commander—led out, in single file, his little army of 468 men to oppose the approaching foe. On the 3rd July he held a consultation with his officers, five of whom were old Continentals recruited from Wyoming, who had just returned home from service when they learned of the danger of attack to their friends at home. These officers gave the information that there was no prospect of immediate aid, and that there was nothing for it but to defend alone their homesteads, their wives and children. On hearing this the Colonel gave the order to his brave, but ill-disciplined and unequal force. He expected to surprise the enemy at Wintermoot, but owing to the presence of some Loyalists in the valley, the approach of the attacking party was notified to Colonel John Butler and he had his forces in readiness for the attack. Colonel John Butler commanded in person the British rangers, and Joseph Brant, an Onondaga chief of the Mohawk tribe, led the Indians. The rangers opposed the right flank of the Americans, and the Indians were opposed to them on the left. The attack was made on a level track partly cleared and partly protected by oak shrubbery and yellow pine. It was four in the afternoon when the conflict began. It was entered upon by both forces with fierce determination. At first the American right was pressing back the British, when suddenly from the swamp and shrubbery a band of Indians with upraised tomahawks rushed upon the rear of the Americans.

Still, although attacked in front and rear, the brave Colonials faltered not in their courage and determination to repel the invaders. But, alas, a fatal mistake occured which changed the whole aspect of the battle. Colonel Dennison ordered his men to fall back lest they might be surrounded ; at the same time Colonel Butler, the British Commander, ordered some of his forces to fall round on the right wing of Zebulon's force. The combined effect of these two movements was to throw the militia into confusion. The melee became general. The "falling back" command of the Colonel was taken as a signal for retreat, and the battle became a mere hand-to-hand contest. The onset of the Indians with knife and tomahawk was hideous in the extreme. It was a battle of extermination, and the result was not long doubtful. Each side was equally bold and daring, but four men, savage and white, were more than an equal for one white, and the battlefield became a mere scene of carnage and butchery. The Indians ran forward with musket and tomahawk upraised, shouting and yelling as they felled the surrounding forces. The end was soon ₁eached ; of the entire band led out by Colonel Zebulon Butler 360 lay upon the field of battle. The remnant who escaped the slaughter were either taken prisoners or fled to the mountains and woods. Flags of truce were sent out from the victorious British ranks to Colonel Dennison—they would offer no quarter to Butler and his remnant of Continentals—to surrender, the condition being granted that the lives of the wives and children would be saved. The Colonel did surrender, but alas! the truce was of no avail to prevent the outrages of the Indians. Colonel Dennison remonstrated with Colonel John Butler against these atrocities. " We have surrendered," he said, " our forts and our arms to you on the pledge of your faith that both life and property should be protected. Articles of capitulation are considered sacred by all civilized nations." The Colonel replied " I tell you what, sir, I can do nothing with them, nothing." "The atrocities," says Colonel Shaffner, " perpetrated by the ferocious allies of Colonel Butler at length exceeded endurance, and the savages are represented as being encouraged by the British soldiers in all kinds of atrocities upon the unfortunate inhabitants. The surrender had no sooner been completed than the ruffians of both nations spread through the valley to plunder and destroy. The village of Wilkesbarre, consisting of twenty-three houses, was burnt, the men were separated from their wives and children and butchered, while the others who could not succeed in escaping were subjected to the grossest treatment by the licentious soldiers. Many of the women and children were mercifully relieved from a life of agonizing despair by being shut up in houses which were immediately set on fire. Others succeeded in escaping from the valley to perish like those who had preceded them amid the swamps, without provisions and almost naked. In short, their flight was a scene of widespread and harrowing sorrow. Their despersion being in the hour of the wildest terror, they were scattered singly, in pairs, or in large groups, as chance threw them on their perilous journey. Many, isolated in quest of food, never regained their companions. Many sank exhausted to die on the journey, and their bones were left to track the dismal path towards the Delaware by which they fled to escape from treatment worse than death itself." The work of desolation and extermination was soon complete, and what a few weeks previous presented an image of paradise now exhibited the blackness of solitary desolation.

We have chosen the Wyoming Valley massacre, not because it is the only recorded case of backwood butchery by the Indians, but because it is a typical case to illustrate the terrors and trials endured on the Indian borders by those patriotic and brave pioneers and continent builders. The horrors enacted in a similar Indian raid, led by one Walter Johnston and the famous Brant, about November of the same year, against the inhabitants of Cherry Valley, in New York State, and some fifty miles from New York city, affords another equally abominable instance of the use made of

these savage allies in the Revolution. In this valley the
inhabitants were overpowered by numbers and butchered
without mercy; their homes and chattels and crops were
plundered or burned. "For months after the destruction
of Cherry Valley settlement," observes Lessing, "no eye was
closed in security at night within an area of one hundred miles
and more around. The desolated village of Tryon county,
as that region of New York was then called, was a dark and
bloody ground for full four years, and the records of the woes
of its people have filled volumes." When news of these
thrilling horrors reached Washington and Congress, authority
was at once given to send an expedition, as already asked
for by Schulyer and Butler, to invade the Indian territory.
General Sullivan, with a force of 4,000 regular troops
and about 2,000 militia, was detached to march direct
to Wyoming and through the Indian territory, and if
possible to penetrate to Niagara. This expedition reached
the Indians, who had been preparing to give them battle, on
the 29th of August, 1779. The Indians, although strongly
fortified, and though they bravely contended for some time
against the experienced general, were, after a few hours engagement, forced to retreat, leaving their old abodes and receding
further inland. Sullivan passed through the now deserted
Indian territory unopposed, and wherever he went he spread
havoc and desolation as a deterrent against future atrocities.
When he considered that he had gained the object of his
campaign he retraced his steps, and returned to headquarters
after an absence of two months.

FRONTIER OPERATIONS IN SOUTH AND NORTH.

HEROISM OF ARNOLD.

CONGRESS did not openly give sanction to offensive hostilities against Great Britain until July 4th, 1776, when the Declaration of Independence was signed by the members of the Continental Congress, and promulgated over the States. Until this important event, America only fought to defend her rights and maintain her liberties, repelling force by force. It is true that here and there, at different points over the Colonies, patriotic bands of militia, on their own initiative, or backed up by individual States, opposed the British garrisons by offensive and defensive warfare. But it was only when the public mind had become exasperated, and when the fruitlessness and hopelessness of petitioning England and her tyrannical sovereign became patent to all, that Congress resolved to fight to a finish It was seen that liberty or slavery were the alternatives. The Colonists saw that to lay down their arms meant slavery for all, and death and banishment for leaders. England was too proud to yield to the demands made upon her by her children over the seas, but Englishmen at home were not so enamoured of the prospects of a Colonial War with their own kindred in America, as to rush at the bidding of George and his minions in the Cabinet and volunteer for the contest. Hence Parliament was compelled to hire Hessian soldiers from Frederick and his petty German Princes, to the number of almost twenty thousand, and it was the employment of these foreign butchers, more than anything else, that convinced America that the utter overthrew of the patriots was the object aimed at by the English monarch. Owing to this misguided step on the part of King George there was soon aroused a universal chorus of public opinion in favour of complete independence and separation, and amongst other agents in uniting and nerving the people were the host of writers, who, by pamphlet and in the press flooded the Colonies with thrilling indictments against England. Amongst those writers the famous Thomas Paine was the most active and patient. He had not then developed his infidel tendencies, and Washington publicly complimented him on the impetus he gave the cause by his " Common sense " and " Crisis " pamphlets.

Whilst Washington was besieging Boston, hostilities were proceeding with varied success in other directions over the States. In Virginia Lord Dunmore was, as Governor, enforcing the Royal proclamations with a high hand. Dunmore was personally a brave man, and not without some good traits of character which recommended him to the people. He had loyally defended them in the last Colonial wars against Indan and French encroachments. He had been for many years in their midst, and was on the most intimate terms of friendship with the leading Virginian settlers, and amongst those who were favourably disposed to him were the Washington and the Halifax families. He, now that the crisis which tried men's souls had arrived, had arraigned himself against the popular cause, and had assumed the role of petty tyrant. He opposed himself to the local militia, who were recruiting and drilling in the cause of liberty, and he placed himself at the head of a band of Loyalists and slaves, to whom he offered freedom in order to tempt them to join him and oppose the Patriots under Patrick Henry who had boldly defied him as Governor and the authority under which he acted. One of the first acts of open warfare in Virginia was the expedition of Henry with a band of militia to Williamsburgh, where he recovered by force some powder that Dunmore had removed from the provincial magazines. This happened about the time of the battle of Concord. Dunmore attempted to seize the reins of government and assert British sway, but popular opinion was too powerful, and he was forced to flee for safety. Soon afterwards he raised a small army around him and openly defied the popular party. He made Norfolk, the chief seaport of Virginia, his headquarters. From this port and fortress he kept up a kind of guerilla warfare against the local militia, but he was forced to vacate the city, and he, in turn, commenced to bombard it from the Bay. His revengeful action in these encounters brought him and his cause into much odium with the State that formerly loved him. He was instrumental, by his base and barbarous mode of retaliation on the people, in turning this hitherto well-disposed colony into one of the most fierce and fearless in the cause of Independence. When the people saw their homes burned over their heads, their property destroyed, their cities and towns razed to the ground, and their families finally murdered by the Loyalist leaders and their band of miscreants and liberated slaves, there was a flame of patriotism and a hate of England enkindled in their breasts that was not quenched until Cornwallis gave up his vanquished army to the great Virginian,Washington, at Yorktown, at the end of the war.

It was the evident plan of the British forces to attack the Colonies at three points simultaneously. We see them, of course, concentrating their chief batteries on Boston, where the rebellion originated, but some of their ablest generals were sent towards the St. Lawrence to keep the Northern ports in subjection, and to seize the positions along the route by Lakes Champlain and Hudson, and co-operate with the forces in the Eastern parts. Thus Burgoyne and Carleton were placed over the forces of the North. In the Southern States a strong fleet was to land at Charleston, led· by Clinton, one of the most active and successful of all the British Generals ; and Admiral Sir Peter Parker, commander of ten ships, had appeared before this important town of South Carolina. Clinton had embarked from Boston, and after a short delay at New York, in which city General Lee had forestalled him with a force of militia from Cambridge, he sailed down to the

Carolinas, in hopes to rouse the strong loyal population there to his banner. The Loyalists in this district were chiefly Scotch settlers who had not been long enough in America to join the patriots against the Motherland. Clinton's forces were too small to risk a battle before the arrival of Parker's fleet. When the British regiments did arrive, however, they found Virginia and the Carolinas organized, and in high spirits over their successes against Dunmore, and their heroic action at Moore's creek in North Carolina, where M'Leod and M'Donald and their Highland Loyalists were routed with great slaughter. When Clinton assumed command of the forces before Charleston, he found himself opposed by an army of Provincials 6,000 strong, led by Lee, who had been ordered to command them. The Southern States were resolute in defence of their important city, and their determination saved them from the havoc and misery of war for some years to come. From the ships of Parker, the forts at Charleston, Johnston and Moutree were bombarded, and in turn the soldiers of these forts cannonaded the ships in the Bay. The effect of the cannons on the forts, thanks to the soft nature of the timber and the courage of the defenders, was slight, whilst the ships of the enemy were much disabled, and many of the men on board put out of action. At last Clinton gave up the bombardment of Charleston, and took off his forces to New York to unite with Lord and Sir William Howe, who were entrenching themselves on Staten Island. The effect of this battle on the American forces was wonderful. It inspired the soldiers with courage, and hastened on the Declaration of Independence. The numbers that perished on the British side were considerable, whilst the Americans only lost a few, and those who fell died bravely calling on their companions to continue in defence of the glorious cause of American liberty.

Whilst the cause was thus progressing in the South, the opposing forces were not inactive in the Northern parts of the country. It is true that the skirmishes we have recorded were rather undertaken by the Colonists in their own defence

than in the way of attack, but if, up to this point, such had been
the spirit of Congress, it soon became necessary that they
should deliberate on other tactics. The enemy was most
aggressive—why should not the patriotic forces also adopt
offensive methods ? Canada was a sister colony—why not
invade it and capture those Northern States and bring them
into line with the other provinces ? Canada was appealed to
by Congress, and the Canadians in response sent expressions
of sympathy to their Southern neighbours. Even old Ethal
Allen, on his own responsibility, had been among the Canadians
rousing them, and the response he received was encouraging to
the American cause, but the English had many strong posts
in New York State, and had complete control across the St.
Lawrence. Hence it was resolved, on the advice of Washington, to send forces to Canada to capture the English garrisons
there. This move was considered by the commander-in-chief
" as of the utmost importance to the cause of the liberties of
America." If the British were left master of Canada, and St.
Johns, and Lake Champlain, they could dictate terms from
these Northern regions, and impede the American arms in the
North and North-Western districts. Washington, accordingly,
sent Generals Schuyler and Montgomery with a strong force
to invade Canada. As it turned out Schuyler was, owing to
sickness, superseded by Montgomery. The latter brave young
general was most successful in the early stages of the expedition.
He captured at Lake Champlain the two strong forts, St. Johns
and Chambly, and after leaving in them small garrisons, he
hastened North to meet Sir Guy Carleton, who was in command
of the British forces in Canada. Carleton, on his way to protect St. Johns, was met by an American force under Colonel
Warner and compelled to flee for safety to Montreal. To this
city Montgomery led his forces, and he soon compelled its
surrender. Carleton, in the meantime, having eluded the
enemy, retreated down the St. Lawrence to Quebec, where he
assumed command, and began to prepare the city for a siege.
As we pointed out in our essay on the capture of Quebec by

Wolfe, that city was the key to Canada, and whatever army was able to hold it was master of the situation.   Hence, Montgomery's next move was to march his forces into Canada.

Benedict Arnold, who at a later stage became so infamous, was entrusted by Washington to proceed during this campaign from Cambridge, with a force of a thousand militia, to take boat down the Kennebec river to Quebec, and there co-operate with Montgomery.   The famous Morgan of Virginia was second in command, with Greene, the De Wett in subsequent stages of the war, and Aaron Burr, who shot Alexander Hamilton in a duel twenty-five years later.   These were all young and ambitious officers, and well suited for a romantic and perilous expedition as this turned out to be.

At the mouth of the Kennebec they floated two hundred boats to carry their little army down towards the St. Lawrence. The journey was a long and dreary one attended by hunger and cold and sickness, and before they reached the landing point at Dead river, their forces by sickness and death had been reduced to nine hundred and fifty.   On landing they were compelled to march through a pathless forest, intercepted at intervals by swollen rivers, some of their number occasionally being lost in the rapids from capsized canoes.   To complete their misery smallpox attacked them and carried off a number. When at last, in the last stages of exhaustion, they reached a friendly village of French Canadians, they rested and received the first nourishing food for many days.   During the toilsome march through the forest an occasional meal of dog's flesh had been hailed as a banquet, and for the last two days they had subsisted entirely on wild roots and water.   Having been rested by a short sojourn at this French settlement Arnold led on his decimated forces towards Quebec, and about the 9th of November, encamped at Point Levi, on the American side of the St. Lawrence.

After some delay he was forced by circumstances to relinquish his cherished hope of immediately seizing Quebec with his army, now reduced to seven hundred men, but had he decided immediately after his arrival to enter the city, there is a belief that it was so ill-guarded on the 14th November, the date he decided to proceed up the river and await Montgomery's arrival, that he would have captured it without difficulty. Montgomery joined Arnold at Point aux Trembles with three hundred men, and after clothing his ragged army he led the united force in December to Quebec.

On the last day of December, in the dark hours of a frosty morning, with snow drifting in wreaths around them, Montgomery marshalled his troops for action. He himself commanded one main division in a separate attack from one end of the town ; Arnold and Morgan were to attack from an opposite point. The brave young General, like Wolfe some years previously, led in person. Rousing his men to action with the brief words, " Men of New York, you will not fear to follow where your general leads," with a wild rush he dashed his forces forward to storm the block house. But alas ! hidden from their sight was a cannon perched on a rock, and as the brave Montgomery came up, the enemy discharged into his ranks a deadly charge of grape shot, and he, along with Captains M'Pherson and Cheeseman, fell mortally wounded. The troops could not be rallied after the repulse. In the attack made by Arnold, though even more daring was displayed by officers and men, a like result followed, but although Arnold had been wounded and put out of action, Morgan did not yield to his adversaries for some hours, and only when he found there was no hope of relief from Montgomery's division did he allow himself to be captured as a soldier of war. Carleton was now master of Quebec and Arnold took off his few remaining troops. The English General was most kind to the prisoners taken in the city, and had the wounded well cared for, and the dead buried in a becoming manner. Soon after this disaster arrivals reached the American camp from Cambridge under Generals Wooster and Thomas, amounting in all to nearly three thousand men. Soon, too, however, large reinforcements under Burgoyne came from

England and sailed up the St. Lawrence to the aid of Carleton, and the American Generals considered it more prudent to leave the Canadian shores and fortify themselves in the forts lately captured by them. But the English General was soon on their track, and St. Johns and Chambly were vacated and fell into the hands of Burgoyne. Wooster joined forces with Generals Gates and Sullivan who were strongly entrenched at Ticondoroga.

Thus ended the Canadian campaign, which at one time looked so hopeful, and thus, for all time, did America lose her hold on a province destined in the near future to be almost her compeer in political and commercial greatness. John Adams, writing to a friend said of this ill-fated expedition : " They were disgraced, defeated, discontented, dispirited, diseased, undisciplined, eaten up with vermin—no clothes, beds, blankets, and no victuals but salt pork and flour."

It was a severe blow to the cause of liberty, the Canadian disaster ; it was not, however, want of valour, but a long chain of misfortunes and accidents that brought about the dreadful result. Than the officers who led in this campaign there were no braver among the many brave leaders of the war for Independence. We will here give *in extenso* a letter from Thomas Jefferson to John Randolph,who was then on a mission to England, to present the last of many petitions from the Colonies, before the final step was taken in the promulgation of the Declaration of Independence. This letter, although more hopeful than the facts warranted, shows the aspirations and resolves of the great minds that led in the crisis, and as it was written by one who took a great part in moulding public opinion, and whose pen worded the great document declaring the United States free and independent of England, it is an admirable supplement to the events recorded above, and a fair index of the trend of the public mind prior to 1776, the year when the Declaration was fulminated from Congress in Philadelphia. The letter is as follows :—

Philadelphia, November 29th, '75.

Dear Sir,

Success attends our arms. Chambly and St. Johns were taken some weeks ago, and in them, the whole regular arms of Canada, except forty or fifty men. This day certain knowledge has reached me that General Montgomery is received in Montreal, and we expect every hour to hear that Quebec has opened its arms to Colonel Arnold, who, with 1,100 men was sent up the Kennebec and down Chauntiere river to this place. Montreal acceded to us on the 13th, and Carleton set out with the shattered remains of his little army for Quebec, where we hope he will be taken by Arnold.

In a short time, we have reason to hope, the delegates of Canada will join Congress (events showed that in this hope Jefferson was too sanguine). Lord Dunmore has commenced hostilities in Virginia. He has burned our town of Hampton, but he has been opposed by our militia and repelled with great loss.

It is an immense misfortune to the whole empire to have such a King at such a time, of such a disposition. He is the bitterest enemy we have. In fact another Pharaoh from whose tyranny the Lord of Hosts deliver us.

By the God that made me I will cease to exist before I yield to a connection with Great Britain on such terms as the British Parliament proposes, and in this I speak the sentiment of America. One bloody campaign will probably decide our future course, and cause us to declare and assert a separation. (The unbloody capture of Boston followed this letter.) We are not mere brutes to crouch under the bands and ties and rods with which we are scourged.

In another place Jefferson adds, " I am one of those who, rather than submit to the rights of legislating for us assumed by the British Parliament, and which late experience has shown they will so cruelly exercise. would lend my hand to sink the whole island in the ocean."

BURGOYNE.

Or the many interesting personalities figuring in the Revolution War, perhaps one of the most remarkable was that of General John Burgoyne, the genial Irishman—more *litterateur*, wit, and man-of-the-world than soldier—who surrendered so ingloriously, albeit gracefully, to the Americans at Saratoga. General Burgoyne's share in the War of Independence is worth recording in any book bearing on the subject, if only for the literary interest imported into it by his high comedy manners, gentlemanly behaviour, and amiable eccentricity under all circumstances.

General John Burgoyne was born in Ireland in the year 1728 and died in 1792. He was supposed to be the natural son of Lord Bingley. We find him mentioned as a Lieutenant Colonel of the 16th Light Dragoons in 1759. In the following year he served at Belle Isle, and in 1762 he commanded a force sent by the British to defend Portugal against the Spaniards. He is mentioned with distinction in the action that led to the siege and capture of Alcantara. In 1761, whilst still in active military service, he was elected member for Midhurst, and in 1768 we find him sitting in Parliament for the city of Preston. He was fined in £1,000 owing to the finding of bribery against his supporters in this election. He contracted a secret marriage with a daughter of the then Lord Derby, and on his father-in-law discovering that he was a man of distinction, as a scholar and a wit, he was openly received as a son-in-law.

He is the author of many works of no mean rank in literature. His play, " The Maid of the Oaks," was written soon after his marriage, but owing to his public service as a soldier and a politician, his early years were too much occupied to

allow him time for his favourite pursuit. It was chiefly after
his surrender at Saratoga that his literary career began.
When he returned to England from America in 1778, he appeared before the enraged King to justify himself, but he
was spurned by his former patrons and refused an audience
with his majesty. Nay, Lord North's ministry would not
allow him to sit in Parliament. It was at this period of his
life, after being soured of public service, and ignored by a
partisan and unreasonable Parliament, that he resigned the
army and devoted his talents to literature. His comedy,
" The Heiress," is considered equal to rank with the work of
Congreve. He wrote, amongst other plays, " Richard Coeur
de Lion " and "The Lady of the Manor," both of which abound
with sparkling wit and a quiet humour, peculiarly his own.
His many experiences in love and war, his travelling and
associations with high life, served to enrich with variety and
information a naturally glowing style.

Towards the end of his days he arose again in public
favour, and just when death called him, he was actively engaged in connection with the trial of Warren Hastings. He
died on the 4th of June, 1792, and was buried in Westminster
Abbey. Had he devoted his entire energies to literature his
place would have been along with Congreve and Byron in
English letters.

There is little doubt he was not the right man for the
important task assigned him in the North American Wars.
Sir Guy Carleton, who defeated Montgomery and Arnold two
years previously, and who still ruled in Canada, was a fit leader
for a successful campaign against a native army on their own
mountain wilds and valleys and rivers and lakes, but Burgoyne
was not a centre of gravity whence authority might emanate.
He was powerfully connected in the Commons and among the
Lords, and hence had little trouble convincing a perplexed
and ill-informed ministry about the feasability of his plans
and his capabilities to carry them into execution. About the
month of May we find him landing on the St. Lawrence with

a fine army, and with the authority of a dictator, to lead the forces which were to conquer the North. Carleton felt aggrieved to find himself placed in a subordinate position, and he refused to serve under Burgoyne. His defection may have accounted for the fewness of the Canadian recruits who joined the new commander, for Carleton was justly popular with the Colonials and Indians on account of his humane administration.

Burgoyne was undoubtedly brave, and one of his supporters in Parliament, the Irishman Barre, who was a consistent friend throughout of the Colonies, said to the opposition in power, " Burgoyne was no coward. Yes, General Burgoyne and his army have been surrounded and captured and cut off from their supplies by those rustics whom you have branded in the House with the epithets of cowards and inhuman. What is the proof ? They have obliged as brave a general as ever commanded a British Army to surrender, and on the most honourable conditions. They might have hurled them into dungeons in chains, but on the contrary," said this brave Irish Commoner, " to show that they are not the lawless band you would dub them they have sent them home as free men across the ocean." " I say," he adds, " it is impossible for you to conquer this brave people, inspired with so high ideals of patriotism, of liberty, and of humanity."

General Burgoyne was little suited, no matter how brave he might be, to carry on a successful war against the bravest and the most daring people on earth, fighting in defence of their homes, their wives and their children, against cruel Indians and inhuman Germans, and reckless ambitious officers and generals who, if successful, would as in Arcadia some years previous under Wolfe, spare neither old nor young in their onward march. It is true that Burgoyne had seen some service in a subordinate post, under Wolfe, but " he was not the man for Galway." He was not the man to supplant Carleton. He was not the man to reconcile the red man to his military sway. He knew nothing about the ways and habits of the

Colonists, except from books. To change generals in such a crisis, and to change them to such disadvantage, presaged no great success for the British cause.

Burgoyne, in some manner, used similar tactics to that of the ill-fated Braddock, under whom Washington served in the last Colonial War. There was with him too much of the glittering tinsel of helmet and tunic, and lance and matlock, too much show and bravado ; too much punctilious manoeuvring and well-defined discipline. He was too slow in all his movements, cutting out roads through pathless forests ; too encumbered by baggage ; he was too confident of success ; and had a too mean and ill-informed idea about the resources, the courage, and the patriotic endurance of the American army under Washington's control. The British commander was known to the patriots as the " General Swagger," on account of his high sounding proclamations to the white natives and the red tribes.

It was the wish of his masters across the channel that all the Indian tribes should be reconciled by him on his march, and made to serve under him where needful. Canadians and loyal Americans were to augment his forces, hence we find him issuing as he proceeded in his march proclamations and addresses, and even calling on the " Sons of Liberty " to bow to the conquering hero. When Burgoyne had arrived as far south on his march from Quebec as the shores of Lake Champlain he was met by a company of Catholic Indians, under a Canadian priest, coming, as they informed him, to join his standard. He seated them down to a sumptuous war feast and then in his most eloquent style addressed them as follows : " Go forth in the might of your valour, strike at the common enemy of Great Britain and America, disturbers of public order, peace and happiness,destroyers of commerce, plunderers of the State."

Then, after praising their courage, endurance, and constancy, artfully flattered them that they were in those things a model for his army to imitate. He then —which was a

humane thing for him to do—entreated them to conform to
the methods of civilized warfare prescribed for their brethren,
and he adds, "I positively forbid all bloodshed when you are
not opposed in arms. Aged men, women and children must
be held sacred from the knife and the tomahawk even in the
time of action. You shall be compensated for prisoners,
but you shall not scalp the dead slain by you. There shall be no
cold-blooded murdering of the wounded or inoffensive."

It is needless to add that all listened with attention, but
just as it is hard or almost impossible to keep hounds from
hunting the fox when once on the trail, so, too, it is hard to
prevent the savage Indian from seeking in war for scalps from
the living, or dead, or dying.

Burgoyne's proclamation to the " Rebel Americans " at
this time was not alone an insult to their patriotism, it was a
blunder from his own point of view, and had the effect of
making them more eager to oppose him. He rated them about
alleged cruelties to their Tory neighbours, and arrogantly
promised them protection if they would submit peaceably to
his authority. Those who remained " disloyal " should have
the red man let loose among them.

After these proclamations he commenced operations with
his force of 9,000 fighting men on the forts around the Lakes
Champlain and George. It was about the end of July that
this ponderous army arrived at Crown Point, which was not
defended by the American garrison, and after taking possession
of it, the British troops divided into three divisions, and proceeded by land and water to Ticonderoga, whither the defenders
of Crown Point had fled. General St. Clair, a brave Scottish
Colonial, was in command of this important fort, with a force
of two thousand men ; too insignificant a number to impede
successfully such a foe.

General Schuyler, who had been in command of the
patriots in these parts, did not, or could not sufficiently
reinforce St. Clair before the approach of Burgoyne. We must
remember that Howe was very actively engaging the energies

of the Commander-in-Chief, and supplies of men were drafted from the Highlands of the Hudson that would have been needful. This fort, a council of war having been held, it had been considered wise to abandon. Firstly, because the stores were insufficient for a protracted seige ; and secondly, because the British had gained possession of a hill beside the fort, which practically gave them command of the position.

Owing to the paucity of St. Clair's forces he could not have easily guarded this hill, to which the enemy had, by extraordinary exertions, drawn up their artillery, and to which they had given the name of " Fort Defiance." Having possession of this hill and Fort Hope, another eminence occupied by General Frazer's forces, the English could not be long restrained from entering and reducing Ticonderoga. When it was seen that it could no longer be considered safe to remain in the fort, the Americans in the twilight of a summer night, sailed down the lake from their fortifications towards the neck of land dividing Lake Champlain from Lake George. They had two hundred batteaux protected by five armed galleys, with ammunition and stores. These soon landed at the neck on which stands Whitehall, the main body of the troops proceeding by land to Castleton.

Owing to the breaking out of a conflagration at the departure of St. Clair, their secret midnight retreat was revealed to the British, who immediately started in pursuit. After midday on the day succeeding, the British fleet, Burgoyne himself commanding, overreached the last of the retreating fleet of St. Clair, but before an engagement had been entered on, the Americans had succeeded in effecting a landing and, burning their boats, and they were successful in reaching Fort Anne at the end of the lake, where Schuyler had collected some militia for opposing Burgoyne. St. Clair's instructions to his subordinate officers were not to lag behind, but a few detachments led by Warner notwithstanding fell behind, and were immediately set upon by Generals Frazer and Rudesel, who were in command of the advance British guard. Had not the

militia given way, and had not the British troops joined
Frazer, this battle at Hubbardton might not have ended in
disaster for the Americans. But, before St. Clair, who was in
advance, could reinforce his flying corps, the British had
completely gained the field, and all that was left of St. Clair's
militia proceeded to Fort Edward to join General Schuyler.

Burgoyne followed up his victory and captured from Col.
Long Fort Anne, but not before this officer had worked severe
havoc on the British columns, as they passed through a ravine
to his fortifications. The Americans, in giving up this fort,
gave a good account of themsleves and had not their ammunition failed them they would have routed the foe.

Up to this point Burgoyne had experienced nothing but
one success after another. Fort after fort fell before him
and the Americans retreated further south. There would
have been little doubt of the final success of this general had
he pressed on by great marches, reached the Hudson and pressed
on to Albany before the Americans could recover from the
panic of defeat. But here Burgoyne blundered. He sat down
to rest himself and to bring up his stores. When the news of
the series of disasters that befel the northern forces reached
Congress, there was much consternation, and St. Clair and
Schuyler were overwhelemd with unmerited reproaches.
The Assembly of delegates, instead of taking the circumstances
of the case into account, instead of bearing a part of the blame
they so profusely heaped on these brave men, rushed to the
conclusion that both were incompetent, or worse, and that they
should be superseded in their commands. Hence General
Gates was raised to the supreme command. Arnold, who
was impetuous and brave, reckless and headstrong, was sent
along with the brave and fearless Morgan to assist Gates in
retrieving the lost prestige of the army. Gates was, as after
events proved, a vain, plotting, timid leader. He had some
powerful friends among the assembly of delegates, especially
those from the New England States. He had, as friends,
officers high up in the army who were plotting against Washing-

ton and his friends, among them the patriotic Schuyler.
Even John Adams, who kept his head well screwed on during
the war, in fair and foul weather, has attributed to him the remark when writing to a friend over the loss of Crown Point
and Ticonderoga : " We shall never be able to defend a post
until we shoot a general." Washington himself was much
perturbed, but he, with his usual prudence, restrained the
overzealous Congress, trusted the wisdom of the Northern
leader, and to placate Schuyler's opponents ordered General
Lincoln, who was a great favourite with the New Englanders,
to proceed also to the seat of war.

The treachery at work against Schuyler did not make
him cease one jot of his exertions to ensure final victory over
Burgoyne. On the contrary it seemed to increase his patriotic
zeal. Whilst Burgoyne was enjoying the success of his late
victories, he took occasion to again issue a proclamation,
calling on all Americans to return to their allegiance. Schuyler
answered him with a counter manifesto, and in it he declared
his intention to dispute every inch of ground with the English
general, and retard his descent into the country from the Lakes
as long as possible. To carry out his threat he took extraordinary pains to sink obstructions in Wood Creek, " by which
stream," says Macay, " the English bateaux must pass to
convey provisions towards the Hudson." In addition to
impeding the watercourse, he strenuously exerted himself to
blockade the road by cutting obstructions and felling timber
along the route. He destroyed upwards of fifty bridges over
rivers and swamps. In addition to this he drove off all the
cattle, waggons, and horses in the vicinity. Hence, when
Burgoyne commenced his march anew through the forest
to reach the Hudson, he found the task so tedious that his
advances were not more than one mile per day, and every day
found him further removed from his base of supplies. From
Whitehall or Shenesborough, as it was then called, to the Hudson river was sixteen miles. Hence we need not wonder
that it was almost August before the lordly Hudson was
reached.

The American army retreated further south to meet the egress of Burgoyne from the woods. They fixed their camp at the junction of the Mohawk with the Hudson, and here they strongly fortified their position, and awaited an attack. The American force were daily increasing, whilst Burgoyne's position was not improving by the delay.

Whilst Schuyler was anxiously watching for the egress of Burgoyne from the forest fastness, some engagements took place to the east and north-west of the line of march. St. Leger, by the plan of campaign, was to join his leader after having conquered and devastated the northern counties of Tryon county (New York State). After a weary march through pathless wilds St. Leger came upon Fort Schuyler upon the Upper Mohawk. This fort was important as it commanded the Mohawk from its source down to the Hudson. The fort was garrisoned by 700 men under Colonel Gansvoort and Colonel Willett. St. Leger was soon joined in his expedition by Guy Johnston, nephew of the famous Sir William Johnston, the warm friend of the Indian chiefs. A Mohawk sachem, a half caste, and probably a relation of Johnston's became an ally, and gathered a band of Indians, and these with a regiment known as Johnston's Greens, joined the St. Leger expedition, to aid in capturing the fort and revenging themselves on the patriots for banishing them as Tories from the Mohawk.

As soon as the British forces laid siege to Fort Schuyler, General Herkimer assembled the republican militia and proceeded to the relief of his friends in the garrison who were, at the same time, ordered to make a sortie and throw the besiegers into confusion. Herkimer led forward his men, and found, on passing through a ravine, that the enemy were posted to meet him. The encounter was fierce. Brant's Indians and Johnston's Greens opened the assault so furiously that the American vanguard stampeded, and the brave General, not able to turn them, turned himself and faced the foe, and after a desperate resistance fell mortally wounded. The death of their General did not, however, end the conflict ; it nerved the patriots to renewed valour, and when Willett's men sallied forth the Tories and Indians fled, hacked and routed in all directions. The republican army did not find itself strong enough at the end of the encounter to relieve the besieged.

St. Leger, like Burgoyne, issued a proclamation to the garrison to surrender, and calling on all loyal men to lay their arms at his feet and give their allegiance to the King. He informed Burgoyne that the fort could not long withstand him. He sent an officer blindfolded, with a flag, to treat with the commander of the fort. He said that Albany was already captured; that they had better yield, as their resistance could not be long, and that it was with difficulty the Indians were restrained from savage ferocity against them and their families. To this lying message Willett, on behalf of his superior officer, made answer : " You come from a British Colonel to the Commander of this garrison to tell him that if he does not deliver it up into your hands, you will send the Indians to murder our women and children. If so, let their blood be upon your heads. We are doing our duty. This garrison is committed to our care and we will take care of it. After you get out of this take the blind from your eyes and view it from without, but never expect to get in again unless you become a prisoner. I consider the message you have brought a degrading one for a British officer to send, and by no means reputable for a British officer to carry."

As the siege was likely to be a protracted one Colonel Willett and Lieutenant Stockwell escaped at great risk and reached the American lines, informing the general of their predicament. Schuyler knew the importance of holding the fort, but it was not in his power to send a force which Arnold, who was to lead them, considered sufficient. Hence a stratagem which had the desired effect was resorted to. A Tory prisoner was released from the American lines on condition he would, in conjunction with some friendly Indians, proceed to Brant's lines and delude the Indians to desert by informing them that the Americans were approaching in great force. The ruse had the desired effect. The Indians left the besiegers, and soon St. Leger, with his handful of followers, returned to Canada, and Fort Ticonderoga was saved to the Americans by Arnold's extraordinary cleverness. St. Leger's aid, and his Indian Tory and Canadian troops, were lost to the Northern army. They retreated so expeditiously that large quantities of stores and baggage, tents and artillery, fell into the hands of the garrison. This retreat occurred on the 27th of August, and Burgoyne was too busily engaged to send out aid sufficient before the desertion of St. Leger.

There was a still more crushing disaster in store for the English commander. His waggons were scarce, and the further he proceeded on his way to the Hudson, the more difficult was it for him to procure provisions from his depot at Fort George. He was at this time informed that, in a friendly district some twenty miles to the east, at Bennington, the Americans had a lot of stores, and that there was hope of gaining not alone provender, but oxen, waggons, and many recruits. He despatched General Baum, a brave officer, with a thousand troops, to carry out this plan for relieving his army. When Baum was seven miles from the New England militia forces, led by the brave old Brigadier Stark, he learned that the Americans were well fortified and in strong numbers around Bennington, and he sent back to Burgoyne for reinforcements.

The Eastern States had now recovered from the panic into which the successes of the British forces had thrown them, and Langoon, speaker of the New Hampshire Assembly, on hearing of Baum's invasion, set an example of enthusiasm to the delegates. "I have," he said, "three thousand dollars in hard cash, I will pledge my plate for three thousand more. I have seventy hogsheads of rum which shall be sold for what it will bring. These are at the service of the State. If we succeed in defending our homes these maybe remunerated, if we fail they will be of no value to me. Our old friend Stark, who so nobly sustained the honour of our State at Bunker's

Hill, may be safely entrusted with the conduct of our enterprise." This inspired the delegates to cease deliberating, and shoulder their muskets in the ranks of Stark's militia who had now reached 1,600. Stark's remark to his army when going up to the enemy is worthy of repetition : "Do you see the redcoats yonder, we hit to-day or Molly Stark is a widow."

Stark divided his forces into four divisions, putting a detachment to the front and rear of the enemy's wings. He himself led the main force in front.

It was shortly after noon when Stark ordered the attack. The militia responded with a wild hurrah and soon the English lines were giving way. At the end of two hours, during which the noise of battle resembled a continuous clap of thunder, the English fled in the direction of the Hudson, leaving Baum mortally wounded on the field of battle. The reinforcements sent by Burgoyne came too late. In this engagement almost nine hundred in dead and dying and prisoners were lost to the English.

It was at this time, when fortune seemed to favour the American cause, that Gates got definite orders to assume command at Stillwater. The news was a shock to the brave Schuyler. He had seen victory in view. His powerful influence and his great wealth were causing men and stores in abundance to reach the Continental lines. It was his judicious obstructions that had wearied out Burgoyne's Indian and Canadian allies, and rendered it so difficult for him to procure the necessary provisions. Schuyler, like a true patriot, though feeling deeply the insult of Congress, spoke thus when giving up his command to Gates :—" I have done all that I could have done as far as the means were in my power to inspire confidence in the soldiers of our own army, and I flatter myself with some success, but the palm of victory is denied me, and it is left to you, General, to reap the fruits of my labour. I will not fail, however, to second your views, and my devotion to my country will cause me, with alacrity, to obey your orders."

It may be interesting to note here, now that the clouds are fast gathering over Burgoyne's head, what were his real opinions regarding the red men, whose barbarism English policy had seen fit to employ in this struggle with their own kith and kin.

To the Secretary of the State he wrote :—" Confidently to your lordship I may acknowledge that in several instances I have found the Indians little more than a name. If, under the management of their conductors they are indulged, for interested reasons, in all the caprices and humours of spoiled children, like them, they grow more unreasonable and importunate upon every new favour. They cannot be relied upon, and were they left to themselves, enormities too horrid to think of would arise, Guilty and innocent, men and women would be the common prey." Stark's victory added to the Indian atrocities had a wonderful effect in rallying the people from far and near to Gates' camp, so that his forces at the time of the surrender in October were computed at 16,000 men.

The critical stage had now arrived with Burgoyne. He was now face to face with the American hosts. How was he going to escape their grasp and join with Clinton ? He collected thirty days' provisions, and in the middle of September resolved to give battle to the enemy.

Kosciusko, the noble Polish volunteer, was not alone a brave soldier but a distinguished naval engineer, and by his instructions the heights of Bemis on which Gates was entrenched were strongly fortified, the English General being encamped to a disadvantage on the plains below. The American fortifications ran from the river's edge over the heights ; on the heights batteries were placed to command the approach of the enemy. Arnold was put in command on the left wing, and on the 19th September, it was determined to give battle to the advancing troops. Burgoyne placed Generals Philips and Rudesel in charge of his left wing, with the heavy artillery along their side, moving by the river's edge. Burgoyne and Frazer advanced over the irregular hills at the head of the centre and right wing. It was the agreed plan that these two advancing columns should join, and then fall on Arnold's troops. Arnold's and Morgan's rifles, impetuous and difficult to be kept back, hurried out to meet the enemy, and after a spirited attack the advance guards of the British lines were forced to fall back. Frazer was ordered out with his light horse to oppose Arnold, and the encounter became furious, each side rallying and falling back in turn. The battle raged fiercest after three in the afternoon. At that hour the artillery under Jones was brought up to protect Frazer who, like Arnold, was here, there and everywhere, where the fighting was fiercest. At last the British advanced with bayonets to the attack, and the Americans fell back into the woods, only, however, to issue forth again and renew the attack.

Night was now approaching and no decisive advantage had been gained on either side. Arnold besought Gates to draw out fresh troops, and assist in driving the enemy off the field, but Gates, instead, ordered his men to go back to their entrenchments, and the day ended without victory being seized by either side. The affair, however, told in favour of the Americans. Burgoyne wished to force his way ahead, and instead he had to be content with camping on the field of battle, in readiness for a renewal of hostilities.

Burgoyne was more than ever convinced that, with the forces at his command, he could not proceed to Albany, notwithstanding his boast to poor Baum when going out to Bennington that he should meet him there and eat his Christmas dinner with him. Baum did not leave Bennington, and Burgoyne had got to face his Saratoga before Christmas.

When Clinton sent up information to Stillwater that it would be the twentieth of October before he should have captured Fort Montgomery, it was hopeless for Burgoyne to expect relief before his provisions were exhausted. Recognising this, he removed to a safe distance from Gates' army, after the first engagement, and for sixteen days remained within his trenches awaiting eventualities. At last, on the 6th October, when no satisfactory news was forthcoming from Clinton, and when the provisions in camp were reduced to three days' rations, after calling a council of war, it was decided to again renew the contest with Gates' swelling forces. On the 7th Burgoyne drew out his right wing with 1,500 picked men, led by himself, Philips and Rudesel and Frazer. The left wing was formed within three quarters of a mile from the left of the American camp. He sent round a band of provincials and Indians to emerge from the woods, and distract the Americans on the rear, and excite alarm in that quarter.

Gates made his arrangements to cope with these designs. Poor, with a regiment of New Hampshire militia, was ordered to meet the enemy's initial advances. Morgan by a circuitous route, gained the high ground above the enemy, with a wood protecting him on his left. Then a bold attack was ordered, and Morgan fired a fierce volley into the front and right flank of the enemy. Another party was ordered out to intercept the retreat of the British. Frazer did yeoman service during this fierce engagement. He was here, there, and everywhere spurring his men to action. Arnold saw that it was necessary to stop him and pointed him out to Morgan. Some of the picked rifles of the Americans got into the trees and the daring general fell mortally wounded.

Burgoyne at last was forced to fall back within his camp and entrenchments, but not before some of Arnold's division had dispossessed the German section of his army of some of their entrenchments. The Americans displayed much bravery, and Arnold himself was carried out of the English fortifications whence he had driven a flying division of Burgoyne's force, wounded in the knee. Colonel Brooks, who led the left wing of Arnold's division, succeeded in ejecting a part of the enemy from their entrenchments, which they themselves retained. Victory on this occasion was certainly on the American side, and before darkness set in the British artillery and 200 prisoners, part of their works, and a great quantity of stores were in the hands of the Americans.

Burgoyne, fearing an attack next morning, withdrew his troops some distance over the river, and, in so doing was, for the time being, removed from the danger of attack. Gates, to prevent the enemy eluding him, had strong guards placed in Burgoyne's front and rear. Burgoyne, at last, retreated by night to Saratoga, leaving behind him some 300 sick and wounded, for whom the Americans made provision. Clearly now there was only one course open to the British—to surrender or be annihilated. After some consultation with his officers it was agreed that the English General should treat for honourable terms of surrender with Gates. This was resolved upon, and Burgoyne sent over one of his officers to Gates to inform him that he was prepared to enter into honourable terms for a cessation of hostilities, and desiring to be informed on what conditions the American General would treat with him. After some preliminary correspondence it was agreed that the British forces should leave the camp with their arms, that these should be taken from them by their own officers, and that the entire army should be kept at Boston as prisoners of war until such time as they might be exchanged or sent home to England, and that they should undertake not to serve during the present war against America.

The Articles of Convention or surrender, entered into between Burgoyne and Gates, are contained under thirteen heads. They are most liberal in terms towards the defeated General, more generous than they might otherwise have been, had it not been known to Gates that Sir Henry Clinton was approaching as a victor up the Hudson, more liberal than they should have been, had it been definitely known that Burgoyne's condition was hopeless. He was reduced to less than 3,000 able-bodied men, two-thirds of whom were Germans, his provisions would not have held out three days, and for a week previous his men were on short allowance. Had the English General delayed in surrendering, hostilities would at once have commenced, and he would, after great slaughter, have been forced to give way before aid could have reached him. Certainly had Gates known that Clinton was laying waste the country along the Hudson, with fire and sword, pillaging and slaying and burning all that came in his way, Burgoyne and his army would not have been so humanely treated as they were.

The capitulation of Saratoga, the loss of this fine army and all their baggage, was a momentous event, and might truly be said to be the turning point in the War of Independence. It roused the spirit of the country to the highest pitch of enthusiasm and patriotism. It struck terror into the British army in America, and into the British nation and Cabinet in England. It quieted the Tories in the Colonies, and roused the hopes of the patriots.

THE CONWAY CABAL.

For some time previous to the end of the year 1777, there had been a plot on foot to undermine the influence of Washington, and this plot had had a measure of success. The State of Pennsylvania, chagrined at losing its capital, and not forgetful of its own backwardness in strengthening the army, supplied many discontented individuals. The faction in Congress who desired a change of Generals were instrumental in promoting the creatures of their choice in the army, and thus we find a new board of war created at this time, of which General Gates was appointed president, supplanting that unpurchasable patriot John Adams, who had held the position since the Declaration of Independence. General Muffin, who was supposed to be one of the discontented faction, was one of its members. General Conway, at the same time, who had joined the faction, was appointed inspector-general, and was promoted over senior brigadiers to rank of Major-General. The factionists had little hold on the affections of the army.

Not even did the victors of Saratoga ever entertain the idea of changing Washington for Gates, and the entire northern forces clung with loving tenacity to the Commander-in-Chief, as the only saviour of their country.

Washington held himself severely indifferent to all the underhand machinations of his enemies. Patriotism over-ruled every other consideration with him. In a private letter from Mr. Laurens, his personal friend, and at the same time President of the Congress, he was apprised of the heavy charges that were levelled against him by anonymous writers. To this communication he replied : " I cannot sufficiently express the obligation I feel towards you for your friendship and politeness upon an occasion in which I feel deeply interested. I was not unapprized that a malignant faction had been for some time forming, to my prejudice, which, conscious as I am of having ever done my duty to the best of my ability, could not but give me some pain on a personal account, but my chief concern arises from an apprehension of the dangers which intestine dissensions may produce to the common cause. As I have no other view than to promote the public good, and am unambitious of honours not founded in the approbation of my country, I would not desire in the least degree to suppress a free enquiry into any part of my conduct that even faction itself may deem reprehensible. My enemies take an ungenerous advantage of me. They know the delicacy of my situation, and that motives of policy deprive me of the defence I might otherwise make against so insidious an attack. They know I cannot combat their insinuations without disclosing secrets it is of the utmost moment to conceal. Why should I complain since such attacks are the unfailing lot of those placed in an exalted station. My heart, however, tells me it has been my unremitted aim to do the best which circumstances would permit. yet I have been very mistaken in my judgment of the means, and may in many instances deserve the imputation of error."

Conway was, it would seem, in constant communication

with Gates and Congress trying to undermine the commander, accusing him of incompetency and of favouritism, especially towards General Greene, and it may be that those plotters were jealous of the influence young Lafayette was supposed to have with the Commander. In justice to Gates we must here admit that he had not been directly involved in the cabal, although he was a willing, if not an active instrument, in the hands of the faction. Washington himself was agreeable to make allowance for his vanity, and to overlook his part in the affair on account of the noble part he played at Saratoga, but he was not prepared to allow the intrigue to wear out his patience as the above letter indicates. This letter brought the plot to an issue. It was to be a trial of strength between underhand faction and the good name and fame of the "father of his country," and now, as ever, the idol of the army. Nor are we to place so charitable a construction on Gates' share in the plot as Washington was inclined to do. We find in Dr. Caldwell's biography of General Greene the following, which decidedly implicates Gates : " Shortly after the surrender of Burgoyne, Gates took occasion to hold with Morgan a private conversation. In the course of this he told him confidentially that the main army was exceedingly dissatisfied with the conduct of General Washington, that the reputation of that officer was rapidly declining, and that several officers of great worth threatened to resign unless a change was produced in that department. Colonel Morgan, fathoming in an instant the views of this commanding officer, replied, ' Sir, I have one favour to ask. Never again mention to me this hateful subject ; under no other man but General Washington as Commander-in-Chief will I ever serve.' Hence from that time Gates treated Morgan with marked coldness and neglect." We may conclude that Gates crept out of this business but very lamely, and that he was in active sympathy with the aims and views of the cabal is beyond doubt.

It was alleged that Washington was too slow, too cautious, and too remiss in pursuing a victory ; too prone to retreat when it was his duty to attack. It was urged that invariably the section of the army which he led personally was less successful than those led by his subordinates. This cabal brewing and fermenting for a long time had supporters of influence, both in the army and in Congress. It seemed to have originated among the northern patriots in the New England States, and included such men as Samuel Adams, Miffin and John Hancock. Amongst the generals the most prominent backers of the cabal were Conway, Lee and Gates—men of great influence, men of talents and culture, and all of them soldiers who had experience in military affairs, prior to the War of Independence.

It was urged at the time the intriguing bubble against the General burst, that he was responsible for the loss of the battle of Germanstown on the 4th October. It would not seem, however, that Congress looked upon Germanstown as a defeat, for they unanimously passed the following resolution:—
" Resolved, that the best thanks of Congress be given to General Washington for his wise and well concerted attack on the enemy's army near Germanstown on the 4th instant, and to the officers and soldiers of the army for their brave exertions on that occasion."

Confirmation of the above and good testimony as to the valour displayed by Washington is afforded by the following extracts from a letter from General Sullivan to the President of New Hampshire : " We brought off all our cannon and all our wounded. Our loss in the action amounts to less than seven hundred, mostly wounded. The misfortunes of this day were principally owing to the thick fog which, being rendered still greater by the smoke of the cannon and musketry prevented our troops from discovering the motions of the enemy, or acting in concert with each other. I cannot help observing that with great concern I saw our brave Commander exposing himself to the hottest fire of the enemy in such a manner that regard to my country obliged me to ride to him and beg him to retire. He, to gratify me and some others, withdrew a little, but his anxiety for the fate of the day brought him up again, where he remained till our troops had retreated. I am, &c., John Sul'ivan "

It was, however, notwithstanding the above, urged against the General that he should not have tarried at the "Chew House," a stone building into which five companies of the enemy had thrown themselves, to impede his march in pursuing the retreating British forces. Washington, in attacking this fortified position, was only carrying out a well-known rule in warfare, not to leave the enemy fortified in the rear. His officers were favourable to the attack, and Knox, one of his subordinates, publically defends the action. It was his prudence and caution, combined with fearless daring and heroic bravery, that won for Washington the renowned name he holds in history as a great General. He feared no danger and, at the same time, he courted no unnecessary risks. His cause was too dear to him to expose his soldiers to dangers through recklessness. His prudence on this occasion, as on many others, exposed him to the taunt of the inexperienced as over-cautious. We saw, from Sullivan's letter that there was no fear—no dread of danger in his mind when the cause of his country, or the army, demanded courage.

Another, and still greater impetus was given to this cabal by the success of Gates at Saratoga. Here, it was alleged, the most glorious, in fact, the first great victory of the war, was gained by Gates—the General whom the intriguers had resolved should supplant Washington. "What," they asked, "was Washington doing whilst the northern army was fighting a superior foe, and capturing a whole army with a great General at their head." Gates was a vain, accomplished, and egotistical commander. He was ambitious of command. By intrigue he induced Congress to make him Commander—over Schuyler's head—of the northern forces. By this act of degrading Schuyler, an admitted injustice had been done him. He said very truly to Gates, when yielding up his command to him : " I have made it possible for you to complete the work begun; yours shall be the honour."

We must not neglect in apportioning the honours for the success of Saratoga, to give due praise to that brave soldier though subsequent traitor, Benedict Arnold. Historians of these battles represent him as a lion spreading death and confusion among the enemy. His reckless courage even against the counsel of Gates contributed in no small degree to hasten Burgoyne's surrender.

Gates had by no means an inferior army at Saratoga. He was stronger in numbers than the enemy by three to one, and his men were patriots from the New England States, the bravest soldiers in the war, while Burgoyne's army were mainly hired mercenaries. Washington had looked upon the passage of the Hudson as of the utmost importance, and had spared, from his main force, some of the best Generals and the flower of his troops to operate against Burgoyne and Clinton. It is a Commander-in-Chief's duty to provide his subordinate Generals with men and material in proportion to the importance of the operation to be carried out, and Washington, undoubtedly, spared more men and officers from the army under his immediate charge than he could afford. He himself, when operating against Howe, had reason to complain that the States from which he should have drawn recruits,—Pennyslvania and Jersey—did not rise to the occasion. But Gates could make no such complaint against the Northern States. They fully supplied men, money and provisions in abundance and Saratoga was the result and the reward of their patriotism. Therefore, while giving all honour to Horatio Gates for the victory of Saratoga we must not take away any of the credit justly due to the Commander who planned the disposition of the forces which led to so happy a result.

That Gates ignored his General-in-Chief is amply shown by the following extract from a letter to Putnam more than a week after Burgoyne's surrender :

"I have not received a single line from General Gates. I do not know what steps he is taking with the army under his command, and therefore I cannot advise what is best to be done in your quarter." On the 30th October, Washington wrote to Gates congratulating the army under his command on account of their success, and, at the same time, adding his regret that a matter of such importance, and having such import to the general operations, should have reached him through other channels than that of a note from him under his own signature."

It was at this point in the intrigue, when matters had begun to take a serious turn, and when what was before but secret plotting became an open topic of conversation among the troops, that Washington wrote the note already referred to to General Conway."

Washington was adverse to noticing the intrigues of the Cabal, as is evident from the following extract from a letter of his to Patrick Henry:—" My caution to avoid anything that could injure the service prevented me from communicating, except to a very few friends, the intrigues of a faction which, I knew, was formed against me, since it might serve to publish our internal dissensions. But their own restless zeal to advance their views has too clearly betrayed them, and made concealment on my part fruitless. I cannot precisely mark the extent of their views, but it appeared in general that General Gates was to be exalted on the ruin of my reputation and influence. This I am authorised to say from undeniable facts in my possession, from publications, the evident scope of which could not be mistaken, and from private detractions assiduously circulated. I have good reason to believe their machinations have recoiled most sensibly on themselves."

This letter was written in March, 1778, before this year's campaign had opened, and some months after the plot had been exposed, and the plotters rightly censured by the public voice. As early as December, 1772, when the intrigue had been laid bare, public censure needed the prudent moderation of Washington to prevent violence to some of the intriguers, and some time later Conway fought a duel with one of the officers in the army, and was so severely wounded that, imagining

himself on the point of death, he thus wrote to Washington :—
" My career will soon be over, therefore justice and truth
prompt me to declare my last sentiments. You are in my
eyes the great and good man. May you long enjoy the love
and veneration and esteem of those States whose liberties
you have asserted by your virtues. Expressing my sincere
regret for my action, I, with the greatest respect, remain
yours, Thomas Conway." Conway was forced to give
up the American cause and emigrate to France. In
pursuing the history of this cabal we are anticipating
events by some months, but it is well that the reader should
have a connected narrative of it from the time it first took
definite shape after the battle of Saratoga to its final extinction
with the court-martial of General Lee after the battle of
Monmouth, in view of the intimate relations between the intrigue and the events of the war.

Thomas Conway was an Irishman by birth, and Irishmen,
almost by instinct, ranged themselves under the banner of
liberty in America. Conway was a mere tool in the hands of
a powerful faction. His letter given above shows that he was
deceived and that he repented of the part he played in the
treacherous game. A letter from General John Sullivan, a
brave New England soldier and lawyer, descended from a
princely Irish stock of colonists, who came over during the
troubled times in Ireland, in the seventeenth century, and
settled in Connecticut, throws some light on the aims and extent
of the cabal. He says, "The faction of 1777, into which General
Conway was unfortunately and imprudently drawn, is not yet
destroyed (1779). The members are waiting to collect strength
to appear in force. Then they shall inspire the people with
sentiments arising from the danger that too much confidence in
you might lead to imaginary evils. They will try to persuade
Congress that absolute power in one man is fraught with
menace to the States, and that three or four Generals, independent of each other, should be in command and responsible
to Congress. In this way the one force would act as a check on

the ambition of the other. They know your claim to the just confidence of the country is too powerful at present, but should a time come that they could further their designs they shall not fail to act against your command."

So ended the Conway cabal, and so ended every attempt to stain the reputation of Washington, and many such insiduous attempts were made from time to time during his honourable career. All efforts of his enemies to fix accusations of any kind upon him either in his public or private, his military or civil character, utterly failed, and in every instance tended to involve the author in difficulties and disgrace. The rank and file of the army adored the Commander-in-Chief, and most indignantly repudiated the factionists. Even the northern soldiers, under Gates, most enthusiastically proclaimed their attachment to Washington, and resisted any attempt to change chiefs. It is not to be doubted that most of them, like Morgan, would have refused to serve under any other. He was the idol of the army, and in him they saw the saviour of their country. They knew he served the cause for no personal gain—for no ambitious motives. They knew that he conscientiously did his best to promote the public good, and that self was never considered. Hence faction was powerless to injure him.

We saw the fate that befell poor Conway. Gates, too, never rallied from the part he played in the intrigue, and two years later, after leading a forlorn expedition against Cornwallis and Cartleton in the South, he lost his army, and fled from the field a hundred miles, with the enemy on his track. Soon after he was degraded from his rank, and left the army in disgrace.

General Lee was in prison from the defeat at New York until exchanged late in 1777, and hence his part in the intrigue was of short duration, but after he regained the army he was by no means an acquisition to the General. He was ever intruding his views in opposition to Washington's, and he was not without talent and prestige to make some headway in his designs. We saw how he refused to obey orders in joining the army before the battle of Trenton. We now know how, in 1778, at the battle of Monmouth, he refused to engage in action, and afterwards, when Lafayette took his command, he sought and gained back his command of the forces Lafayette was leading, and we see him ordering a retreat when he should have been attacking the foe. Washington publicly upbraided him for his disobedience and took the command in person. This action of Lee's led to a public investigation, to a court-martial, and finally to his expulsion from the army, and to his death in disgrace some years later.

THE TREATY WITH FRANCE.

BURGOYNE surrendered on the 7th October, 1777. One year previous to this event Commissioners Franklin, Henry Lee and Silas Deane had been in France for the purpose of negotiating an alliance with the court at Versailles. Their mission at first was not crowned with success. They were courteously received in the French capital, and they were assured of private aid, but officially it was not considered opportune to enter into any open alliance. The King of the French was a youthful prince, but prudent and cautious. His country had been involved in much debt of late owing to the Colonial wars. He needed money himself to fill his much impoverished exchequer. He was advised not to risk, at present, an open rupture with England. No doubt, France indirectly aided the States by private help. She furnished such men as Lafayette, De Kalb, and Thaddeus Kosciusko; and many other volunteers left her shores, prior to the Saratoga surrender, and did gallant service under Washington.

There was no doubt that France felt the humiliation of

losing Canada, and a strong party was rising at Court which was not averse from striking a blow against English prestige. Saratoga gave this party its opportunity. Soon after that success to American arms France openly offered alliance with America. Franklin, the leviathan of these negotiations with foreign powers, was a wary diplomat. Whilst negotiating with France, he offered to open an alliance with Lord North and his nation on similar lines of mutual goodwill and commercial agreement, on condition, of course, that hostilities should cease, and that the Independence of the States should be made a necessary preliminary. His parleying in this manner with Lord North had the desired effect of hastening the longed-for treaty with the French, and after that with the Spanish government.

It was wonderful how soon the tone of the English bullies changed towards the United States envoys, and the hitherto despised farmer soldiers. British ambassadors at European Courts would not negotiate with the "envoys of rebels" before the great General Burgoyne was humiliated; now North, the Prime Minister, was willing to enter into friendly negotiations with Congress, with Washington, and the different States. He was willing to grant all that America petitioned for; he was willing to give them every liberty, short of independence. But the die was cast. There was no use in the great Chatham shedding crocodile tears over the abomination of employing Indians in the war. "Such a use of these savages," said the great statesman, "as butchering women and children and the wounded in warfare, was a principle abominable and abhorrent to religion and humanity." The British Parliament appointed delegates to proceed from London to America and communicate, by proclamation, the amicable designs of Great Britain towards her unruly subjects. They were empowered with high authority to cause cessation of hostilities—to treat with the States individually or collectively. They had powers to grant all pardons, to establish govern-ments in every State willing to acknowledge the supremacy of

England. Their object was the mischievous one of trying to alienate any disaffected State from the whole. They offered bribes to any Congressmen who should aid them, and one Mr. Reid, was offered ten thousand pounds if he would work for conciliation on their lines. His answer was noble, and it was also typical of the whole Congress : " I am a poor man but all the gold of the King of England could not buy me." The mission of the British Commissioners proved a fiasco, and they were glad to return to England as they came.

The French Cabinet, now that things looked so propitious, lost no time in entering into a treaty with America. Not alone did they agree to a commercial alliance, but they openly entered into a mutual alliance during the war of offensive and defensive operations. The alliance agreed upon bound France and the United States to a common cause, and it stipulated that the States were not to enter into a truce with Great Britain without the formal consent of France and *vice versa*. Moreover, they mutually engaged each other not to lay down their arms until the Independence of the United States should have been formally or tacitly assured by the treaty or treaties that should terminate the war. That this alliance was no " hole in corner " agreement was soon made patent to the world: The Marquis de Noailles was commissioned to officially announce the fact to the British Cabinet, as soon as ratified by the signatures of M. Gerard, on behalf of France, and Franklin, Lee, and Deane, on behalf of the United States. The document conveying the intelligence to the Court of London is worthy of reproduction. As a piece of shrewd diplomatic sarcasm it is inimitable.

" In making this communication to the Court of London the King is firmly persuaded that it will find in it fresh proofs of his Majesty's constant and sincere dispositions of peace, and that his Brittanic Majesty, animated by the same sentiments, will equally avoid everything that may interrupt good harmony, and that he will take in particular effectual measures to hinder the commerce of his Majesty's subjects of the United

States of America from being disturbed. In this confidence the underwritten ambassador might think it superfluous to apprise the British ministry that the King, his master, being determined effectually to protect the lawful freedom of the commerce of his subjects, and to sustain the honor of his flag, his Majesty has taken, in consequence, eventual measures in concert with the United States of America."

The above document was dated 13th March, 1778, and when it reached the British Court it cast the ministers into a state of alarm. It now became painfully evident to King George and his advisers that the issue was widening, and that their ancient rival had thrown down the gauntlet once again to England. On the 17th March a message from the King of Great Britain announced to both Houses of Parliament that, in consequence of the receipt of an offensive communication from the Court of France, referring to his Majesty's revolted subjects in America, the King had ordered the withdrawal of his ambassador from France, and that he relied upon the patriotism of his people to enable him to exert all the resources of his kingdom to resent the insulting and provoking aggression of the French King.

Both Houses pledged themselves to exert every energy at their command to vindicate the honour of the Crown, and protect the rights of the kingdom. With the Americans single-handed they might have treated for peace and cessation of hostilities, but at the dictation of their old rival, Never!

Lord Chatham, with Burke and Barre and Conway, had been all along strenuous advocates for peace and reconciliation. Many were the speeches these orators delivered against the justness of the war, and the causes that led to hostilities, but now that America, through her French ally, had demanded peace and Independence, Chatham had himself carried down to the Assembly of Peers to deliver his last public speech against American Independence. He was almost dying, and died four days after he uttered his memorable oration, from which we may be excused for quoting largely, as it truly voices the sentiment of the nation in this crisis :

"I have made an effort," he said, "almost beyond my strength, to come down to this House on this day, to express the indignation I feel at an idea which I understand has been proposed to you of yielding up the sovereignty of America. My Lord, I rejoice that the grave has not closed upon me, that I am still alive to lift up my voice against the dismemberment of this ancient and most noble monarchy. Pressed down as I am by the hand of infirmity, I am little able to assist my country in this most perilous conjuncture, but my lords, while I have sense and memory, I will never consent to deprive the royal offspring of the House of Brunswick, the heir of Princess Sophia, of their fairest inheritance. Where is the man that will dare to advise such a measure ? His Majesty succeeded to an empire as great in extent as its reputation was unsullied. Shall we tarnish the lustre of this nation by an ignominious surrender of its rights and fairest possessions ? Shall this Kingdom, that has survived whole and entire the Danish depredations, the Scottish inroads, and the Norman Conquest ; that has stood the threatened invasion of the Spanish Armada, now fall prostrate before the House of Bourbon ? Surely, my lords, this nation is no longer what it was. Shall a people that seventeen years ago was the terror of the world now stoop so low as to tell its ancient inveterate enemy, ' Take all we have, only give us peace !' It is impossible. In God's name it is absolutely necessary to declare either for peace or war, and if the former cannot be preserved with honour, why is not the latter commenced without hesitation ? I am, I confess, not informed of the resources of the Kingdom, but I trust it is sufficient to maintain its just rights. But, my Lords, any state is better than despair. Let us at least make an effort and if we fall let us fall like men."

England was flaming with indignation at the French alliance. She accordingly formed her plans to checkmate her ancient rival. On the announcement of the alliance the joy of America was unbounded, and when the French fleet arrived at the mouth of the Delaware in the spring of 1778, accompanied by their ambassador, and under the command of Admiral the Count D'Estaing, with 4,000 troops to take part in the war, and act under the instructions of Washington and Congress, hopes of final victory sat upon the souls of all. The soldiers at Valley Forge were exultant when the glad tidings reached them. A day was set apart for feasting and jubilation ; Washington gave a public banquet to his long-suffering soldiers. He himself, surrounded by his officers, and with bands playing French and American airs, dined in the midst of the army on the public holiday for the festivities. Patriotic toasts were drunk, and cheering, tossing of hats in air, and wild huzzas were fully indulged in to express the pleasure all felt at the glad event.

The cause of American liberty now entered upon a new chapter of hope and confidence of final success. Where doubt reigned among many over the States new hope and determination and certainty of final victory replaced the despondency. The sun of American Independence had already began to glimmer on the horizon. The union of Stars and Stripes with the Fleur de Lis was all that was required to bring about their emancipation.

VALLEY FORGE.

Our retrospect over the striking scenes of the Revolution would be incomplete without a glimpse of Washington's army in winter quarters after the battle of Germanstown. The careful Commander-in-Chief had chosen for it the high grounds, twenty miles up the mountains from Philadelphia, where he might have a commanding and safe position in the large protected valley for resting his wearied and shattered forces, recruiting and disciplining them for the campaign of '78. Here he hoped to be able to intercept the foraging parties that might go out from the cooped-up forces of Howe, in and around Philadelphia.

The condition of the troops was truly deplorable. Here you had an army of 10,800 men, enduring privations so severe that, in the history of wars. there is not recorded a parallel. Nothing but the most exalted patriotism, and a restless craving for Independence could possibly have kept them together during the severe winter months that intervened from November until the Spring of 1778. Patiently, with calm determination, and amidst penury, hunger, and cold, these brave men waited without a murmur for the necessaries to come into camp, often famishing in their patient endurance from hunger and cold. "Such," says Warren, "was the deficiency of horses and waggons that the men, in many instances, yoked themselves to carriages of their own construction, while others carried burdens of wood or provisions on their backs for the day's supply."

The soldiers were subsisting for days at a time without the necessary provisions to render them fit and efficient for an emergency. Many of the common soldiers were without shirts and boots. Washington had to endure the common lot of Generals so situated, of seeing many of his men deserting him. He had to allay murmuring and complaints among the disaffected. Some of his officers, wearied with the hard lot of camp, handed in their commissions that they might return to home and social ease. The vacancies in important positions in the army were often left unfilled for a long interval, and some of the officers were essential, so that organization and discipline could not well be maintained.

"A large army," says Lessing, "was concentrated at Valley Forge, whose naked footprints in the snow, converging to that bleak hill-side, were often tracked with blood. Absolute destitution there held high court, and never was.the chivalric heroism of patient suffering more tangibly manifested than was exhibited by that patriot band within those frail huts that barely covered them from the keen wintry blasts. Many were sitting without shoes or stockings and nearly naked, obliged to sit night after night shivering round their fires in quest of the comforts of heat."

Washington, who kept Congress constantly supplied with information about every detail of his army, thus wrote from his camp to the President of Congress on the 23rd December, 1777 :

" I am now convinced, beyond doubt, that unless some great change suddenly takes place in the commissary department, this army must inevitably be reduced to one of two things —starvation, or to disperse and procure provisions in the best way they can."

The latter mode of gathering in provisions from the farmers had to be resorted to, before the winter was over, and Congress passed resolutions sanctioning it.

Again, at a point later than the above letter, we find Washington thus addressing Congress : " For some days there has been little less than famine in the camp. Naked and starving as they are, we cannot enough admire the incomparable patience and fidelity of the soldiers that they have not ere this been incited to a general mutiny by their sufferings. Strong symptoms of discontent have, however, appeared in particular instances, and nothing but the most active efforts everywhere can long avert so shocking a catastrophe."

The general, to add to his difficulties, often found that those in authority were slow to move to supply his wants. " I declare," he said, " that no man, in my opinion, ever had his measures more impeded than I have, not alone by the vulgar, but by every department. Many of my men are confined to the camp, and unfit for duty for want of shoes, many are in hospital from one cause or another. We have from a field return made early in the winter some 2,898 unfit for duty because without shirts and barefooted."

It is strange that, notwithstanding these urgent appeals, Congress for months delayed coming to the aid of the harassed army. The hope and determination of the Commander, under the many crosses and trials he endured, never failed him. He kept constantly before him the fact that in him and his army the liberties of the country were placed. Hence he

I

never failed to plead for his soldiers, and he shared with them
the toils and heats of battle, and the colds and privations of
winter quarters, still steadily looking forward to the spring
when he should have a force strong and equal to take the
field against the well-fed, well-housed forces of General Howe.

It is worthy of note that the three winters the British
army had been operating up to this in America, they lay
inactive, cooped up in large cities, where there were no enemies
but old people, women and children, and only ventured out
when burning and foraging compelled them to harass the
neighbourhood around. It was thus in Boston in the winter
of '75-'76, and was thus in New York in that of '76-'77,
and it was in this inactive manner Howe in the year following
held confined an army of almost 11,000 from December until
May. Doing nothing, attempting nothing, unless when fresh
food for horses and men was necessary. when pickets would
be detached to capture forage, and to annoy the neighbourhood.
It seems also worthy of note that Howe seemed to be acting
under advice from the Home Government in this course of
inactivity, and when he refused to act on such instructions
from civil authorities. His successor, Sir Henry Clinton, seemed
to have no other immediate policy in the May of 1778 than to
evacuate one city and march to New York, and thus like
" hare whom hounds and horns pursue, return to the spot
from whence at first he flew," almost two years previously.

During these winter months, besides feeding and clothing,
and drilling his forces, and keeping a sharp look-out on flying
parties, Washington was not unmindful of the brave men
who were prisoners of war in the hands of the enemy. Many
of these men suffered much in land prisons and in ships anchored
at sea. In the beginning of the war, no exchanges were
allowed by General Gage, but when complaints and remonstrances were made to Howe, he denied that there was any
ill-treatment to his knowledge, and undertook to exchange
man for man and officer for officer. A committee of inspection
was formed to go to the barracks or prisons of each army and

see and hear for themselves how matters stood. In this way, by protest and negotiations, much reform was worked in the treatment of prisoners confined in English dungeons.

We may here mention that the forces led by Gates and Putnam were quartered around the Hudson, and along the north-east seaboard, after the British forces led by Clinton the previous autumn had returned to New York, leaving as they did, the forts they so successfully captured in October in the hands of the Americans.

When the news of the alliance between France and America had reached the British forces at Philadelphia, it spread con-sternation throughout the ranks. It was already evident that the Commissioners sent out by Lord North were a failure. Reconciliation, short of Independence, was not to be heard of, on the part of the Americans, and, as yet, England could not think of yielding up her title of sovereignty in America. It was dishonourable of England to go around endeavouring to induce the States to break their solemn oath and treaty with France, and a writer at this time thus speaks of the English : " What sort of men or Christians must you suppose us Americans to be. After you rejected all our humble petitions with insults the most galling, after you declared war upon us and called in brutal Germans and savage Indians to butcher our women and children, after having starved in stone dungeons our prisoners, harassed the people, burned their homes, and pillaged and plundered their property, you ask us to become reconciled with you and break faith, after our sworn declara-tion to be faithful, to our French Alliance. Such a request argues corruption and infidelity in the proposer. It exhibits you as a nation without faith with whom a solemn promise or oath is a trifle."

The intention of England, when news of the Alliance was known to them, was to proclaim war against France. Hence it was not judicious to have a large army cooped up in Phila-delphia. But were they to reach New York by land or water, for to New York Clinton was ordered to transfer his forces ?

It was soon made known to the British General that a large naval force was setting out from Toulon, and that its destination was in all likelihood America. Clinton feared, and with good reason, that if he delayed at Philadelphia this fleet might arrive on the Delaware, co-operate with Washington, and treat his army to a second Saratoga. He despatched a great part of his baggage and some of his regiments by water to the east, whilst he prepared his main body to cross by Jersey to Sandy Hook. Washington, well posted by his scouts of every movement of the enemy, sent forward detachments of his army to hang on his flanks, keeping themselves safely on the heights. The Pennsylvania militia and Lafayette, with an active corps of the main line, were sent off for this advance work. Washington himself followed up with the main line some distance in the rear, and held a council of war as to the advisability of giving battle to the enemy by a general engagement. It was argued by General Lee and most of the officers that it was not advisable to risk an action with the enemy, that it was better to wait the arrival of the French fleet, and then give them a crushing blow that should end the war. Washington was at first inclined to yield to this advice, but being pressed by Wayne, Greene and Lafayette, and other brave and enthusiastic leaders, he determined to give the enemy battle at Monmouth, to the east of Delaware, whither they were now marching. Of course this decision of the General was subject to the condition that circumstances should prove favourable for attack. It seemed to be the wish of the English General to bring about an engagement, so slow was his forward movement.

It was June the 28th when young Lafayette set out with 5,000 troops, to give battle to the enemy from the heights above Monmouth. General Lee, who at first was opposed to lead, though it was his privilege to supersede Lafayette, later on repented of this, asked the General for orders to lead the advance forces now in command of the Frenchman. Lee had his wish granted, but on coming up with the enemy, instead of leading an attack he ordered a retreat and brought back his forces some two miles, with the enemy in hot pursuit. Washington, arriving on the scene with his contingent, sharply censured Lee, rallied the retreating forces, changed the fortunes of the day, and turned the British pursuit into a retreat. After rallying and rearranging his troops he placed Greene in temporary command. The encounter was fierce and well sustained. Many fell on both sides, and not until darkness did the contending armies desist from battle. The Americans stood to their arms during the night, determined to renew the contest by daybreak, but Clinton was satisfied with his share in the encounter and during the night, unobserved by Washington, marched off towards the Hook. He thus eluded the pursuit of the Americans, because it would not have been safe to follow him further east. Washington, after the battle of Monmouth, withdrew his forces across the Delaware, and camped on the borders of the Hudson. The losses on both sides were pretty even, being computed at about 300 in killed and wounded on each side. The gain, however, was all on the American side, as the engagement proved to the enemy the courage of the Continentals, and the waverers and stragglers to well nigh the number of a thousand abandoned the British on their slow march from Philadelphia to the sea at Sandy Hook. Washington, in his report of this battle to Congress, gave a high meed of praise to both officers and men. General Lee was, soon after this, placed under arrest and court-martialled for disobeying orders, for shameful retreat before enemy, and for writing insulting letters to the General after the battle. He was suspended and retired in disgrace, and it is now believed he was a traitor to the cause of American liberty.

The details of the battle of Monmouth, with all the circumstances and particulars as to the disposition of his men, and the bravery of his officers, especially Wayne and Greene and Morgan, were duly after the battle communicated according to his practice by Washington to Congress, but we have selected a private letter of the General, dated 4th July, from

Brunswick, to his brother John Augustine Washington, as a more suitable account of the engagement in a history for readers now one hundred and thirty years removed from the times about which we write. He writes :—" Dear Brother—Before this will have reached you, the account of the battle of Monmouth will probably get to Virginia, which, from an unfortunate and bad beginning turned out a glorious and happy day. The enemy evacuated Philadelphia on the 18th June. At ten o'clock that day I got intelligence of it, and by two o'clock, or very soon after, I had six brigades on their march for the Jerseys, and followed with the whole army the next morning. On the 21st we completed our passage over the Delaware at Coryell's Ferry, about thirty miles from Philadelphia, and distant from Valley Forge about forty miles. From this ferry we moved down towards the enemy and on the 27th got within six miles of them.

General Lee, having command of the van of the army, consisting of four thousand chosen men, was ordered to begin the attack next morning, so soon as the enemy began their march, to be supported by me, but strange to tell, when he came up with the enemy a retreat commenced, whether by his order or from other causes is now a subject of inquiry, and consequently improper to be descanted upon, as he is under arrest and a courtmartial is sitting for his trial. The disorder arising from their retreat would have proved fatal to the army had not the bountiful Providence, which has never failed in the hour of distress, enabled me to form a regiment or two in face of the enemy and under fire of the pursuing enemy, by which means a stand was made long enough to form the troops that were advancing upon an advantageous piece of ground in the rear. Here our affairs took a favourable turn, and from being pursued we drove the enemy back over the ground they had followed, and recovered the field of battle and possessed ourselves of their dead. But owing to the nature of the ground surrounding the enemy, owing to the fatigue

of our men from want of water and heat, and because of darkness setting in, we found it impracticable to do anything more
that night.   In the morning we expected to renew the action,
when, behold, the enemy had stolen off silently in the night,
after having sent on their baggage and wounded in advance.
We accordingly judged it expedient, considering that they were
only ten miles from a strong fort, to move to the North river,
lest they should have any design upon our posts there."

Clinton marched his army into New York without any
opposition after the battle of Monmouth.   He was well advised
to evacuate Philadelphia at the time he did.   His fate, had he
delayed much longer, might have been that of Burgoyne, for
he was no sooner clear of the Delaware than the French fleet
under D'Estaing, with a force amounting to 4,000 men on
board, reached the mouth of the Delaware.   Had not the
French Admiral been delayed on his journey, owing to adverse
winds, it can hardly be doubted that the British General,
hemmed in by two armies, would have been forced to surrender.

Washington, not knowing what might be Clinton's object
in choosing New York as his destination, sent word to General
Gates, who was guarding the Hudson, that he was marching
to join him, so that he might be able to checkmate any movement of the enemy against the American lines on the North
river.   He encamped his army across the Hudson at the White
Plains, and sent instructions to Count D'Estaing to sail to
Newport in Rhodes Island, to aid in expelling a British force
of 4,000 stationed in that seaport.   Admiral Howe, commander
of the English fleet, followed the French commander with a
fleet of four men-of-war, in order to allure him to a sea battle.
It had been arranged that the Continentals, under Sullivan,
should, simultaneously with the French forces, make an attack
on the 9th August on Newport, but Howe appeared on the
scene and upset all their arrangements.   The two fleets cruised
about, sparring with each other, but did not come to any serious encounter until a storm arose at sea lasting for some days,
which separated and buffeted the vessels about and did much

injury to them, so that both Generals were compelled to run to ports of safety for repairs ; the British to New York ; D'Estaing to Boston.

Sullivan who, with John Hancock, was in command of the American forces around Newport, appealed to the French to allow his men to co-operate with the Americans and effect the expulsion of the British before he should retire to Boston, but all entreaties and remonstrances failed to move the French Admiral to change his resolve. Laurens, Lafayette, and Greene joined Sullivan in entreating the sensitive Frenchman to send his troops ashore to co-operate with the Continentals, but in vain. There was but one course open to Sullivan and that was to make sure of a safe retreat from the Island on which his 6,000 men were posted, as it was deemed inadvisable to attack Newport without the French auxiliaries now that Howe and Clinton had come to their aid with a force of four thousand from New York.

The conduct of the French Admiral gave much chagrin to the American Generals, especially Sullivan, who, it seems, used some very uncomplimentary expressions about the fleet, and the value of the French Alliance. The feelings of the common soldier in the lines of both American and French forces were not by any means the most friendly. There were old animosities coming down from the Colonial days, when French and Americans were opposed to each other in the border wars. The refusal of D'Estaing to yield to the wishes of the American Generals at Newport had renewed the old sores, and matters at this time looked so serious that it took all the diplomacy of Congress, all the tact and prudence of Washington, and the powerful intermediary influence of Lafayette to reconcile the two nationalities, and bridge over the rising indignation that the unfortunate occurrence at Newport engendered.

Some extracts from correspondence of Washington's at this time will best disclose how matters stood. On the 1st September, 1778, he thus wrote from White Plains camp to General Greene :—

" I have not now time to take notice of the arguments that were made use of for and against the Count's quitting the harbour of Newport, and sailing for Boston.   Right or wrong it will probably disappoint our sanguine expectations of success, and what I esteem a still worse consequence, I fear it will sow the seeds of dissension and distrust between us and our new allies unless the most prudent measures are taken to suppress the feuds and jealousies that have already risen.   I depend much upon your temper and influence to conciliate the animosities which I plainly perceive, by a letter from the Marquis, subsist between our army and officers and the French in our service.

To the Marquis de Lafayette at this time Washington writes asking him " to use his best endeavours and the great influence which undoubtedly his high rank gives him with the Count and his fellow countrymen, to bridge over the opening chasm of disaffection and jealousy and distrust created by the Newport affair."   He says, "We appreciate the importance of the alliance, and the impetus a French fleet on our shores gives to our arms, but in a free republican government you cannot restrain the voice of the multitude.   Every man will speak and think as he judges right, without often weighing the consequences.   You can afford a healing hand to the wound that unintentionally has been made, and I have no doubt." he adds, " you will use your utmost endeavour to restore harmony, that the honour and glory and mutual interest of the two nations may be promoted and cemented in the firmest way."

To General Sullivan at this critical juncture he wrote : " Permit me to recommend in the most particular manner the cultivation of harmony and good agreement, and your endeavours to destroy that ill humour which may have got into the officers."

We may be permitted to add one more extract from the numerous letters of Washington written at this time. He says, speaking of the present position of affairs : " It is not a little pleasing nor less wonderful to contemplate that, after two years manoeuvring and undergoing the strangest vicissitudes that, perhaps, ever attended any one contest since the creation, both armies are brought back to the very point they set out from, and that the offending party at the beginning is now reduced to the use of the spade and the pickaxe for defence. The hand of Providence has been so conspicuous in all this that he must be worse than an infidel that lacks faith, and more than wicked that has not gratitude enough to acknowledge his obligations. But it will be time enough to turn preacher when my present appointment ceases, and therefore I shall add no more on the doctrine of Providence."

There was little real warfare on American soil for some time after the Newport expedition. The English at home were busily discussing American affairs. The general opinion and the heart-felt wish in England was to come to peace at any cost with America; short of granting independence, both sides of the house were prepared to concede anything. The one enemy to be punished was the French, the historic rival of England's greatness. There is no doubt that much chagrin was felt that the Americans, descended as they were from Anglo-Saxon fathers, who had hated and fought the French in Colonial and Continental wars, should now turn round so soon after having by petition and proclamation assured the English monarch of the love for his person and patronage, ally themselves with the descendants of the Catholic line of Bourbons, and bring over to their shores a French army to banish for ever the monarch of their fathers. But there were not wanting English statesmen in Parliament to remind Lord North and his ministry that they first had brought in the subjects of a foreign prince to butcher his American subjects. North was reminded of how he spurned all the entreaties of the Americans for a peaceful alliance on honourable terms, before hostilities commenced, how he had outraged them by bringing in Indian savages to tomahawk defenceless men, women and children ; how the country was made to groan under pillage, butchery and burnings, and how the quondam subjects of the King had been called rebels, and chased from their desolated country to seek refuge in open hostilities in the army of their countrymen arrayed under the banner of Washington. The tactics of the British army and government from the commencement of the war till the end of 1778, the time of which we speak, could have only one effect on the American people: it exasperated both patriots and loyalists. Many of the latter were still found in the country whom it certainly was the interests of the English to conciliate and strengthen in their loyalty, but when they found—as was the case in Jersey, and around New York—the wicked soldiery, German and English, indiscriminately burning, pillaging, and destroying houses aud villages without distinction, timid friends were very soon converted into bitter enemies, and the people of America united in a solid phalanx to resist the common oppressor.

But desperate as were the military atrocities which were of so frequent occurrence along the seaboard, they fall into insignificance when compared with the horrors and barbarities perpetrated on the inland frontiers, where Indians were the chief agents in the brutal warfare. There can be no doubt that the war party in England was directly accountable for the use of the red savages, whose only thirst is for booty, blood and scalps. The instructions the Generals operating in the West and North-Western territories received were to use the Indian chiefs and tribes as scouts and allies against the " rebel " American subjects. It was no wonder that some of the opposition statesmen in Parliament denounced, in some of the most famous orations in the English language, this inhuman mode of warfare. It will be interesting and appropriate in this place to give some extracts from the speeches delivered in the debate on the use of Indians and Germans in these wars.

The Earl of Chatham in moving an amendment to the address from the throne said :—

" Conquest is impossible. You may swell every expense and every effort, pile and accumulate every assistance you can buy or borrow, traffic and barter with every little pitiful German prince that sells and sends his subjects to a foreign prince. Your efforts are vain and impotent, doubly so from the mercenary aid on which you rely, for it irritates to an incurable resentment the minds of your enemies to over-run them with mercenary sons of rapine and plunder, devoting them and their possessions to the rapacity of hireling cruelty. If I were an American, as I am an Englishman, while a foreign troop was landed in my country, I would never lay down my arms—Never ! Never ! Never !

Your own army is infected with the contagion of these illiberal allies. The spirit of plunder and of rapine is gone forth among them. I know from authentic information that our discipline is deeply wounded, and while this is notoriously our sinking situation America grows and flourishes ; whilst our strength and discipline are lowered theirs are rising and improving. But, my lords, who is the man that, in addition to these disgraces and mischiefs of our army, has dared to authorise and associate to our arms the tomahawk and scalping knife of the savage, to call into civilized alliance the wild and inhuman savage of the woods ; to delegate to the merciless Indian the defence of disputed rights ; and to wage the horrors of his barbarous war against our brethren ? My lords, these enormities cry for redress and punishment."

The American Congress was not able to reconcile the Indians to their government, nor to win them over to any great extent to their cause. They could not supply them with those European articles which they were accustomed to use. Seeing that conciliatory means were of no avail to prevent the savage incursions of the red neighbours into ill-protected, isolated Colonies on the borders, and considering, also, that these savages were organised and armed by Brant and other leaders in the interests of the British forces, who were operating from Detroit and the Lakes, it was deemed advisable by Congress to entrust an American General, named M'Intosh, with a force, to march from Pittsburgh against the organized British, Indian and

Canadian troops, who, from information to hand, were meditating early in 1778, a general attack on the frontier. Unfortunately, the American expedition was neglected, but the enemy carried out, in a most inhuman manner, their meditated attack.

COLONEL GEORGE RODGER CLARKE.

Colonel George Rodger Clarke, a youthful Virginian farmer and relative of Thomas Jefferson, distinguished himself in the frontier wars for Independence, subduing the Indians and British in the Ohio, Wabash, and Mississippi territories, and the tracts of land lying north-west of the present city of Pittsburgh. In his youthful days Clarke, like the immortal Washington, and many other illustrious Americans, followed the occupation of surveyor. He had also been at an early age trained in the local militia, and held the position of captain. He served, like Washington, in the Colonial wars, which were brought to a close in 1764, and which gave to the English undisputed control of those North-Western territories. Clarke, like many a bold and ambitious youth in those early colonizing days trekked out in the year 1774 from his North Virginian plantations across the Ohio, and into the territories now known as Kentucky and Illinois. Here he soon distinguished himself amongst his fellow-colonials. He was not like many of his companions in this unreclaimed region, devoid of education; his wider range of knowledge of men and movements made him looked up to among his compeers. He was of a daring and venturesome disposition. He knew not fear, and he saw far ahead for one so far removed from Eastern civilization. It may truly be said that these Western squatters were completely cut adrift from the Eastern States by the pathless Alleghany mountains, with their forest-clothed peaks and winding rivers shutting them off. They, in some sense, were at the mercy of the Indian tribes, and their British masters who directed them from the Forts across the Ohio and the Lakes.

The transmigration of planters was slow across the borders into the unknown regions occupied by wandering tribes of Indians. After the capture of Montreal, when the French lost Canada, the Indians on the west borders did not cease to harass the planters, and beat them back from their westward encroachments into their territory east and west of the Ohio. From the year 1755, when Braddock was defeated by the Indians, until 1774, when Lord Dunmore, then Governor of Virginia, gained a decisive victory at Fort Pleasant against a superior number of Indians, the Indian tribes never gave the " big knives," as they called the planters, any peace on the borders. Although this battle was gained at the cost of the loss of many brave Virginians, yet it so terrified the Indians that they gladly signed a treaty of peace with the British Governor.

An epistle sent by one Logan, a chief of the tribes, to Lord Dunmore at this time reflects very characteristically the undying hate in those frontier days, that the much abused Indians had for the Paleface. " I appeal," says the chief, " to any white man to say if ever Logan's cabin was shut against the hungry ; if a white man entered he gave him what meat he had ; if ever he came cold and hungry and naked Logan clothed him. During the long war Logan remained at home idle in his cabin—an advocate for peace. Such was my love for the white man that my countrymen pointed as they passed and said, ' Logan is the friend of white man.' I have even thought to have lived with you but for the injuries of one man. Colonel Cressy, the last spring, in cold blood and un·provoked, murdered all the relations of Logan, not even sparing women and children. There runs not a drop of my blood in the veins of any living creature. This called on me for revenge. I have sought it ; I have killed many ; I have fully glutted my vengeance. For my people I rejoice at the beams of peace, but do not harbour a thought that mine is the joy of fear. Logan never felt fear. He will not turn on his heel to save his life. Who is there to mourn for Logan? Not one."

Soon after this peace was signed the Revolution began. The peace was then of little avail to the backwoodsmen, since almost all of them had joined the cause of liberty. The Indians looked on themselves as bound, more or less, by the treaty, as far as they respected rights under a treaty. As a rule the Indian looked upon it as a duty to keep back the pale-faces, and those roving and venturesome spirits who left their homes in Virginia, North Carolina, and Pennsylvania had little concern with treaties or Indians further than to shoot the latter down like rabbits if they came their way. The Indians, like Logan, too, were legion who deemed revenge a sacred duty, and in their turn they lay in wait and murdered the squatters and frontiersmen in their homes, at their work, in the corn fields, on the rivers and on the chase, wherever, in short, a paleface was to be found in the neighbourhood of the Indian hunting grounds.

Notwithstanding the constant danger that attended the life of a pioneer in those days, many venturesome individuals trekked out into those pathless regions now known as Kentucky and Illinois, so that about the years '77, '78 and '79 there was a formidable array of backwoodsmen in these territories. These men were organized and commanded by George Rodger Clarke and by Daniel Boone and Simeon Kenton, mainly for use within their own borders. Clarke saw things in a broader light than Boone and Kenton, and hence, after he organized those pioneers and became their advocate and deputy at the House of Burgesses in Virginia, he led them against the combined forces of British and Indians across the frontiers from Ohio to Mississippi, and north to Detroit. Boone and his companion were men who might be called the local defenders of the settlers of Kentucky. They fought hundreds of engagements against the Indians in defence of their homes and forts, and friends. They were fearless of danger. They loved the wild and romantic life of a pioneer in those forest regions. The beauty of the forests, the variety of foliage and scenery attracted them ; the towering oaks, the rivers, and the hills and valleys of the West had fascinations and charms for them. The " dark bloody ground," as designated by the Indians was their paradise. Boone was a remarkable figure in his time. He was feared for his reckless valour by his cautious and cruel red neighbours. They seldom took him by surprise. He shrank from no danger. He was a kind of local general with a loyal band of sure riflemen, and was a match for the Indian in his own territory. He had learned their habits and modes of attack, and he became, like his deadly foes, circumspect, cool and deliberate, but firm in the hour of danger. It might, without exaggeration, be asserted that no whites in these years could have lived in Kentucky had it not been for the fear among the Indians of Boone and Kenton. Through them the Indians were kept at bay. The Indian tribes of the north-west were remarkably energetic in their efforts to expel the whites, and they constantly harassed them on every possible occasion. The most ordinary duties had to be performed at the risk of life. Collins, in his history of Kentucky, says, " While ploughing their corn they were waylaid and shot ; while hunting they were pursued and killed ; and sometimes a solitary Indian would creep up near to the fort during night, and fire upon the first of the garrison who appeared in the morning."

We will quote a long extract from Colonel Shaffner's history of America, giving in detail the life, manners, customs and industry of those early pioneers whom Boone so bravely defended, often at great loss, and whom Clarke organised into a civil form of government, subject to the Virginian Legislature, from whom also he recruited that gallant band of militia who struck terror into the Indians, captured the British forts, and made prisoner of the General of the forces in those parts.

"The vast domain lying to the West of Virginia," says the historian, "was a land of enchantment to Virginians and North Carolinians. The climate was excellent, its scenery was beautiful, its forests grand, its soil productive, the game of every class abundant. Permanent settlements had never been made in that vast unexplored wilderness. The dismal forests, thickly matted, were only imperfectly known to the savage tribes. On the south side of Kentucky dwelt the Cherokee, Creeks, and Catawba tribes, and on the north side were the Shawanees, Delawares and Wyandots. These respective northern and southern tribes sectionally considered were enemies to each other, but they presented a united front against the Colonists who came to drive them back westward. Every foot of ground attempted to be occupied by the Virginians was stubbornly contested by the roving savage tribes from the north and south.

Not alone did it behove the settlers to be brave and guarded, but they required to build themselves forts and stockades, into which and around which they might congregate for safety and support. The chief forts in the settlements were Louisville, Boonsborough and Horrodstown.

It was the custom of the settlers to build themselves cabins of log around the forts, and in case of isolated squatters, when danger was imminent, to remove to the forts for protection. The frontiermen accustomed themselves to the Indian mode of warfare, taking aim at the enemy from behind trees and logs, and each man able to fight carried his rifle by his side and in his girdle a tomahawk and a knife. In case of attack in one of those isolated Colonies by a combined band of Indians, the settlers hurried off to the fort—man, woman, and child, and took up their abode as long as the savages remained in the neighbourhood of the fort, which was built on an open plain, and occupied about an acre of ground. The fortification around was parallelogram shaped and had a blockhouse at each corner, with lines of stout pickets about eight feet high standing from one blockhouse to the other.

Within the enclosure were store-house, barrack rooms, garrison well and a number of cabins for the use of families. In these forts muskets and ammunition were kept in readiness for emergencies. There were port holes at intervals, for aiming at the enemy, and the ground around the fort was cleared of all obstruction for the distance of a rifle shot, because the Indians invariably fought from behind a fence or tree. The scenes of valour recounted in the pioneer history of Kentucky would fill volumes, and to dwell on such details would be out of place in the limited scope of this work. We will, however, give the reader an idea of the life and primitive shifts those settlers were forced to have recourse to to procure the comforts and conveniences as well as necessaries of life.

"Almost every family," says Shaffner, "contained its own tailor, shoemaker and artisan. Their shoes were made for service, plainly sewn together, and when finished they were in construction partly shoe and partly mocassin. The women did all the tailor work. They could cut out and make hunting shirts, leggings and drawers, and these articles of clothing were made from the dressed or tanned deer skin. The tan-vat was a large wooden trough sunk to the upper edge in the ground, and the bark was taken from the trees in springtime, when the men were clearing the lands. This bark was broken to pieces by the women with small axes and mallets. Ashes from the hickory wood were used in place of lime for taking off the hair. Bear's fat, hog's lard or tallow answered for oil. The skins were dressed with rude knives made from hoop iron, and the leather was blackened with soot and hog's lard. The mills for grinding meal were of the tub water-mill construction, though most of the families depended upon their hominy-block for bread. This block was a log about four feet long with one end burnt out evenly to an edge in a bowl form, so as to hold about half a bushel of corn. The maize was placed in this mortar and beat with a pestle to hominy. Some of the families had small stone mills rudely made, which resembled the mills still in use in Palestine.

There was generally some one in the neighbourhood or settlement more skilled than others, who did many ingenious things in mechanical and handicraft work. Thus wooden ploughs, vessels for milk and butter, looms and benches were constructed. The houses were made of round logs, the chinks were closed with split wood and for mortar clay mud stiffened with straw finely cut was used. There were no windows except holes between the logs. The roof of the cabin was made of rived boards, some two feet long, weighted to the rafters by heavy logs extending from one end of the house to the other.

The doors were also made of rived boards and fastened to battens with wooden pins. The hinges were of hickory wood and the chimneys were made of split pieces with fine beds of stone and clay mortar. The floors were of logs split into halves called puncheons, and these were hewn smooth with the axe and laid with the flat side uppermost. The bedstead consisted of one post with side rails extending at right angles from the post into the logs of the side of the house. The seats were plain stools or logs, sawn in short lengths. The whole family occupied but one room, and thus, in simplicity, but with the purest virtue these noble pioneers lived scattered over the dark and bloody ground of the great west. In the cabins port holes were left for the rifles which were always loaded lest an Indian might be lurking near. The dogs which the frontiersmen kept always gave the alarm when Indians were near. Wolf traps were also set near the cabins so that in the dark Indians were in dread of falling into them, and hence kept away from the cabins."

We have made a somewhat long digression in our survey of events on the Virginian frontiers, but if we have to any extent succeeded in arousing interest in the life of a backwoodsman that digression will not have been without its use. Those were the men who made it possible for John Adams and Franklin to hold out for better terms in the treaty at the end of the war. Those were the men who gained to America that vast territory, bounded by the Mississippi, the father of waters, when the infant States might otherwise have been cribbed, cabined and confined to the east of the Alleghany Mountains, or at farthest, could not have their boundaries further west than the Ohio. These were the men who defended almost alone 700 miles of frontier when the Revolution forces in the East were fighting for all they knew against a powerful enemy that showed no mercy and knew no defeat. These were the men that with a small force, ill-provided with necessaries for war, hunted a strong Canadian and Indian combination from the north-western regions back to the Lakes. This feat in tactics and valour is the more remarkable, when one considers that nearly all the Indian tribes were in the pay of, and well supplied by the commander of the British forces at Detroit, their headquarters, with all the munitions for war. The British forts, from Detroit to St. Vincent's, were depots for supplying the Indians with ammunition and rifles. They were marts where the red men received European luxuries, such as tobacco and whiskey, in exchange for furs and buffalo flesh and skin ; nay, the British general, horrible to relate, pandered to the savage thirst for blood and scalps, and at the forts, a premium was given for every scalp carried in by the Indian allies. The price paid varied in proportion to the fighting value of the frontiersman slain ; for infants and women the price was less than for grown-up males. It may, then, be truly said that every backwoodsman lived on the borders in those troubled days at great peril, and often a few score of brave men were forced fo fight for their lives and the lives of their neighbours, against ten times their number of Indian warriors. So skilled in the arts of war, and so well informed in the tactics and stratagems of the Indians were the frontiersmen that invariably they forced them to retreat and always with a great loss of men.

The Indians rarely made incursions among the white settlers during the winter. It was a code with them to fight from under cover. The woods in winter were without foliage, and besides the summer was the time when invasion was most profitable. The killing of whites and attacking their forts was not their only ambition ; no, they burned and pillaged corn and houses, and carried off cattle and horses, and summer was the best time for this work when the people at the stations were busy here and there at their work.

The Canadians, as we saw, early in the war refused to throw in their lot with the Americans, and notwithstanding the fact that the Colonials south and west of the Lakes and Detroit and Niagara were French who had no love for England, and whose country had allied itself with America, yet they acted, even in the years '78 and '79, under the directions of Governor-General Hamilton, the cruel commander of the British in these parts. The entire British force stationed at the different forts was about 2,000. The chief forts at which they were stationed were Detroit, near Lake Erie, St. Vincent's situated on the Wabash, about sixty miles from the Ohio. The two other military posts under Hamilton in these parts were Kaskaskia and Cahokia, near the Mississippi. These forts were all across the Ohio. The forts belonging to the Continentals on the south of this river were forts Pitt, Henry, Point Pleasant, Boonsborough, Logan and Harrod. These forts, with the exception of Pitt, were very weakly garrisoned, and they were mere blockades to which the people in the neighbourhood could flee in time of danger. Fort Pitt had a garrison of about 300 militia.

When George Clarke, who was one of the brave leaders in Kentucky, became convinced that a combined Indian and British attack was meditated on his border, and that the aim was to push back the frontiersmen, if possible, across the mountains, he immediately set off to Williamsburgh, in Virginia, the parent State, to solicit and to defend their rights and save his friends from the barbarous invasion on foot. Clarke had himself well informed about the designs of the enemy, their strength, and the power of the Indian alliance. He knew each fort and how it was guarded and garrisoned,

He determined, if he could get men and money and ammunition, to attempt to capture the forts of the enemy before they should let loose the red hell hounds of war on his people. After much toil and delay Clarke gained the approval of the Virginian Governor and his private council to carry out his object. The commission he received was to be kept private, so that the enemy should not know his designs. The commission is dated 2nd February, 1778, and signed by P. Henry, Governor. It may here be mentioned that although Washington was Commander-in-Chief, and had a right to direct all warlike expeditions, yet, in cases of emergency, and where expedition and secrecy were required, the particular State affected could, as Henry did, send off an expedition for military purposes in the State or on the borders. The orders which Clarke received empowered him to raise 350 soldiers by recruiting around Pittsburgh and in Kentucky. He was to receive boats and ammunition at Pittsburgh, as well as military stores. He was ordered to be humane with his prisoners. The soldiers to serve under him were to receive the pay and allowance of militia. He says himself in the journal he kept during his campaign, and from which the account here recorded is mainly taken, that he was clothed with all the authority he could wish.

The task assigned Clarke was an onerous one; it was similar to the work George Washington, as a youth, was commissioned to fulfil during the Colonial wars. It was more momentous, however: Washington was nearer the parent State, was better equipped with men and money. The energies of the parent State were not divided and distracted and almost exhausted as was Virginia during the long continued wars for liberty, at the time that Clarke, a burgess representative from Kentucky told to their faces the Governor and Congress at Williamsburgh, that " if Kentucky and Illinois were not worth defending, they were not worth claiming," and that " he would be better employed organizing for defence at home than coming over mountains and rivers 800 miles to a State which was the parent State, but which disowned her children." Such a brave man and bold speaker was irresistible before the Demosthenes of America, Patrick Henry.   Clarke was one of those spirits which only a wild and unclaimed wilderness like America one hundred and fifty years ago could produce. In such a crisis as the Revolution it was impossible to keep him in the background.   He was born to lead men to victory· Before he placed his plans before the Virginian council he had weighed well the possibilities of a successful encounter with the British.   He knew their weak and strong points; the Indians also he had weighed and studied.   The result of his campaign will disclose that he possessed some of the characteristics which go to make up statesmen and diplomats as well as those of the soldier and commander.

Clarke, as we have seen, was empowered to raise a force, a few hundreds in all, ostensibly to defend Kentucky, but, in reality, to capture the British and Indian forts across the Ohio.   Had the real goal of the expedition been known at Pittsburgh and Kentucky, it is possible that more men and ammunition might have been, and with less difficulty, procured by Clarke at Pittsburgh; but for the hard task assigned him, he was poorly equipped indeed.   He set off down the Ohio with an army somewhere about two hundred strong, four small cannons, and four swivel guns, flat-bottomed boats and provisions.   The flag for the party was some red flannel tied to a pole.   The expedition might be said to be starting out on a mission which, in all human probability, would end in disaster— from which not one of that warlike band would probably ever return.   But they were not down-hearted.   They loved their young leader, and were prepared to follow where he should lead ; their life, in any circumstance, was in constant peril from their red neighbours.   Many if not all of this band of Clarke's, loyal as they proved to their chief, were young men who lived in the woods and mountains and rivers.   Hunting was their occupation and their passion, and when such an ideal venture presented itself as the Western expedition to Kaskaskia it seemed to them they were going to fight for American liberty, and all, with one voice, raised a wild hurrah for freedom.

This expedition sailed down the Ohio on the 29th June, 1778, and by the 4th of July they arrived outside the town of Kaskaskia, the chief town in Illinois. Clarke, although he made the distance between his own territory and this important British settlement in four days, did not rashly venture himself among enemies without feeling his ground and paving his way. He captured some French hunters *en route*, who not alone acted as his guides for part of the journey, but gave him some valuable information which he turned to the best advantage. He did not lie long before the fort. Once he arrived in view of the town he immediately entered in two divisions, completely surrounded the town, called on the garrison to surrender, and on the townspeople to keep within their homes. There was no opposition from any quarter to the peaceful occupation of the town and fort. M. Rochblave, the governor, surrendered at discretion. There were few militia in the fort, and the Indians had departed the settlement some time previous. The inhabitants, to the number of 700, renounced the British flag, and swore allegiance to the American cause and State of Virginia. The inhabitants in this settlement of Kaskaskia were mostly of French origin. Their priest, Father Gibault, was their guide, philosopher, and friend ; whatever he said would be of much weight with such simple people. He asked, in company with some of the leading citizens, to have an interview with Clarke. The Kentuckians were very much feared and dreaded by the British and Indians—more dreaded than their more eastern friends. It was to the Kentuckians, in a special manner, that the names '' Palefaces,'' '' Long Hunters,'' and '' Big Knives '' were applied. They were fond of sport, splendid marksmen, said to never miss their aim. They generally put the ball through the eye of the Indians. Hence those French settlers were expecting a rough handling from their captors, and Clarke surprised them when he informed them that they were not savages. He said, " I am almost certain you look upon us as such from your language. Do you think that Americans intend to strip women and children, or take the bread out of their mouths ? My countrymen disdain to make war upon helpless innocence ; it is to prevent the horrors of Indian butchery upon our own wives and children that we have taken arms and penetrated into this remote region of British and Indian barbarity, and not the despicable prospect of plunder." The King of France, he went on, had united his powerful arms with those of America, and war would not in all probability continue long, but the inhabitants of Kaskaskia were at liberty to take which side they pleased, without the least danger to their property, or families. Nor would their religion be any source of disagreement, as all religions were regarded with equal respect in the eyes of American law ; so that any insult which should be offered to it should be immediately punished. "You have been misinformed and prejudiced against us by British officers," he said. "We will at once release your friends as a proof of our humane dispositions." The villagers were overjoyed at the above declaration, and the people with one accord assembled in the Church to give thanks to Almighty God for their deliverance from the horrors which they were led to expect. Major Bowman was sent off, as soon as peace was proclaimed in Kaskaskia, to order the fort at Cahokia, some 60 miles distant on the confines of the Mississippi, to surrender. The inhabitants of Kaskaskia asked permission to join the expedition, as they had many friends at the fort, and they assured the Colonel that he would meet no opposition. The result of the expedition was as the French inhabitants had said, and on the 6th July the second outpost of the British line of defence fell without the shedding of one drop of blood, and the British influence died for ever in these regions east of the Mississippi. St. Vincent's, a fort lying more to the west, still remained south of the Lakes in the hands of the British, and Mons. Gibault asked for permission to accompany Captain Helm from Kaskaskia and procure peace to the citizens and possession of the fort which at that time was without a garrison. The result was all that could be desired, and thus by the kind assistance of the French colonists, who took the oath of allegiance to the American cause, the three forts for defending the country and organising the Indians of Illinois and Kentucky were lost to the British General, who directed operations from Detroit, which alone was still safe in the enemy's hands.

Clarke had now performed, in a short space of time, a great work without loss of blood or waste of powder. He now sat down to organize the district from Kaskaskia, and he sent a detachment to build a fort and storehouse where now is Louisville. Clarke had one obstacle yet to overcome ; he had to reconcile the Indians to his rule, and his presence in their midst. He knew the Indians well. He studied their character, noted the treatment meted them by British and French in times past, and saw the results. The British had no hold on these savages. The French had always the allegiance of many of the tribes, and if they were now against America in many localities, it was from circumstances similar to those which leagued the Canadians against America and their own King, but not love for the English. And yet the British had ever tried by bribes and inducement to placate the red man, not knowing that the wily savage never trusts the kindness of the Palefaces. The French missionaries did make some impression on them, as the Catholic religion in a special manner appealed to them and captivated many of the chiefs and tribes. Clarke knew them and did not try to placate them, but they, when it became evident that the Kentuckians were the power in Illinois, sent a deputation to plead for peace and friendship. Clarke received them coldly, but agreed to treat with them. The various parties assembled, white and red. The chief who had been selected to open the council advanced to the table at which Clarke was sitting with the belt of peace in his hand, one of the officers sitting near him holding the sacred pipe, and a third the fire to kindle it. The pipe in silence was lighted, presented to the heavens, then to the earth, and after it had completed the circle of those assembled it was presented to all the spirits, invoking them to witness what was about to be done. The pipe was again presented to Colonel Clarke and afterwards to every person present. This ceremony took half an hour, and was performed in silence in reverence for the Great Spirit, and then an Indian chief spoke thus to the warriors assembled :—" Warriors, you ought to be thankful that the Great Spirit has taken pity on you, has cleared the sky, and opened your ears and hearts so that you may hear the truth. We have been deceived by bad birds flying through the land (meaning the British emissaries), but we will take up the bloody hatchet no more against the Big Knife, and we hope that as the Great Spirit has brought us together for good, as he is good, so we may be received as friends, and peace may take the place of the bloody belt." At the end of this speech the chief, before he sat down, threw into the middle of the room the bloody belt of wampum and flags which he had received from the British, and stamped them under his feet in token of complete surrender into the hands of Clarke and the offer of friendly alliance.

Clarke in reply said he had carefully heard what was spoken and would give a reply next day, when he hoped the hearts of the people would be ready to hear the truth. He advised them to keep away from the big knives in the meantime and prepare not alone to give the hand but the heart as a guarantee of peace. All were well pleased with this meeting, and the formal reply of Clarke was much appreciated by the warriors. On the next day, when all had assembled as arranged, Clarke with great dignity arose in their midst and delivered the following eloquent and appropriate address which we append here. Although it is rather long it will serve to bring out in bold relief the talents of Clarke. It shows forth the hopes and fears, passions and prejudices, as well as the weak sides of the Indian character which Clarke had so thoroughly studied, and which he indirectly touches off in the address. Thus he addressed them :—" Men and Warriors, pay attention to my words. You informed me yesterday that the Great Spirit had brought us together, and you hoped as he was good it would be for good. I have also the same hope, and expect that each party will strictly adhere to whatever may be agreed upon, whether it be peace or war, and henceforward prove ourselves worthy of the attention of the Great Spirit. I am a man and a warrior, not a counsellor. I carry war in my right hand and peace in my left. I am sent by the great Council of the Big Knife and their friends to take possession of all the towns owned by the English in this country, and to watch the motions of the red people ; to bloody the paths of those who attempt to stop our course, but to clear the roads from us to those who desire to be in peace, that the women and children may walk in them without meeting anything to strike their feet against. I am ordered to call upon the Great Fire for warriors enough to darken the land, and that the red people may hear no sound but the birds who live on blood. I know there is a mist before your eyes ; I will dispel the cloud that you may clearly see the causes of the war between the Big Knives and the English. Then you may judge for yourselves which party is right, and if you are warriors, as you profess yourselves to be, prove it by adhering faithfully to the party you believe to be entitled to your friendship, and not show yourselves to be squaws." This and much more he told the assembled Indians. The warriors and braves and their chiefs listened with rapt attention, and at the conclusion of the oration, in the midst of universal approbation, the Indian chief arose in the midst of the assembled council and said he believed all that Clarke had spoken. He was not like the English : he did not speak with a forked tongue; and if hitherto his people, meaning the red men, had been enemies of the Big Knives, it was owing to evil birds who spread bad reports among them and told them lies about the wicked deeds of the Kentuckians against their people. They were prepared to ratify the treaty by smoking the pipe of peace, and to throw the tomahawk into the river where it could never be found. After the chieftain's speech was concluded the pipe of peace was lighted in the usual manner and presented to all the spirits in the four winds of heaven ; to the spirits of earth, forest and water. Finally all present in succession smoked the pipe, and at the conclusion all present shook hands, and the peace between the red men and the palefaces was concluded.

Clarke had now achieved a marvellous succession of victories in a short space of time without the loss of a single soldier, and without any considerable diminution of his slender resources. He could not, however, conceal from himself the fact that his position, notwithstanding, was extremely critical, for although he was for the present master of Kentucky, Illinois, and the north-west ports of the Mississippi, the Father of Waters, and the key to the west, yet he was isolated in a wilderness, far away from Pittsburgh, the nearest arsenal for supplies. He had three forts to protect, a wilderness to guard, and the British troops from Detroit to ward off. Whilst Clarke was cogitating matters of such moment to his cause, Hamilton, the British commander-in-chief, had already, in the month of December, at the head of a great force from Detroit, arrived in St. Vincent's. We saw how the French inhabitants readily, through the agency of their priest, Pere Gibault, transferred their allegiance to the Americans, and when Captain Helm and his man Henry arrived from Kaskaskia to claim the place in the name of Virginia, he met with no opposition. Now, when Hamilton with eight hundred soldiers arrived at Vincennes, they commenced to bombard the place, not knowing the strength of the garrison. "As soon as the attack began Captain Helm placed a cannon in the open gate of the fort, which was charged by the soldier Henry, while Helm himself stood by with a lighted torch ready to touch it off. When Governor Hamilton and his troops were within hailing distance, Captain Helm cried " Halt! " The Governor demanded the surrender of the garrison. Captain Helm demanded with an oath that no man should enter until he knew the terms of surrender. The answer was " You shall have the honours of war." The conditions were accepted, and the entire garrison, consisting of one officer and one man, walked out of the fort as prisoners of war. Intimation of the surrender of St. Vincent's was carried, inside a month after, to Clarke, and although it was midwinter, and a most inclement season, inactivity on his part would have meant annihilation of his forces in the spring, the capture of the forts now in his possession, and the horrors among his people of the Indian tomahawk. He resolved, therefore, on a bold course of action. That was no other than at once to organize a band of soldiers and volunteers, and surprise Hamilton before the winter should pass by. Clarke says, " I collected the officers, and told them the possibility I thought there was of a chance of turning the scale in our favour. They were all eager for the undertaking, and all hands set about getting ready for an enterprise that to the eye of cool calculating persons would have appeared not only hazardous but foolhardy." The French settlers, and especially the ladies of Kaskaskia, with whom young Clarke was a general favourite (he was somewhat of a gallant and a hero in their eyes) raised companies. Standards were presented, and a large boat called " The Willing," under Lieutenant Rogers, with two four pounders, four swivels, and an abundant supply of ammunition and provisions, was launched with forty-six men on board. She was to sail down the river Kaskaskia to the Mississippi, down to the Ohio, and up that river to the mouth of the Wabash ; and from this river they were to co-operate with a band of one hundred and thirty Kentuckians and Frenchmen under Clarke who set out by land on the 7th February, 1779. This expedition is memorable in the annals of war. Neither Caesar nor Hannibal, nor Napoleon himself, in all their campaigns, have recorded of them any military feats to surpass this daring expedition of the backwoodsman Clarke. The march lasted twenty days, and the distance covered was 250 miles, or a little over twelve miles per day. The discipline of the journey has been graphically penned by Clarke himself, and Captain Bowman, one of his officers, who also kept a journal of the march. We can here only give a meagre and truncated account of the march, made up of the extracts which follow from the diaries referred to :—On the 8th—We marched through the waters which now began to meet us in those level plains. Our men are keeping in great spirits although much fatigued. On the 15th—We ferried over the muddy Wabash, now nine miles broad, and came to dry lands on the opposite hills, where we camped. It was raining heavily. 16th—March all day through water and mud ; our provisions are becoming short. 17th—We are still wading through deep water and as darkness falls we are not yet reached a dry place to camp upon. 20th—We are almost in despair for want of food. 22nd—Clarke exhorts his men to persevere ; tells them that soon the water will abate and that the end is near. Men becoming faint from fatigue and hunger ; no provisions ; no help. 23rd—Waded for four miles to the breast in water across a place called the Horseshoe plain. Here Clarke expected to lose some of his gallant band from hail which fell during the night and froze up their soaked garments. Hunger of his men intense. The end of the journey was now within reasonable view, but let us give the final day's march in Clarke's own words :—" The last day's march through the water was superior to anything the Frenchmen had any idea of. . . . A canoe was sent off and returned without finding that we could pass. I went on myself and sounded the waters and found it deep as to my neck. I returned with the design to have the men transported on board the canoes to the sugar camp, which I knew would spend the whole day and ensuing night, as the vessels would pass slowly through the bushes. I would have given a great deal now for a day's provisions or for one of our horses. I returned but slowly to the troops, giving myself time to think. On our arrival all ran to hear our report. Every eye was fixed on me. I unfortunately spoke in a serious tone to one of the officers. The whole were alarmed without knowing what I said. I viewed their confusion for one moment, whispered to those

near me to do as I did, immediately put some water in my
hand, poured in powder, blackened my face, gave a war whoop
marched into the water without saying a word. The party
gazed, fell in one after another like a flock of sheep. I ordered
the men near me to give a favourite song of theirs. It soon
passed through the line and the whole went on cheerfully.
They reached a sugar camp in which there was about half an
acre of dry ground. Hungry and weary the men lay down
and slept till morning. This was the coldest night we had.
The ice in the morning was from one half to three-quarters
of an inch thick near the shores, and in still water. A little
after sunset I lectured the whole force, telling them that when
we reached the opposite woods our fatigue would be over, and
at once I stepped into the water. All followed me with a
huzza. We marched in a single file. I called back just as we
entered the water and told Major Bowman to put to death any
man who refused to march. The whole band gave a cry of
approval, and on we went. This was the most trying experience we came through. I generally kept fifteen or twenty of
the strongest men near me. When we were about the middle
of the plain I found myself sensibly failing, and as there were
no trees or bushes for the men to support themselves I feared
that many of the most weak would be drowned. I ordered the
canoes to make the land, discharge their loads, and ply back-
wards and forwards and pick up the weak and fainting, and
to encourage those behind that land was beyond. This
stratagem had the desired effect ; the men struggled on, the
weak holding on by the strong. When we reached the woods
we had the water as high as the shoulders. The smaller men
clung on to the trees and floating trunks, and in this manner
reached the shore."

In this way the journey was made. The armed boat with
provisions did not arrive, but a canoe was captured at this time
from some Indians which contained buffalo flesh, corn and
kettles. By this fortunate chance was appeased the hunger
of the almost despairing band. The fort was now in view, and

some French hunters came in to camp and gave details about the strength of the enemy, and the weak points in the fortifications. When Clarke settled down on the enemy on the 24th February, in view of the fort, his followers were beyond themselves with joy at their deliverance from the fatigue of the journey. Every man feasted his eyes on the scene before him, desiring to be led against the enemy, forgetful of all the previous suffering. They were in raptures with the good generalship of their commander, and said that a soldier could desire no better fortune. The situation now demanded all the bravery and skill that Clarke could bring to bear upon it. There was no hope in retreat. It they were unsuccessful there would be no mercy from the Indians. They must then face the issue, prepared to conquer or die. Clarke and his men saw the issue in this light. The first move of the young commander was to issue a note to the townspeople not to fear, but to keep within their homes. He then by marching and countermarching, changing colours, passing around hillocks and in front of the enemy with a variety of flags and ensigns, magnified, like to the bold M'Cracken on the Collin peaks in '98, the numbers of his forces, so as to overawe the British Governor. His next move was to send in a peremptory order to the garrison to surrender at discretion, and when this was unheeded he at once commenced to bombard the fort through the portholes. After three days skirmishing, Clarke again demanded the surrender of the fort, and at last Hamilton surrendered on conditions, *sic.*, " 1st—Lieutenant Colonel Hamilton engaged to deliver up to Colonel Clarke, Fort Sackville, as it at present was, with all its stockades, etc. 2.—The garrison was to be allowed to march out with their arms, etc., and deliver themselves up as prisoners of war." On the 25th February, Hamilton surrendered the fort, and the firing off of thirteen cannons signalised the passing of authority from the British to the American commander. Two days after the capitulation the armed bateau from Kaskaskia arrived. Clarke now, with his long expected stores and the 50,000 dollars worth of stores surrendered, was beyond

L

immediate want for the needs of his men. Hamilton and Major Hay were sent to Virginia with very bad credentials from Clarke. The horrors perpetrated by the Indians on the frontiersmen, on innocent children, and old people and women were noted, and these two officers were, by the authority of Thomas Jefferson, confined in irons in a dungeon ; but, on a appeal being made to Washington, they were later treated as prisoners of war. The indictments made against Hamilton by Jefferson in a letter to George Washington, reveal a barbarity in the war, sanctioned by England, that cannot be equalled in the annals of warfare in pagan times. Clarke's ascendance in the revolution practically ended with the capture of Vincenne. He failed, some two years later, to capture Detroit with a superior force, and after a few years guarding the frontiers, he was rewarded by Governor Harrison with a tract of land near Louisville, where he lived practically in retirement for thirty-four years and died in 1818. Governor Harrison thus wrote him in 1783, at the end of the war, when recalling his commission as Brigadier-General on the frontiers :—" Belore I take leave I feel called upon in the most forcible manner to return you my thanks and those of my council for the very great and singular services you have rendered to your country by wresting so great and extensive a country out of the hands of the British enemy, repelling the attacks of their savage allies, and carrying on so successful a war in the very heart of their country."

THE TREASON OF ARNOLD.

WEST POINT, in the years 1780 and 81, had became the most important stronghold in the country. It had been judiciously chosen by the Commander-in-Chief as a fortress, on account of its commanding position. From it the British army in New York was easily held in check, and as it commanded the Hudson, the object of the British General's ambition, it gave Washington not alone free communciation with New England, as well as the central and north-western districts, but free communication also with his forces in the south. To this camp the American General had removed most of the stores and necessaries of war. It had been fortified with the greatest care, and some of the foremost engineers in two continents had been engaged in perfecting it. It was a prize that Sir Henry Clinton valued very highly, and to obtain possession of it, he was prepared to pay a great price. To capture it by fair means he deemed himself unfit. To find a traitor who should betray it into his hands was much desired by him, and such a degenerate—a son of liberty—he found in the already famous General Benedict Arnold, commander of the fortress. Arnold held command in this important fortress. He had some time previously, at his own request, been placed there by Washington. Arnold was amongst the bravest, the most daring, and the most brilliant leaders on the American side. He had seen service in different parts of the Continent, from Canada to Saratoga, and around Philadelphia, and the laurels he gained and the wounds he received, made him an object of admiration to the army and nation. It will be remembered by those familiar with the history of the Canadian expedition, led by the brave but ill-fated Irishman, Montgomery, what heroic sacrifices Arnold made during the winter of 1775 to capture Quebec, and none can deny him a lion's share of the honours for the capture of Burgoyne at Saratoga in 1777. He was, on account of his dashing reckless valour, the terror of his enemies, and the idol of the army he led. His manner as a soldier was most erratic, and had he not been invariably successful in his headlong charges, or had he been a less idolized soldier, he would have been long before courtmartialled for violation of orders. Owing to his recklessness in the hour of danger, and his impetuous conduct on all occasions, he was never entrusted with supreme command, where prudence and caution are more than anything else needed ; yet, in the estimation of his country, he was looked upon as a brilliant asset to the army. The wounds he received at Quebec and on Behmus heights rendered him for a time unfit for active service, and as he had no temporal possessions in his native Connecticut, which gave so many brave men and only one traitor to the cause of liberty, he was, soon after the evacuation of Philadelphia by Howe in 1778, placed in military command over the troops in the congressional city. His duties in this place did not entail much active military service, hence, whilst occupying the position he found an outlet for his free and reckless nature, by living a somewhat riotous and extravagant and luxurious life. He mixed much in high Tory society, and revelled in dissipation, and he soon became a favourite in high circles of the wealthy loyalist society of Philadelphia. He took to himself a wealthy loyalist's daughter as wife, and through her became a great favourite with certain officers in the British army. Amongst his correspondents were included Sir Henry Clinton himself, and one Major Andre—a brave and accomplished young officer, and favourite aide to the British Commander-in-Chief. Whilst enjoying the responsible position assigned him at the then capital of the Union, and mixing in society which dragged him into pecuniary embarrassments, he found himself unable to meet his liabilities. His affairs becoming desperate, he railed against his hard fate. He con--

sidered his merits were not appreciated, nor his reward equal to the service he had rendered his country. He had recourse to extortion and speculation to enable him to meet the pressure of his debts. He proved unfaithful to the confidence reposed in him by his general and Congress, and it was not long until the outcry of the citizens became so loud against his extortions that a military tribunal was called into requisition to try him for his offences against the public. The result, though lenient, was more than his sensitive and ungovernable nature could endure. He was ordered to be reprimanded by the Commander-in-Chief. The rebuke administered by the General was conveyed in the kindest and gentlest manner in the following words :—" Our service is the chastest of all ; even the shadow of a fault tarnishes the lustre of our finest achievements. The least inadvertence may rob us of the public favour, so hard to be acquired. I reprimand you for having forgotten that in proportion as you had rendered yourself formidable to your enemies, you should have been guarded and temperate in your deportment towards your fellow-citizens. Exhibit anew those noble qualities which have placed you on the list of our most valued commanders. I will myself furnish you as far as may be in my power with opportunities of gaining the esteem of your country." Weighed down by pressing debts, despised by the people who once adored him, and mortified at what he considered the ingratitude of his country, he tried every expedient to procure money to meet his increasing demands. He turned his attention towards the French minister to the States to procure a loan from his country, but in return, only received the gentlemanly rebuke that such a request supposes the recipient to become the obedient servant of the French, as only on such conditions could the ambassador act on his behalf. Then he secretly entered into negotiations with the British Commander at New York to sell his country. The correspondence in both cases was carried on under an assumed name, and some say, with the co-operation and assistance of his young and accomplished wife, who was a great favourite with the officers of Clinton, although Washington and most historians of this sad affair acquit her of any share in or knowledge of the treason. His next step was to make it known to Washington, through friends, that he desired the position of commander of the garrison at West Point. Washington, not in the least suspecting any treasonable designs on Arnold's part, granted him his wish, although he, personally, would have preferred that so brave a servant should be engaged in a more active service, and accordingly, the perfidious Arnold succeeded to the position at West Point evacuated by General Howe, about whose competence the General had some doubts. No sooner did this base man receive the appointment than he entered into negotiations with Sir Henry Clinton to betray the fortress and the Commander-in-Chief into his hands for ten thousand pounds.

Major Andre was selected as the intermediary to meet Arnold and receive his plans and instructions on behalf of his chief. John Andre was a brave and fearless soldier, and most devoted aide of Clinton. He was only 30 years of age at the time he entered on this unfortunate affair. He was born in England in the year 1749. His father was a native of Geneva, and carried on extensive business as a merchant. Young Andre, after his education had been completed in Geneva, spent some time in his father's business before he joined the English army in 1771. In 1774 he joined the forces as lieutenant and sailed for service in America. He served in Canada, in Boston, and in Pennsylvania. In 1780 he was appointed aide to Clinton, and was promoted to the rank of adjutant-general of the British army in America. The work of aiding the traitor Arnold in selling his country could not have been very agreeable to so high-minded a man as Andre proved himself to be ; yet, in obedience to his master and in the interests of his country he bravely undertook it, and in the month of September he set out from his camp at New York, with civil garb over his military dress, to meet Arnold on neutral ground up the Hudson and to receive from him the plans he had prepared. To facilitate the design the *Vulture*, a British sloop, with the Major on Board, ascended the river as far as Point. She cast anchor below West Point, at midnight, on the 21st September, at the time when Washington was at Hartford, in Connecticut, concerting plans with the French commander about the future operations of the combined armies. Andre was rowed from the vessel in a boat sent by Arnold, manned by a soldier named Smith. Arnold met him in the woods at midnight, and both retired to Smith's cabin hard by, and there, during the night, settled the details. Day, however, dawned upon them before everything was finally agreed upon, and Arnold returned to headquarters. Andre, owing to the removal of the *Vulture* to a safer distance from the American lines, was compelled on the night following to set out by land for his camp. Smith was ordered to accompany him part of the journey. In his possession he carried the treasonable papers, as well as a pass in Arnold's handwriting to admit him through the American lines. However, although he had reached neutral ground outside the American lines, thanks to the pass, he was not out of all danger. The neutral ground for twenty miles between the opposing armies was infested by quasi-militia, "Cowboys" and "Skinners," the former friends of the British, the latter Sons of Liberty. These men were mainly freebooters, who robbed the passersby and carried on a profitable traffic with the armies. It happened that Andre was met by three of the Skinners, at once held up, carried into the woods near at hand and there searched. In his socks were found the papers given him by Arnold, and at once one of them, brave John Paulding, examined the documents and surmised that Andre was a spy. The three patriotic Skinners rode off to the nearest camp on the American lines, and although every offer of reward was made by Andre for his release, they spurned them, and safely placed their prisoner in the hands of Colonel Jameson, who commanded the forces at North Castle. The papers found on Andre were forwarded to Washington, and the prisoner himself was conducted, under a close guard, to West Point. Washington was on his way to West Point in company with Lafayette. He had just returned from Hartford and intended calling at West Point, breakfasting with Arnold, and inspecting the fort and magazines. He, however, delayed on the way, and two of his aides-de-camp were sent forward to explain the cause of the delay. Seeing that the General and his suite would not arrive for some time, Arnold and his wife sat down to breakfast with the aides. Whilst they were at table a letter was handed Arnold by Lieutenant Allen, written by Colonel Jameson apprising him that "Major Andre of the British army was a prisoner in his custody." Jameson was only carrying out his duty in so informing Arnold and was entirely ignorant of the treason of his superior officer. When Arnold received the letter and read it, controlling his agitation he rose hurriedly from the table, excused himself as if called away on urgent business, ran upstairs to his wife's room, called her to him, and in a few words explained the imminent danger he was in. She, learning of his treason being discovered, and told that they might never meet again, swooned upon the floor. He had no time to soothe her sorrow, and kissing his child he fled the house, entered a six-oared boat, carrying a white flag, rowed away to the *Vulture* and thus escaped. Washington was soon after informed of the treason of Arnold, but too late to intercept his flight. When Hamilton, who carried the documents from Jameson, placed them in the hands of Washington, and a letter from Andre, disclosing his rank and mission, he was deeply distressed, and was heard in sorrowful accents to exclaim, "Whom can we trust now?" As might be expected, Mrs. Arnold, on the arrival of the General at her house, was in great agony, but she received the sympathy and consideration of all around her, no matter how much they abominated her husband. Not long after Arnold was safe on the decks of the British sloop, he forwarded a note to Washington :—" I have no favour," said the hardened traitor, " to ask for myself. I have too often experienced the ingratitude of my country to

attempt it, but, from the known humanity of your excellency,
I am induced to ask you protection for Mrs. Arnold from
every insult and injury that a mistaken vengeance of my country might expose her to. It ought only to fall on me. She is
as innocent as an angel, and incapable of doing wrong." Of
course Washington, with the gentlemanly instincts natural
to him towards the fair sex, required no reminder from the
heartless Judas of his country. He had Mrs. Arnold safely
conducted to her husband at New York.

Andre was sent forward from West Point to Tappan
under Major Tallmadge. At first the prisoner did not realize
the serious nature of his offence, and on his way to the place
of confinement he became very inquisitive," says Tallmadge,
" to know what should be his fate." His conductor recounted
to him the following incident :—" I had a much-beloved class
mate at Yale College by the name of Hales who entered the
army in 1775. Immediately after the battle of Long Island
Washington wanted information respecting the strength of
the enemy. Hale tendered his service, went over to Brooklyn,
and was taken just as he was passing the outposts of the
enemy on his return. Do you remember the sequel of the
story?'" " Yes," said Andre, " he was hanged as a spy. But
you do not consider our cases similar." " Yes," said Toll-
madge, " precisely similar, and similar will be your fate."
Andre, cultured and gentlemanly and honourable man that
he was, pleaded not to be considered as a spy, but rather as
an officer obeying the orders of his superior. He confessed
fully the part he took in the transaction.

A courtmartial, with General Greene as presiding officer,
was held to try the prisoner, and every care was taken to find
out had Arnold any or many accomplices in the ranks which
he was going to betray. Andre's own confession of the manner
in which he was implicated in the affair was proof sufficient
without anything further to convict him. The finding of the
board was " That he had come on shore to hold a secret interview with Arnold, had changed his dress within the American

lines, passed the guards in a disguised habit and name, having about him papers containing information for the enemy. These circumstances, they considered, justified them in regarding him as a spy and condemning him to die by hanging." It is needless to add that, notwithstanding every protest and strong appeals for mercy from Clinton and others, the law was carried out in all its rigorous justice. On the 2nd October, in the presence of the army, Andre was hanged on a scaffold. His noble bearing, manly indifference and resignation to his fate, impressed every one, and not a few were the tears shed amongst the silent spectators of his sad fate. "His death," says Dr. Thatcher, an eye witness, "was a tragical scene of the deepest interest. During his confinement and trial he exhibited those proud and elevated sensibilities which designate greatness and dignity of mind. Not a murmur nor a sigh ever escaped him, and the civilities and attentions bestowed on him were politely acknowledged." Having left a mother and two sisters in England, he was heard to mention them in terms of the greatest affection, and in his letters to Sir Henry Clinton, he recommended them to his particular care. He betrayed no want of fortitude, but smiled and bowed complacently to several gentlemen whom he knew. His last words were :—" I am reconciled to my death, but I detest the mode. I pray you to bear witness that I meet my fate like a brave man." His remains lay for over fifty years at Tappan, until a movement was got on foot to have his dust conveyed to a tomb in Westminster among the immortals. The King was not unmindful of his name nor his dying wish. He fixed a pension on his mother and he conferred a knighthood on his brother, to honour the death of the Major. Washington was very much grieved that no other course was open to him but execute the brave Andre. The cause of liberty required that condign punishment should be meted out to all spies and traitors. The death of Arnold would have been preferred a hundred times over to that of Andre. Washington offered to exchange his prisoner for the traitor, but no matter how

Clinton despised his new friend, Benedict Arnold, honour forbade him to give him up to death. " Andre," says Washington in a private letter, " has met his fate with that fortitude which was to be expected from an accomplished man and a gallant officer. But I am mistaken if at this moment Arnold is not undergoing the torments of a mental hell. He wants feeling. From some traits of his character which have lately come to my knowledge he seems to have been so hackneyed in crime, so lost to all sense of honour and shame, that while his faculties still enable him to continue his sordid pursuits, there will be no time for remorse." Although Arnold had escaped a traitor's death, his fate was infinitely worse than that of Andre. He was doomed to perpetual banishment from his native land, which he so basely sold. He was loathed by those who sheltered him ; his countrymen held his name in execration, and the stigma of his treason descended on his children down the generations. His life was a living hell to his latest day. He stipulated for £10,000 as the price of his treason ; he received only a part. " Sir Henry Clinton received him," says his biographer, " with measured cordiality, appointed him Colonel of a regiment of British soldiers, with the brevet of Brigadier-General, and shortly afterwards wrote to the minister for foreign affairs, " I have paid to that officer (Arnold) £6,315 sterling as a compensation for the loss which he informs me he has sustained by coming over to us." The British army, of all forces, detested the new commander. Far different was the memory of the unfortunate Andre. Of him Sir Herny Clinton thus spoke when announcing his death : " The unfortunate fate of this officer calls upon the commander to declare that he ever considered Major Andre a gentleman of the highest integrity and honour, and incapable of any base act or unworthy conduct." The general officers under Greene, who condemned him, deeply regretted the course that duty pointed out to them in handing him over to the executioner, and had it been known that there were no Arnolds but one in the American service he probably would have been spared the extreme penalty of his crime.

Arnold afterwards issued a proclamation, attempting to justify his treason, and calling on his late soldiers in arms to do as he had done. His proclamations had one effect only, and that was to blacken with a deeper dye the traitor in the public eyes. They showed to the world how heartless and callous was the man. One fact stands out prominently from the treason of Arnold : no instance is recorded of any soldier from the highest to the lowest in the American army deserting the cause of liberty after this act of treason. A prize was offered by Congress for any one who should deliver the traitor Benedict Arnold into the hands of the American Commander.

THE CAPTURE OF CORNWALLIS AT YORKTOWN.

WASHINGTON had been forming his plans during the weary months he waited in the Northern Highlands for a sufficiency of men and baggage. In this retreat, removed from the scenes of active warfare in Virginia and Carolinas, he was contemplating a grand assault by the combined forces of Count de Rochambeau de Borras, commander of the navy, and his own forces. From the arrival of the French forces the previous year no active fighting had been accomplished by them. They had remained shut up in and around New Port in Connecticut. The British navy had the port blocked, and the land forces were tied to their positions on shore to protect the fleet in the bay. At last relief came ; the British Fleet was scattered and badly damaged by the storms that swept the seas early in the year, and news had reached Count Rochambeau that Count De Grasse might shortly be expected to reach American waters with a superior fleet, having on board troops amountng to three or four thousand, under the famous Marquis

Saint Simon. Washington now saw the opportunity arriving which would enable him to strike the blow he so long dreamt of, against Clinton at New York. Accordingly, an order was sent to the French commanders to hasten with much expedition towards New York. A note was also despatched to intercept De Grasse on his arrival, and cause him to besiege New York by water and block the ports, thus effectively co-operating with the land forces which were to assault the fortress from the Hudson. It was expected that a strong blockade and active assault by the combined sea and land forces would prove too much for Sir Henry, and that he and his troops and arsenals would fall into the hands of the allied torces. De Grasse had received his instructions from the court of Versailles prior to embarking at Brest where he had been blockaded. It would seem that Lafayette had been in communciation with the French court, and of course with Washington, under whose directions he was conducting his campaign. To both parties he made known how hard he was pressed by a superior force. Washington, whilst willing to send him all the aid he could, was not prepared just then to carry out the wish of the Marquis, namely, that he should come down to Virginia and lead in person, as nothing else would rouse up the country to a true sense of their duty, but the presence of the General. He considered the capture of New York of the first and most pressing importance. However, the instructions given to De Grasse from Versailles overturned all the General's calculations, and no doubt these instructions, happy in their result, were prompted by Lafayette's appeal for aid in Virginia.

We may well conceive the chagrin and disappointment it was to Washington to receive the intelligence that the fleet and land forces from France were to proceed to the Chesapeake, that they would arrive there at end of August and were under orders to reach the West Indies towards the end of October. It is said that the Commander-in-Chief was so intensely grieved and so excited, that although of a naturally cool and calm disposition, he shut himself up in his room for some time and refused to see anyone. But he was too level-headed and prudent to ruminate long over what could not be remedied, and it was not long until he had resolved on his future course of action under the changed circumstances. His new plans were to evade Sir Henry Clinton, and hide from view his ulterior object, and so to arrange that by quiet stages he might reach the Southern forces under Lafayette, before the British in New York could have time to recruit Lord Cornwallis, now engaged strongly entrenching himself in Yorktown and Gloucester Point, at the mouth of York river in Virginia. Accordingly, after the junction of the land forces of France under Count De Rochambeau, Washintgon sent instructions to Lafayette to lead in person a force of 6,000 troops—4,000 French and over 2,000 Americans—to form a junction at Williamsburgh with the troops under Reuben and Wayne, to enter into communication with De Grasse, and instruct him to wait the arrival of the allied land forces at the mouth of the Chesapeake, where he was to effectually block the egress of the troops and hold up the fleet stationed in the bay to protect the troops of Cornwallis, now 8,000 strong, on the two points at the mouth of York river. Whilst these plans were being perfected Clinton counteracted the order some time previously sent to the southern General that he should send off some of his forces to New York, owing to the arrival of a few thousand fresh troops in the eastern city from Europe. Immediately after the project was formed, the combined forces were marched from the Hudson into New Jersey, and to keep up the delusion that still their object was New York, a part of the forces were ordered to throw up entrenchments and raise fortifications, giving Clinton the idea that their object was to turn round by a circuitous route on New York. Washington wrote letters so worded as to lead Clinton (into whose hands they were allowed to fall) to believe that he was eager for the dreaded attack on the British on the north, whilst all the time he was by quiet stages hastening towards the Delaware and Philadelphia. Clinton, misled by the false information he gained from the intercepted letters, smiled at the knowledge he thought he possessed of the enemy's intentions, and rested securely in his well-fortified camp on Manhattan Island.

Cornwallis was not idle at Yorktown. He divided his forces after their arrival, and sent about 2,000 to the Gloucester side of the Chesapeake, on York river, whilst he remained at Yorktown on the south with his main forces. Yorktown was, previous to the war for independence, a village of considerable trade, the houses for the most part being built on the edge of the cliff overhanging the river. The buildings covered a small area, and the approaches to the town were intercepted by creeks and ravines. Redoubts were placed on the various roads, some distance from the village on the main highway leading from Williamsburgh to Yorktown. Fortifications were erected on plans, approved by the army engineers, and advanced forts were posted on the outskirts to protect the workmen busy securing the fortifications and entrenchments. It may here be mentioned that between Washington and the French commander, Count Rochambeau, the most cordial relations existed, and both Generals used every effort to infuse harmony, mutual respect, and confidence into their officers and men. To show how mutual was the co-operation of the Generals one instance will suffice. Some of the New England troops under Washington were unwilling to march south in this campaign unless Congress advanced their salaries. There was a jealousy that caused northern soldiers to serve in the south with difficulty. Rochambeau, to remove the cause of their revolt, advanced money from his own resources, and on the other hand, we are told that the American army, to show their appreciation of the allies, supplied them with the best provisions and tents, and even gave them their own horses, whilst they were content to walk, to subsist on rougher diet, and, without a murmur, lie in the open without tents. The ruse of the American commander worked so well that the forces were setting sail at Philadelphia before Clinton became aware of their object, and so quickly did the Commander-in-Chief effect his march, that on the 25th September the army had arrived at Williamsburgh, and the two Commanders who had reached this town some days previous, had the fleet of De Grasse in readiness without any delay to transport them by water to Yorktown. Washington, on this journey down from Philadelphia, took occasion to pay a flying visit to Mount Vernon. This was his first visit for many years to his Virginia home.

Whilst these movements were proceeding by land and along the Delaware, Admiral Hood, a British commander, had been despatched by the commander of the English fleet, Lord Rodney, to intercept De Grasse at the Chesapeake, to which place Baron De Borras, commander of the fleet at Newport, had sailed to join him. Hood, on arrival at the Chesapeake, found that De Grasse had not then reached American water, and accordingly he sailed back to New York. But he was not long departed when De Grasse arrived with twenty-four sail, and three thousand troops to act by land. He took up a strong and commanding position at the mouth of the York river, off Cape Henry, where he anchored his fleet. The British fleet, on returning to encounter the French, were surprised at their superiority in numbers, and after some slight skirmishing off the coast, De Grasse desisted from following Hood, who returned to New York. Cornwallis now found himself in a most embarrassing position. The British fleet had deserted him ; De Borras had blocked the entrance of York river, and De Grasse was hovering around to protect the allied forces now coming down to besiege the British General in his entrenchments. Everything was now in readiness for operating offensively by sea and land against the besieged forces. By a marvellous feat of generalship, Washington had covered a distance of four hundred miles, from the Hudson to Yorktown, in less than twenty days, carrying with him, without loss, his implements of warfare, ammunition, artillery, and stores. He was in a fit condition by the 1st October to set about active operations on the fortifications, and accordingly he arranged his forces and disposed his plans to commence at once to carry by assault the works so strongly built and bravely defended by Cornwallis. The time had arrived for striking a final blow at British ascendancy in America, and in the cause of liberty in the United States. The troops of both French and Americans were in high hope of success. The people around on the Virginian borders were joyous, and prepared to co-operate in every way. All that the State legislature could perform to keep the army well provided was performed. The allied forces well nigh amounted to 16,000 men. Those under Cornwallis did not exceed 8,000. It was only a matter of time until the besiegers would be forced to yield unless reinforced from New York. It behoved Washington not to delay lest Clinton should reach his besieged friend before he submitted. Plans were, therefore, at once put into execution to reduce the fortress. When Clinton learned of Washington's destination he wrote Cornwallis that if he could hold out until 6th October he would reach him with reinforcements ; these promised helps did not come, however, until the last week in October, a week after Cornwallis had capitulated. Cornwallis, from the time he determined to take his stand in a life and death struggle at Yorktown, made superhuman efforts to strongly entrench himself, and improve the natural advantages of his position. The right wing rested on a swamp which covered that side of the town. Beyond this, and near to the river road leading to Williamsburgh a redoubt was built. He had several armed vessels moored opposite the swamp on the right, and he caused two redoubts to be erected, one on each side of the main road from Williamsburgh. The centre of the position was protected by a thin wood. On the left of the centre a field work was erected and mounted with cannon to command the Hampton Road; a deep ravine and creek running down to York river covered the left. In addition to these defences trees were felled, and batteries were raised at vulnerable points. Excellent field artillery were placed along the line of defence to the greatest advantage, which could act on the open plain in front of the morass, against the enemy. Gloucester Point, about a mile across the Bay from York river, was a strong position, and on this eminence he had located a swift corps of cavalry. On the 29th September Cornwallis wrote as follows to Clinton, and from the tenor of his note, we learn that he had no fear but that he would be able to hold out until relief reached him. He says, " I have ventured these last two days to look General Washington's whole force in the face, in the position on the outside of my works, and I have the pleasure to assure your excellency that there was but one wish throughout the whole army, which was that the army should advance. I have this evening received your letter of the 24th, which has given me the greatest satisfaction. I shall retire this night within the works, and have no doubt if relief arrives in any reasonable time, York and Gloucester will be both in the possession of his majesty's troops." As soon as the outer trenches and forts were abandoned by the enemy, the allied forces entered them, and the same day the Duke de Lauzen, with his legion and a body of Virginian militia, took a position in front of the British post at Gloucester, and kept it blockaded until the termination of the siege. The besiegers were duly positioned by the Commander-in-Chief. On the Gloucester side the entire force, French and American, were placed under the command of General de Choise, whilst Count Rochambeau, who commanded on the York side, had general control over the French troops, subject to the supervision of Washington, who directed in person all the operations. Lafayette and Colonel Hamilton were placed in prominent command in the line of attack over the American forces at York.

It was the chief concern of Washington to restore confidence and harmony and good feeling among the French and American forces. Up to this engagement the Allies had rendered no very material service in the field to the American cause. This, no doubt, was accounted for, not so much from any unwillingness on the part of the French to expose them-

selves to danger, or from any want of enthusiasm in the cause
of American liberty, but rather from ambitious generals
acting on their own initiative, or on orders received prior to
coming over to America. Now the case was different. Washington was in supreme authority, not alone so placed by his
own countrymen, but so recognised by the King of France and
the Court at Versailles, and by the French Generals. The
wish of Washington was to give the allies due honour, and suitable opportunities to gain glory on the field of battle, and he
encouraged a healthy rivalry between his ambitious allies and
his own soldiers. Soon a hundred cannon were mounted by
the besiegers, and they began to shell with sure aim and destructive effect the redoubts of the British, and then the word
was given for a general attack. Lafayette led in the charge,
at the head of the Americans, and Baron de Viominel had
command of the French detachment. The trenches were gained
with little loss ; the Allies entered, erected their batteries at
close range, and had the inner entrenchment at their mercy.
On the 11th October, Cornwallis wrote again to Clinton, and this
time, it is evident, his courage was beginning to fail him.
" Nothing," he says, " but a direct move to York river,
which includes a successful naval action, can save me. The
enemy made their first parallel on the night of the 6th at the
distance of six hundred yards, and have perfected it, and constructed plans of arms and batteries with great regularity and
caution. On the evening of the 9th their batteries opened,
and have since continued firing without intermission with
about forty pieces of cannon, mostly heavy, and sixteen
mortars. Many of our works have been considerably damaged.
We cannot thus hope to make a long resistance." Cornwallis
saw, at last, that to remain as he was after the second parallel
had been carried, and the enemy were making holes in the
inner fortifications, meant speedy defeat and surrender. He
accordingly resolved as a last and desperate resource, to attempt
to cross over his troops to Gloucester during the night in boats,
mount his own cavalry and that of De Choise and make a race

for life across the country towards New York. In this bold attempt he was foiled owing to the storm which arose on the night he launched his boats, and he was glad, with much danger and difficulty, but little loss of men, to regain his entrench- ments. The disastrous attempt to cross over without baggage occurred on the 16th October. The attacking parties of Cornwallis, in this desperate crisis of their affairs, when a hundred cannon were playing at once on their works, and their own artillery were almost silenced, made some heroic sallies against the assailants, and in one of these succeeded in spiking eleven guns and killing a hundred French soldiers. It was all, however, to no purpose, and to save a further loss of lives, and a useless continuation of the siege, Cornwallis, on the 17th October, under a flag, sent the following note to Washington : " Sir, I propose a cessation of hostilities for twenty-four hours and that two officers may be appointed by each side to meet at Mr. Moore's house, to settle terms for the surrender of the forts of York and Gloucester." Washington, fearing to lose the well-merited prize now in his grasp by any temporising or delay, knowing, as he did, that Sir Henry Clinton would strain every nerve to forward the relief of his brave general so hard pressed in Yorktown, sent a message, that in two hours, the terms of surrender should be forwarded him in writing. The conditions stipulated by Washington were that the troops should lay down their arms and surrender themselves as prison- ers of war, until the end of the war. The Tories in their ranks were to be handed over to the civil powers of the States, to decide their fate. However, most of the objectionable Tories or Loyalists were, by tacit connivance on both sides, allowed to sail to New York in the *Bonetta*, a vessel which Cornwallis was allowed to despatch to New York to acquaint Clinton of the surrender. The army of Cornwallis consisted of somewhat over 7,000, including both land and sea forces. The surrender was considered of the greatest moment and excited the wildest enthusiasm over the States. It was justly considered the turning-point in the war for Independence. The successive stages of the whole project, beginning with the march of the combined forces from New York, and ending with the rapid march south, and the final surrender of the most formidable general the British possessed on the American continent, were carried into execution with such military skill and accuracy, with such tact and judgment, that not alone were the allied armies dazzled with its splendour, but friend and foe alike were forced to exclaim that Washington, the American General, was entitled to rank amongst the greatest military leaders that any age or race had ever produced. The patriot statesman and sage, Dr. Franklin, in a letter to his friend Washington, from Paris, thus wrote : " All the world agree that no expedition was ever better executed. It has made a great addition to the military reputation you have already acquired, and heightened the glory that surrounds your name, and that must accompany it to our latest posterity." General Lincoln, who had been so unfortunate in the previous year in losing the southern capital, and the Continental army was specially mentioned with Reuben, Lafayette and others, both French and Americans, by Washington, for the heroic part he took as senior officer in the siege, and his wounded feelings were requited by the honour paid him in being privileged to lead the conquered army to the field where they laid down their arms. Washington, with his usual prudence and tact, and fine sense of honour, gave strict orders for no display to be made by the victorious armies. " My boys," he said to them, " let there be no insults over the conquered foe. When they lay down their arms don't huzza ; posterity will huzza for you." The following vivid picture of the last stage in this Yorktown drama is given us by an eye-witness, Abbe Robin, military Chaplain to the Count de Rochambeau. " The two lines of the allied army were drawn out for upwards of a mile, the Americans having the right. The disproportion of heights and ages in their men, and their soiled and ragged clothing might be unfavourably contrasted with the neater and more soldierly appearance of the French; yet, under such circum-

rather be looked upon as an enhancement of the triumph they had gained. I was struck with many indications of the fact how much more keen at that moment was the animosity between the English and Americans, than betewen the English and French. Thus the English officers, when they laid down their arms and were passing along the enemy's lines, courteously saluted every French officer, even of the lowest rank, a compliment which they withheld from every American, even of the highest rank."

Washington, on the date of the surrender, wrote a detailed account of the whole transaction to Congress. In this document he praised the emulation of the allied forces, and the good feeling that happily existed between the men of both forces. He mentioned a number of officers and leaders who distinguished themselves, and in a special manner conveyed the thanks of Congress to Count de Rochambeau and Count de Grasse and his fleet for their distinguished aid and support. To the above account of the successful capture of Cornwallis and his army we will add a short extract from a long detailed despatch from the defeated General to Sir Henry Clinton, after the capitulation. He says, " I sincerely lament that I could not obtain better conditions than the articles of treaty enclosed, but I must say that the treatment in general we have received from the enemy since our surrender has been perfectly good and proper. The attention to our needs by the French officers in particular has been admirable, their delicate sensibility of our situation, their generous and pressing offers of money, both public and private, to any amount has really gone beyond what I can possibly describe, and will, I hope, make an impression in the breast of every officer, whenever the fortunes of war should put any of them into our power."

Congress voted their unmeasured thanks to Washington, and the officers and men of both armies under his command. It was resolved that the 24th October should be set apart for public thanksgiving in all the churches of Philadelphia. Trophies and medals were ordered to be presented to the different commanders. An obelisk, commemorative of the victory, was ordered to be erected in Yorktown, and every testimonial of national gratitude was rendered to the victors. The following account of the joyous effects of this victory is graphically given by Chief-Justice Marshall in his *Life of Washington* :—" The exultation manifested throughout the States at the capture of this formidable army was equal to the terror it inspired. In Congress the intelligence was received with joy proportioned to the magnitude of the event, and the sense of that body on this brilliant achievement was expressed in various resolutions, returning the thanks of the United States to the Commander-in-Chief, the Counts De Grasse, De Rochambeau, the officers and men of the allied forces generally, and to the corps of artillery and engineers particularly. In addition to these testimonials of gratitude, it was resolved that a marble statue should be erected in Yorktown, in Virginia, with emblems of the alliance between the United States and his most Christian majesty, and that a succinct narrative of the surrender of Earl Cornwallis to his Excellency General Washington, the Count De Rochambeau, and Count De Grasse, be inserted thereon. Two stands of colours taken at Yorktown were presented to General Washington, and two pieces of field ordnance to Counts De Rochambeau and De Grasse. A proclamation was issued appointing the 13th December for a day of general thanksgiving and prayer on account of the signal interposition of Divine Providence. Everywhere throughout the Union, public joy at the great event was most enthusiastic. The praises bestowed on Washington were genuine and universal. The most flattering addresses were affectionately presented to him from every state on the Continent. Senate and city, town and village, learned professors and humble peasants, vied with each other in testifying their sense of gratitude and indebtedness to him for the signal service he had rendered to their country and to the cause of liberty. Some time after the departure of the French fleet which sailed away, as instructed, from Versailles to the West Indies, Washington led his army north and the captured troops proceeded under General Lincoln to Philadelphia.

AFTER YORKTOWN.

AFTER the surrender of Cornwallis the fighting in the Southern States was of a fitful and desultory nature. The English forces were mainly confined within their sea coast fortresses in Charlestown and Savannah, their circuit of operations did not extend more than a radius of twenty miles inland, and they only traversed the neighbourhood in search of forage for their troops and plunder from the inhabitants. The condition of the American forces at this time, under Greene, was most deplorable, and Washington, mindful of the wants of his favourite general, proceeded to Philadelphia, not alone to receive the personal thanks of Congress on his late victory, but also, as he wrote Greene, to stir up the Congress to call forth aid for the sorely tried southern army. At this time he wrote the following note to General Greene : " I shall attempt to stimulate Congress to the best improvement of our late success, by taking the most vigorous and effectual measures to be ready for an early and decisive campaign next year. My greatest fear is lest, viewing this stroke in a point of light which may too much magnify its importance, they may think our work is nearly closed and fall into a state of languor and relaxation. To prevent this error I shall employ every means in my power, and if, unhappily, we sink into this fatal mistake, no part of the blame shall be mine." For twelve months General Greene, the Fabian Commander, and his army had been marching and counter-marching, attacking and re-treating, and driving the British before them to their sea-side strongholds. That some idea may be formed of the trials of the army under Greene we will let one of his letters to the Secretary of War speak for itself : " I would order the returns you require, but we really have not paper enough to make them out, not having had for months past paper enough to make provision returns, or to record the necessary returns of the army. Since we have been in the lower country, through the difficulty of transportation we have been four weeks without ammunition, while there was plenty of this article at Charlotte. We lay within a few miles of the enemy without six rounds a man. Had they known our position they might have ruined us. You can have little idea of the confusion and disorder that reigned throughout the southern States. Our difficulties are so numerous and our wants so pressing, that I have not a moment's relief from the most painful anxieties." Greene was, as has been already remarked, a great favourite with the Commander-in-Chief, and like Washington, he had most inveterate enemies, one of whom was the Secretary of War, to whom the following letter, in the midst of his trials, was addressed : " My military conduct," he tells him, " must speak for itself. Let it suffice to say I have had more embarrassments than it is proper to disclose to the world, and that this part of the United States has had a narrow escape. I have been seven months in the field without taking off my clothes for one night." In this communication he alludes to a plot formed against him by his own soldiers to take his life. He executed the ringleader and thus infused fear into those who might in future have treasonable ideas against him. Greene was truly a great general, neither sparing his men nor himself. When asked in the heat of the conflict to disband his army and desist from an attempt so hopeless as to regain with a handful of men the lost Southern States, he made answer "he would regain them or die in the attempt." This remark was the key to his character and his success. It will suffice, as far as the lingering campaign waged by Greene after the surrender in October is concerned, to say that before the end of 1782 the British forces bade adieu to the Southern States, and Greene and his ragged band of soldiers entered triumphantly into Charlestown after it had been two years in the hands of the enemy. It is needless to add that he received an ovation from the terrorized inhabitants, and the honours paid him by Congress and his country were only second to those bestowed upon Washington himself.

The Southern States were truly grateful to General Greene for his superhuman struggle for their emancipation. Not alone did they reward him by public acclamation, numerous addresses, and festive entertainments, b .t they bestowed substantial rewards in gifts of land. From South Carolina he received an estate valued at ten thousand pounds ; from Georgia and North Carolina he also received extensive tracts of land. The war was now at an end. Arrangements were soon entered into for the evacuation of New York, and on the 25th November. 1782, the last of the British fleet and army sailed away from the verdant shores of the infant Republic, defeated and disgraced, and Washington and his army were left in sole possession of the United States of America.

King George, the relentless foe of American liberty, was still in hopes that the proud prestige of the British arms would not be tarnished by his rebellious American subjects. He was prepared to sacrifice everything—and some were so bold as to say even the crown itself—rather than lose America. He urged Lord North to procure a vote in Parliament to continue the war with renewed force and vigour. The sentiments of the King, and his determination to pursue his headstrong and foolish policy, in spite of all opposition in both House of Parliament, in spite of addresses from the people of London, headed by their Lord Mayor, calling for a cessation of hostilities ; in spite of appeals from the merchants and men of property over the country, in spite of protests from his other Colonies, were plainly made known to his Parliament and nation in the address from the throne, delivered a few days after the defeat of his forces in Virginia was announced to him. The warlike spirit of the King and his ministers was well summarized by Mr. Fox in an eloquent oration in moving an amendment to the address. He said that if the King " had listened to the voice of the nation, before urging on the war after the defeat of Cornwallis, instead of being led by his present advisers, he should have thus addressed himself from the throne : ' I have been deceived and imposed upon by misinformation and misrepresentation, and in consequence of this delusion, the parliament has been deluded, but now the deception is at an end. I and my people have been in error ; the nation has suffered long enough ; our error and our sufferings are at an end.' Instead of language like the above we have listened to speeches from the government, breathing vengeance, rancour, blood and misery." " It expressed," says Fox, " exactly these sentiments : " Much has been lost ; much blood, much treasure have been squandered ; the burdens of my people are almost intolerable ; but my passions are ungratified—my object of subjugation and of revenge is yet unfulfilled, and therefore I am determined to persevere." To delude the Parliament and the people they then described the contest to be a mere squabble. It was only " Hancock and his crew " with whom we were at war, and not the entire people of North America." " Yet," continued the great statesman, " Every period of this disgraceful contest on our part has been marked with disaster, but the last misfortune was such as took away the final hope even of the most violent abettors of the war. The honorable gentleman who had seconded the address had said that we could not blame the unfortunate and gallant lord who commanded the army in Virginia ; that we must receive him with praise, for victories had been the preludes to the surrender of his army. He would join that honorable gentleman in bestowing the warmest praises on that noble lord, for not to him did he impute disaster, but to the ministry by whose savage obstinacy he was ordered to persevere in an expedition against the evidence of both fact and reason. But had not all the transactions of this war been of the same sort ? Had not all the generals been brave and all unfortunate ? The conquest of Ticonderoga had concluded in the surrender of Saratoga. The victory of Brandy-wine had ended in the recall of Sir William Howe, and the triumph of Camden to the capitulation of York. It had been with Earl Cornwallis as it had been with General Burgoyne :

" The path of glory leads but to the grave."

General Burgoyne had been brave ; General Burgoyne had failed ; and General Burgoyne had been reviled, persecuted, and proscribed. So had General Sir William Howe ; so, perhaps, in his turn, would the brave and unfortunate Earl Cornwallis. Their dirty literary engines would be set to work, and calumny would come forth in all the insidious garbs that inventive malice could suggest. They would place the blame anywhere but in the right place—their own weakness, obstinacy, inhumanity and treason."

Lord North, after King George himself, was the chief instigator of the war, and we must not omit here in giving extracts from the expressions of public opinion in England, to quote a passage from an oration of the Prime Minister in reply to Mr. Fox. " We have," he says, " been unfortunate, and a melancholy disaster has befallen our arms in Virginia, but must we, therefore, lie down and die ? No, it ought to rouse us into action ; it ought to impel and urge us and animate us ; for by bold and united exertions everything might be yet saved ; by dejection and despair everything must be lost." Let us listen next to Edmund Burke in reply to Lord North : " The language of the minister," he said, " froze his blood and harrowed up his soul. Good God ! Mr. Speaker, are we yet to be told of excellent rights ? Oh, valuable rights ! valuable you should be for we have paid dear at parting with you. Oh, valuable rights ! that have cost Britain thirteen provinces, four islands, one hundred thousand men, and more than seventy millions of money. Oh, wonderful rights ! that have lost to Great Britain her empire on the ocean, her boasted grand and substantial superiority, which made the world bend before her. Oh, inestimable rights ! that have taken from us our rank among nations, our importance abroad, and our happiness at home ; that have taken from us our trade, our manufactures and our commerce ; that have reduced us from the most flourishing empire in the world to be one of the most compact, unenviable powers on the face of the globe. Oh, wonderful rights! that are liable to take from us all that yet remains. What were these rights? Can any man describe them? Can any man give them a body and soul answerable to all these mighty costs? We do all this because we had a right to do it, that was exactly the fact, and all this we dare do because we dare. We had a right to tax America, says the noble lord, and as we had a right we will consult no ability, we will not measure our right with our ability : but we will have our right; we will have our bond. Next your heart we will have it ; the pound of flesh is ours and we will have it. That is the language of ministers. Oh, miserable and infatuated men ! Miserable and undone country, not to know that right signified nothing without might— that the claim without the power of enforcing it was nugatory and idle." . . . . " The Americans have money," he goes on again, " we want it, we will have it. They resisted the claim : they fought the battle for a time themselves. At last they called in an ally ; they are joined by the French, and conjoined ; they have forced your armies to surrender ; and yet, the noble lord comes down and tells the parliament of the nation that he has ruined—insolently tells them—that we are fighting for a right. He trusted a day of reckoning would come, and whenever that day came he should be able by impeachment to bring upon the heads of the authors of their unhappy affairs, the punishment due to them. He had looked cautiously at the conduct of Lord Cornwallis ; his gallantry he attested ; but what had his operations been but marching and counter-marching from north to south, from the mountains to the sea, and from the sea to the mountains? This had been done to deceive the people here, and make them believe we had a proportionate interest in the country to the extent of territory traversed. When real generalship was to be manifested the Americans had shown it. Nor was the capture of Cornwallis the only instance of captured armies. Give us back our armies and no longer protract this disgraceful war." After much preliminary debating, and voting and counter-voting on resolutions proposed by the opposition, the issue was brought to a test—whether or not the present policy of continuing the war was acceptable to the house—by a resolution proposed by General Conway, a consistent friend of the Colonies. He moved that any further attempt to reduce America by force would be ineffectual and injurious. The voting power of the Ministerials was still strong, although the eloquence of the opposition, and the overwhelming voice of the country for peace were effectual in lessening the hitherto safe majority, which always voted solid for Lord North's war policy. The vote was lost by a majority of forty-one in a house of near four hundred members. It was becoming evident to the ministers that Parliament was heartily sick of the war, when the personal appeal of the King and a powerful ministry could only carry a vote for war by such a majority. But did the Parliament represent the real mind of the nation ? By no means ! The country from end to end raised a determined howl of protest against the war and the government. General Conway proposed another resolution of protest against the present advisers of his Majesty, as public enemies of their country, and this time the government only succeeded in escaping disaster by one vote. Soon after this the ministry of North resigned, having reigned in the Cabinet of the nation for twelve years. Lord Shelbourne took up office after the unexpected demise of the Marquis of Rockingham, who was opposed to the continuance of the war and favoured American Independence.

It is said that King George urged the new Prime Minister to yield a treaty for cessation of hostilities and enter into negotiations for peace with the American Commissioners ; but he had one proviso, viz., he was on no account to formally grant Independence to the Colonies. The good offices of Catherine of Russia failed to bring about peace some time previous, owing to her leaning toward the same proviso. Dr. Benjamin Franklin, who was one of the American Commissioners deputed by Congress to negotiate the treaty, said that among George's papers were found instructions to Lord Shelbourne as follows : " I will be plain with you. The point next to my heart and which I am determined to resist, be the consequences what they may, is never to yield a total unequivocal recognition of the Independence of America, unless with my crown and life. Promise to support me and I will grant you full and uncontrolled powers as Prime Minister of the Kingdom. Shelbourne accepted the terms of his King, but the American delegates were firm, and refused to negotiate unless in conjunction with their French allies. The tide of popular feeling in England ran too strong in favour of American Independence to be indefinitely postponed by the King or his Ministers. Mr. Oswald, the English plenipotentiary, met in Paris the American delegates, Franklin, Joy; and Laurens, and after much preliminary debating regarding boundaries, fishing rights, a common basis was arrived at. The right to fish on the Newfoundland banks was a point that Dr. Vergennes, the French Minister, was at first unwilling to concede to America. The American and British delegates signed a preliminary treaty, recognising the disputed fishing rights, and determining imaginary boundaries, embracing the territory in the north-west as far as the Mississippi, acquired by Clarke. The Mississippi waters were contended for by John Adams, and without this concession he threatened, on behalf of America, to break up the negotiations. Although he was strongly opposed by the French in his contention, yet Dr. Vergennes at last acquiesced, and on the 3rd of September, 1783, the treaty was duly signed by the three powers, through their delegates, and the fundamental basis of the treaty was the recognition of the sovereign Independence of the United States of America.

THE AFTERMATH OF WAR.

EARLY DIFFICULTIES OF THE REPUBLIC.

THE United States had gained freedom and had had their independence recognized by treaty, but their territories lay prostrate from the ravaging effects of the war; they were bankrupt in men and money. When the war commenced in Boston eight years before, the Colonies were without an exchequer; during the war the financial difficulty was constantly recurring; now that war was ended an almost hopeless financial state stared the nation's leaders in the face. The resources of the country had been neglected, or left to the aged, the young and the female portion of the population. The demands on the State were enormous. Rich and poor, farmer and labourer, merchant and artisan, felt that the country, now that peace was proclaimed, owed them not alone gratitude, but something more substantial to repay them for their losses in the war. It was truly a critical period, and the difficulties in the way of national regeneration seemed well-nigh insurmountable. Washington writing to his friend, James Warren, in 1785, puts the condition of affairs at this period pretty clearly. He says: " The war has terminated most advantageously for America, and a fair field is presented to our view, but I confess I fear we do not possess wisdom or justice enough to cultivate it properly. Illiberality, jealousy, and local policy mix too much in all our public counsel for the good of the Union ; in a word, the Confederation appears to me a shadow without the substance, and Congress a sham whose deliberations are ignored. To me it seems inexplicable that we should confederate, as a nation, and yet be afraid to give the rulers of that nation—who are the creatures of our own making, appointed for a limited period, and amenable to us for their action in Congress—sufficient powers to regulate our affairs. ˙ By such a policy the wheels of government are clogged, and our highest expectations frustrated. From the high ground on which we stood we are descending into a vale of confusion and darkness. That we have it in our power to become one of the most respected nations in the world to my mind is beyond doubt, if we pursue a wise, just, and liberal policy towards one another, and keep good faith with the rest of the world. That our resources are increasing none can deny, but while they are grudgingly applied or not applied at all we give a vital stab to public faith, and we shall sink in the eyes of Europe into contempt. It behoves us to establish just principles, and this cannot be done by thirteen heads, differently constructed and organized. The necessity, therefore, of a controlling power is obvious, and why it should be withheld is beyond my comprehension." We may here conveniently make a slight survey of the historical causes which militated against the bond of Union, and the strengthening of a central government. When the war broke out in 1775, all the thirteen Colonies were commonwealths, separate and distinct one from the other. Each had its own constitution, governors, assemblies of representatives, and counsels, or senate ; each levied its own taxes, developed its own resources, made its own laws and administered justice by its own judges. When the Motherland began to oppress by taxing them without their consent, they formed themselves into a league to defend their rights wherever attacked, and deputed delegates from each State to meet for deliberation for the common defence. In 1776, as the war assumed serious proportions, they called together a Convention in Philadelphia, and drafted the Declaration of Independence, which set at defiance the authority of George III., and bound each to persevere in union until the British troops should leave for ever their beloved land. This convention of 1776 deputed a committee to draw up " Articles of Confederation." These

N

Articles aimed at uniting the Colonies of North America in a
" perpetual union," and these States were in future to be
known as the United States of America. Certain definite
powers were given by these Articles, similar to a constitution,
but those powers, though loyally observed during the war, were
more by way of recommendation to the different States than
in the nature of a binding constitution. The principle running
through the Articles shows how tenacious each State was of its
own sovereignty. Article 2nd says, " Each State retains its
sovereignty, freedom, and independence, and every power,
jurisdiction and right, which is not by this confederation
expressely delegated to the United States in Congress assembled," and Article 3rd states that " these thirteen States
enter into a league of friendship with each other for common
defence, the security of their liberties, and their mutual and
general welfare, binding themselves to assist each other against
any force offered, or attack made upon them, or any of them,
on account of religion, sovereignty, trade, or other pretence
whatsoever." The union thus formed continued during the
war, but the Articles, when sent for ratification to the different
States, were not adopted by all until 1781. After the final
ratification of these Articles in 1781, the constitution, thus
drafted, became the bond of Union between the States. It
worked harmoniously until after the Treaty, but, as we see
from the above letter of Washington, was very inoperative
after the Revolution storm.

When the soldiers were disbanded, and the Colonies, or
different States, settled down to the serious work of recon-
structing their domestic affairs, little attention was paid to the
Articles of Confederation. Each State relapsed into the old
groove that was so familiar before the war. The uppermost
idea of patriotism, in the mind of the ordinary citizen, was the
sovereignty and independence of his own State. The affairs
common to the entire confederation were little heeded, and
the appeals made to the State Legislature had little effect.
Yet, if there was to be stability for their Union, if there was to

be permanency for their liberties, if the war for freedom was to be a reality, a patriotism that embraced the entire Union, that advocated the fulfilment of the conditions of the Treaty with Great Britain, acting under the Articles of Confederation with Great Britain, was urgently required over the Union, Congress, acting under the Articles of Confederation, was very weak. It could declare war, but it could not raise or support an army. It could not raise a dollar on taxation. It had no power to control and direct commerce, or impose tariff to aid in government. Commerce with foreign nations and between the States was under the control of the States. All that Congress could do was to make known to the State legislatures the financial and other difficulties common to the Union, but individual States might refuse to listen to their petitions. It could not compel a State or a citizen to do anything before the State Assemblies had given their approbation. Not alone were matters of domestic and national interest in a precarious state at home, but foreign nations were beginning to lose respect for the Colonies. England, mistress as she was of the seas, and never having been noted for tenderness of conscience or an aversion to piracy and dishonest practices, refused to give American merchants fair play. She sheltered herself behind her " Navigation laws," restricted the free imports of the States, and otherwise by dumping her produce among those Colonials prepared to pay, aided in impoverishing the struggling States and embittering the feeling in America against England. Each State, as we saw, regulated its own commerce at this time, and one State trafficking with another put tariffs on goods, &c., imported, and different States had different imposts for the same articles with foreign traders. New York, for example, laid a duty on chickens and dairy produce from New Jersey, and on firewood from Connecticut. New Jersey, in turn, retaliated on New York, by laying a tax of 1,800 dollars annually upon a lighthouse which New York had erected on the Jersey shore. This process of retaliation caused bitter feelings over the States, and rendered the people more jealous and unfriendly towards each other. This was one of the causes that led to the framing of the Constitution, and the founding of the Republic, this necessity for a strong central authority to regulate commerce. Another cause, and one which more closely affected the States, aided the patriots in hastening the consolidation of the Union into a Federal Republic, and that was the financial difficulties which pressed severely on the individual States and on the National Congress. When war was declared in 1775, three million dollars of paper money were issued. At first these bonds were equal to and accepted for their gold or silver equivalent. Before the end of the second year of the war, they had fallen in value one half, and before the end of the war, they had depreciated to one hundredth part of their original value. The amount of the issue of these paper notes during the war was reckoned at over two hundred million dollars. So plentiful had they became after the war that the squatters out west used them, we are told for papering the interiors of their log-built cabins. Besides the two hundred million dollars issued by the Union Congress, the separate States, on their own account, for State circulation had issued almost a similar amount. Congress, in addition, had borrowed from France, and other friendly nations, about forty-four million dollars. The cost of the war was supposed, in round numbers, to have reached the sum of one hundred and forty-four million dollars. Interest, as well as principal of the borrowed debt, had to be paid, and foreign creditors were becoming insistent on having their loan refunded. Of course, we must not confound the amount of paper money issued with the real debt or cost of war. This money depreciated year by year, and each succeeding holder of the bills lost as much as they depreciated whilst in his hands, and in this way, indirectly, the bills were a tax on the holders. The depreciation of the paper money naturally created a public clamour among creditors, and they kept " ghosting " the State legislatures and Congress for payment in specie. The individual States considered their own liabilities more pressing than the national credit of

Congress, and soon little or no attention was given to Congress and its demands. Over the Union, great opposition was shown to the officials and taxgatherers for State and Federal purposes, and litigation became universal. It was the harvest time for the legal profession, and the "limbs of the law" were everywhere detested among the Colonists. In Massachusetts matters became so agitated that the military were ordered out to put down an insurrection, led by Daniel Shays, a former captain in the Continental army. General Lincoln, of Revolution fame, was placed at the head of a few thousand troops, and after some feeble resistance the rebels dispersed. This rising in the heart of the New England States caused patriotic men over the Union to reflect and take council for common defence, to secure peace and harmony at home, and to raise the dwindling credit and hampered commerce abroad. This year, 1786, becomes memorable in the critical period of American history, not alone from the rebellion which took place, but from the fact that its quick suppression showed to the world, which was jealously watching the infant Republic, that there was vitality—a latent power in reserve in the States. Credit and trade and prosperity leaped ahead from this period. It was in this year that the Virginian legislature, perceiving the necessity of some revenue for the Federal government, and believing that Congress ought to be able to protect the commerce of the Union, appointed Commissioners and invited other States to meet them by delegates in Annanopolis, to consider these matters. The opinion held by Virginia, that more power should be placed in the hands of the Federal government, was almost universal amongst thinking and patriotic men over the Union. A letter from Washington to John Jay attests to this : " Many are of opinion that Congress have too frequently made use of the suppliant humble tone of requisition in application to the States, when they had a right to assert their imperial dignity and command obedience. Requisitions are a perfect nullity where thirteen sovereign, independent, disunited States, are in the habit of discussing and refusing compliance with them at option. Requisitions are actually little better than a jest and a byword throughout the land. If you tell the legislatures they have violated the treaty of peace and invaded the prerogatives of the confederation they will laugh in your face. What then is to be done ? Things cannot go on in the same train for ever."

The patriotic delegates assembled in Annanopolis solved the difficulty by drawing up a resolution, to be put before Congress, asking that assembly to request the States to meet in the following year at Philadelphia to consider how the Articles of Confederation might be revised to meet the new necessities of their country. The States were duly notified, and each State appointed delegates to assemble in May of 1787, in the then capital of the Union, to deliberate and finally draft the famed constitution of the United States. In this Assembly, presided over by Washington, there were fifty-five delegates present, amongst them being some of the most distinguished patriots of their country. Franklin, the sage and scholar, the Nestor of the convention, sat side by side, now an octogenarian, with Samuel Adams, John Adams, Hamilton and Carroll. The ablest and best men of the nation were in the constitution at Convention—men who, in army and senate at home, and at foreign courts, had spent themselves in the cause of their country's liberty. They came together for the greatest and most important public work of their lives, the work which was destined to make their nation feared and loved, respected and powerful, among the nations—the framing of the Constitution. The scope of convention and the impediments it had to contend against cannot be better stated than by that ripe scholar, worthy son of a worthy father, John Quincy Adams, who was President of the U.S. about the year 1825. " In most of the inspirations of genius," he says, " there is a simplicity which when they are familiarised to the general understanding of men by their effects, detracts from the opinion of their greatness. That the people of the British Colonies who, by their united counsels and energies, had achieved their independence, should continue to be one people and constitute a nation, under the form of one organised government was an idea in itself, so simple, that it at once forcibly addressed itself to the reason and the imagination of every thinking man from Maine to Georgia. But, no sooner was it conceived than it met with obstacles innumerable. They resulted from the existing social institutions, diversified among the parties to the projected national union, and seeming to render it impracticable. There were chartered rights, for the maintenance of which the war for independence was waged. There were State sovereignties, corporate feudal baronies, tenacious of their own liberties, impatient of a superior, and jealous and disdainful of a paramount sovereign, even in the whole democracy of the nation. There were collisions of boundary, and of proprietary right—westward in the soil—southward in its cultivation. In fine, the diversities of interests and opinions, of manners, of habits, and even of extraction, were so great that the plan of constituting them one people appears not to have occurred to any of the members of the convention before they were assembled together." Hume, the historian, speaking of the difficulties that have to be contended with in constitution building says, " To balance a large state or society, whether monarchial or republican, on general laws, is a work of so great difficulty, that no human genius, however comprehensive, is able, by mere dint of reason and reflection, to effect it. The judgment of many must meet in the work, experience must guide their labours, time must bring it to perfection ; the feeling of inconveniences must correct the mistakes which they inevitably fall into in their first trials and experiments."

The State House in Philadelphia, where the historic Declaration of Independence was signed, was chosen for the convention. In this hall, those delegates held their sessions from May 25th until 17th September, five months less one week. The debates were carried on with closed doors. Newspaper men were debarred their meetings. Absolute secrecy was enjoined on every member present. Charles Wilson, a famous Ulster man, was appointed Secretary. The records of the debates were taken down *in extenso*. Thirty years elapsed before the documents were ordered to be published by Congress, at a time when nearly all the performers in the Convention had died. Washington, in the year 1796, placed the records in the archives of the nation under strict custodianship. In this procedure wisdom and prudence suggested, we see, a precedent for the secret methods of the abortive conference which lately sat at Westminster. It is a consummation devoutly to be wished that our British statesmen would carry further their imitation of the proceedings of the fathers of the American constitution. And viewing the progress of democratic ideas at the present time it may well be, as is the opinion of many wise heads to-day, that circumstances unerringly are hastening events and shaping the way in these islands for a constitution on the American plan. James Bryce in his work on the American Commonwealth " says : " They (the Americans) are believed to disclose and display the type of institution towards which, as by law of fate, the rest of the civilized mankind are forced to move, some with swifter, others with slower, but all with unhesitating feet." Slow though it be the progress of events in the United Kingdom is certainly in that direction. The difficulties confronting the Philadelphia convention were local and historical. Each State, historically considered, stood out from its sister State as an isolated and concrete entity. Some sort of gradual union or spasmodic alliance occurred, of course, amongst the most of the States for pur. poses of mutual self-defence from Indian raids and French encroachments. Each State or settlement came over from Great Britain and Europe fortified, before arrival, or soon after, with Royal charters or letters patent, giving them, under the English crown, certain territories and certain privileges. Some of the States had more liberal terms granted them than others, just as the different sovereigns desired to be more or less liberal to their exiled compatriots. We find that most of the English, Scottish and Irish who sailed to America as

Colonists, with the exception of the militia, who were superfluous at home after the wars, and who were placed in possession of large tracts in the southern and midland states, and
some of the useless nobility also, who were favourites at Court,
were lovers of civil and religious liberty, as conceived by them
jn those backward ages. They placed these benefits above king,
or prince, or prelate. In Charles the First's time many emigrated to escape tyranny at home, and the terrors of the Star
Chamber. After the Cromwellian wars, and the fall of the
Roundhead administration, large numbers of fearless, brave,
and republican-loving Puritans came over to colonize the New
England and middle states. The Presbyterians from North
of Ireland and Scotland rebelled at home against high rents
and taxes, and religious disabilities, and sailed for the land of
liberty. Maryland, settled by dissatisfied English Catholics,
under Lord Bellemore, became the home of freedom for all
creeds and classes as early as the year 1634. Its constitution
was most liberal and its charter was equally generous. Penn
received a liberal charter,and his broad-minded policy towards
all but infidels, rendered Pennsylvania one of the favourite
colonies for all, but chiefly for Quakers, who were detested by
the Puritans. Penn's principle of government would seem
to be that expressed by his favourite dictum, " Liberty without
obedience is confusion, and obedience without liberty is
slavery." The form of government, from the days of Penn,
was republican and democratic. The Colonies over the union
were democratic, and some more so than others. In each state
or colony there was a Governor, a Council, and representatives.
Some colonies elected their own governors and council, and
some were elected by the Crown. Those States that elected
their own governors were more democratic than the Royal
States, whose governors were court favourites sent over from
London. In Rhode Island and Connecticut, the people
elected the governors. In Pennsylvania, Delaware, Maryland the proprietary electors elected the governor, and in the
rest of the states royal governors were appointed. The

governors in all the states except the elective States were most unpopular, and the constant friction between them and the people showed the spirit of the people antagonistic to English interference in their domestic affairs. It was in the heart of New England that the most ardent spirits of the Revolution were nurtured, in the land that sheltered the Pilgrim Fathers, who sailed to Plymouth on the *Mayflower*. Around Boston and Rhode Island many who fled Ulster in Queen Anne's reign, or from the effects of her laws on their religion, settled in and around Boston. Their descendants were not sleeping, we may believe, on the morning of Bunker's Hill fight. There were such ardent republican preachers as Williams and Rodgers and Anne Hutcheson, who, whilst they preached the reformed creed, propounded republican principles that produced fruit in the Revolution ; seed too that was still fructifying in the constitutional Convention. Let us in imagination transplant ourselves to those distant times, and scenes, and surroundings, and see how isolated one state was from another. In each State, after the Revolution, there was a dread and fear of kingly power, or any power over them, approaching to kingly domination. There was the fear amongst them of delegating any power which might recoil on themselves. They loved their state independence, each was jealous of its sister state : in fact they had little intercommunication in this sparsely-populated country, owing to their slow means of travelling and their little rivalries and distrustfulness of each other. Hence one of the chief obstacles that barred and retarded a closer union and fusion and some sort of alliance, was the jealousy of State sovereignty and State rights and long independence of control by any body or union. It was this state rights question that later brought about the civil war, in conjunction with the slavery question, another difficulty which also troubled the ingenuity of the Constitution builder to settle. In these states interested in the Union you had agricultural and commerical interests clashing ; you had the seaboard states with their fishing interests, their shipping interests ; and you had the more inland states, mainly depending on the land. You had the tobacco and cotton interests and their slaves. It was no wonder that Franklin, during the din of conflict in their prolonged and perplexing deliberations, asked that heaven might be invoked in prayer to give light and guidance to hasten a propitious ending to their Convention,

It need not be wondered that the Convention lasted many months—anxious months for the members within doors, and anxious also for the nation outside. It would take larger space than we have at our disposal to record the hundred and one points that came up for discussion and for voting upon. How should the President be elected, or should there be a President at all ? The Swiss have no President. Should his term of office be long, or for a year, or seven years, or for life ? What should be his title ? Should he have a salary ? Could one not native born be President ? Should he be above all law or be liable to impeachment ? What powers should he have and what his relations with the Congress ? Then discussion was long and animated on the composition and powers, privileges, salary, mode of election of the Senate and House of Representatives. Who should have votes and what should be the qualifications of voters ? Should the central power be supreme or the state supreme ? Could a state secede or could a state refuse to accept the legislation of the new government. Was it any wonder that it took five months to bring forth the document known as the American Constitution ? A document, too, which is so comparatively short   It is plainly and simply written, and easily understood. It was truly a relief to those weary delegates when the time approached that each should vote on the draft parchment and sign his name to the Constitution. Little time was wasted, after the Convention closed, in having it sent through Congress to the separate States for discussion and ratification. Franklin made a final appeal to the entire delegation to unanimously affix their names to the document which ended with these words : " Done in Convention with the unanimous consent of the States present on the 17th day of September, A.D., 1787, and the 12th year of the Independence of the United States of America. In witness whereof we have hereunto subscribed our names." There were fifty-five members in convention, of whom thirty-nine signed.

Washington forwarded the Constitution to Congress with a letter signed by himself together with some resolutions passed in Convention, viz., " That Congress forward document to state legislatures, and that when nine States ratify it the new government in agreement with constitution should be formed." The following letter of Washington's on the subject of the Convention cannot be omitted :—

In Convention, September 17th, 1787.

" Sir,—We have the honour to submit to the consideration of the United States in Congress assembled that Constitution which has appeared to us most advisable.

The friends of our country have long seen and desired that the power making war and peace and treaties, that of levying money and regulating commerce and the correspondent executive and judicial authorities, should be fully and effectively vested in the general government of the Union, but the impropriety of delegating such extensive trust to one body of men is evident. Hence results the necessity for a different organization.

It is obviously impracticable in the federal government of these states, to secure all rights of independent sovereignty, and yet provide for the interests and dignity of all. Individuals entering into society must give up a share of liberty to preserve the rest. The magnitude of the sacrifice must depend as well on situation and circumstances as on the object to be obtained. It is at all times difficult to draw up with precision the lines between those rights which must be surrendered and those which may be reserved, and on the present occasion this difficulty was increased by a difference among the several states as to their situation, extent, habits, and particular interests.

In all our deliberations on this subject we kept steadily in our view that which appears to us the greatest interest of every true American, the consolidation of our union, in which is involved our prosperity, felicity, safety, perhaps our national existence. This important consideration seriously and deeply impressing our minds, led each state in the Convention to be less rigid on points of inferior importance, and thus the Constitution which we now present to you is the result of a spirit of amity and of that mutual deference and concession which the peculiarity of our political situation rendered indispensable."

That it will meet the full and entire approbation of every State is not to be expected, but each will doubtless consider that had their interests alone been considered, the consequence might have been particularly disagreeable or injurious to others ; that it is liable to as few exceptions as could reasonably have been expected, we hope and believe ; that it may promote the lasting welfare of that country so dear to us all, and secure her freedom and happiness, is our most ardent wish.

With great respect, we have the honour to be, Sir,

Your Excellency's most obedient and humble servant,
(Signed)
George Washington, *President.*
By unanimous order of Convention.

His Excellency the President of Congress.

THE IRISH IN THE REVOLUTION.

EARLY ULSTER EMIGRANTS.

It would be ungracious for an Irish writer, and still more so for an Ulsterman, to touch, however lightly, on the history of the American Revolution, without referring to the part played therein by the early emigrants from the North of Ireland. The share of Ulster in the Revolution forms most interesting reading. Plowden in his "Historical Review," Vol. I., p. 458, says that "most of the early successes in the Revolution in America were immediately owing to the vigorous exertions and prowess of the Irish emigrants from the North of Ireland, who bore arms in that cause." Dr. Reid, in his History of the Presbyterian Church in Ireland, speaking of the great flow of emigration in the eighteenth century from Ulster, says that "poverty pressed heavily on the members of the Church in Ireland, and in the seventies all the efforts of their ministers were unavailing to keep down lawlessness and sedition and plunder." It was poverty and oppression that produced the Hearts of Oak and the Hearts of Steel, two anarchical secret associations. It was amongst the farming and labouring classes that poverty and discontent were keenest. Disorder and sedition were repressed with the firm hand of the law, but there was no legal redress immediately forthcoming. Murmurings of discontent and rebellion were silently brewing against the rulers. Thousands were annually crossing the Atlantic, and in the years of the Revolution appeared in arms against the motherland as assertors of the Independence of the American Republic. It has been asserted by historians that from the year 1719 till 1776 as many as 200,000 emigrated from Ulster to the American Colonies. These emigrants were mainly Presbyterians. Arthur Young in a letter written from Portrush in 1776, while on a tour in Ireland, says that emigration to America " seems to be confined to the Presbyterians, and chiefly to those Presbyterians in the linen trade." Of the Catholics, at this time, he says " they seem to be so firmly wedded to their homesteads that none emigrate, and few even pass from one parish to another." From reliable sources we find that this flow of emigration for fifty years was constant, and averaged annually about 4,000. There must have been some deep-rooted causes to drive out one-third of the hard-headed, industrious race of Scottish Presbyterians from their homesteads in half a century. There must have been some serious injustice that could make the sons of men who fought with Cromwell, who put the Crown on William, and defended Derry with such courage and bravery, fly from Ireland. Yes, the Presbyterians were treated unjustly, from Anne ascended the throne until they wrenched their civil and religious rights from an unwilling government, through fear of an armed and disciplined force of volunteers, 100,000 strong. These brave peasant soldiers, like the soldiers of Cromwell, stood firm, until a corrupt Irish Parliament unwillingly listened to their grievances and redressed them.

A bird's eye view of the history of Presbyterianism in Ireland will show with more clearness the unequal treatment meted out to them in Ireland. The North of Ireland Presbyterians, who were mainly of Scottish origin, did not transplant themselves at one time, nor to one place. Arthur Young in the fifth of his twelve letters written from Portrush village in 1776 says of the Scottish settlement in and around North Antrim—" During the time England was endeavouring to extend her pale in every direction from the capital, our desperate but disunited enemy, the Scottish clan M'Donnell had, by intermarriage in Ireland, got footing and began their ravages on the northern coast of Antrim, and finally established themselves over a tract of country near forty miles in length. The native Irish betook themselves elsewhere, and thus the Scotch-Irish got rooted in the soil. These settlers are in general, an industrious, thrifty race of people. They have a great deal of substantial civility without much courtesy to relieve it and set it off to advantage. The bold ideas of rights and privileges which seem inseparable from the Presbyterian Church, render them apt to be ungracious, and litigious in their dealings. On the whole the middling and lower class of the people in this quarter of the kingdom are a valuable part of the community." Many Presbyterians came over to Ireland after the wars of Cromwell, and settled on the land leased and rented to them by the planters. The Test Act, which was in force from the time of Charles II. in England and Scotland, had not been enforced in Ireland until 1704, after Anne had ascended the throne. Many Nonconformists, therefore, went from Great Britain to Ireland that they might evade the detested sacramental test and enjoy more civil and religious liberty. William was friendly to the Presbyterians of Ireland for their bravery at the battle of the Boyne, and to a great extent he gave fair play to all denominations, but contrary to the High Church party's policy towards the Presbyterians. Anne detested the Presbyterians and Catholics alike. The law was enforced in 1704. The consequences of the Act were galling to the Dissenters. Unless they conformed, and received the sacrament according to the rites of the Church of England, they were debarred from all civic rights. They could not be an office-holder under the crown, a Justice of the Peace, a school teacher, an income tax gatherer, or excise officer. Their marriages were null and void; their dead had to be buried according to the Church of England rites. Their ministers were in a kind of bondage, and the doctrines they taught were strictly scrutinized; the mediums of redress with the Crown were chiefly the Primate of Dublin or Armagh. No wonder that after repeated attempts to have this Act repealed, and after repeated failures to get any relaxation of their grievances, these sturdy Presbyterians sailed away in multitudes from tyranny, and with vengeance and hate in their hearts against the English rulers. No wonder that an historian of note had said that the men from the North of Ireland were the first to unsheath the sword, and the last to leave it down in the cause of American freedom.

The spirit of these stout Ulstermen is well illustrated in the following incident from the history of the Revolution : Colonel Polk, grandfather of President Polk, was the leader of an Irish regiment in North Carolina in the war for Independence. (Polk was born in Donegal, Ireland.) In 1776, when reading the Declaration of Independence from the steps of the Courthouse in Charlotte one afternoon to his soldiers and the citizens, he showed the courage of his countrymen by adding a little speech of his own in which he used the words : " Whosoever directly or indirectly abetted, or in any form or manner countenanced the unchartered and dangerous invasion of our rights, as claimed by Great Britain, is an enemy to our country, to America, and to the interests and inalienable rights of man, that nation which had invaded and trampled on our rights and liberties and inhumanly shed the blood of American patriots at Lexington." Archbishop Boulter in the year 1728, some years after the Toleration Act was passed, writes to the Secretary of State in a most doleful strain giving a " melancholy account " of the extensive emigration from the northern province to America." He says : " We have had for several years some agents from the Colonies in America, and several ship captains, that have gone about the country and deluded people with stories of great plenty and estates in America, to be had for the going thither, and they have been the better able to delude the people by the necessities of the poor of late. The people that go from hence make great capital of the oppression they suffer here, the dearness of provisions. There were about 3,100 emigrated last summer, and of these about one-tenth were men of substance ; of the rest most are so poor that they have to hire themselves as quasi slaves to the undertakers and shipowners to pay their passage money." " At present," he adds, " the whole North is in a ferment and everyone is talking of emigrating."

Amongst those who emigrated there were many ministers who, disgusted with the intolerance of the Test Act, and owing to the poverty and fewness of their flocks from emigration and decline of the linen trade, found it impossible to support themselves. A minister from Templepatrick wrote, at this time, saying that there were two years stipend due to him, and that for over a year he had not received twelve pounds from the congregation. The High Church party in Ireland and the House of Lords were the great enemies of the Presbyterians of Ireland during the eighteenth century. Several times did the Irish Commons pass a Bill to remove the religious and civil disabilities of the Dissenters, and as often were these Bills rejected by the Lords. The moving spirit, moulding public opinion against them, was that versatile writer and vehement satirist, Dean Swift. The liberal party, with substantial majorities, sent up to the Lords Acts of Toleration for Dissenters in 1728, 1733, 1741 and 1758, to be each time spurned and rejected. A quotation or two from Swift will show the animus of the Established Church at this time towards Presbyterians. He says that "they, the Dissenters, had oppressed and persecuted the Conformists in those parts where their power prevailed, had invaded their congregations, propagated schism in places where it had not the least footing formerly;" that "they refused to take Conformist apprentices, and confined trade among themselves;" that, "in their illegal assemblies they had prosecuted and harassed these people for marrying according to law ; that they had thrown public and scandalous reflections upon the Episcopal order, and upon our laws, particularly the Sacramental Test Act, and had misapplied the Royal bounty or regium donum of £1,200 per annum, in propagating schism, and undermining the church, and had exercised an illegal jurisdiction in their presbyteries and synods, and assemblies, &c." Is it any wonder that the Established Church and the Dissenters at this time were deadly foes ? Swift even goes further in his charges against them, when he compares them with Papists, towards whom the great man had little affection.

"The Papists," says Swift, "aimed at one pernicious act, which was to destroy the Protestant religion, wherein by God's mercy and the assistance of our glorious King William, they absolutely failed. The Presbyterians attempted the three most infernal actions that could possibly enter into the hearts of men forsaken by God, which were the murder of a most pious King, the destruction of the monarchy, and the extirpation of the Church, and succeeded in them all." "Have," he concludes, "ever yet any of these sectaries in a solemn manner renounced any one of these principles upon which their predecessors then acted ? " The woollen trade of Ulster in the eighteenth century was chiefly in the hands of the Presbyterians and French dissenters. England became jealous of their growing prosperity, and as she goaded on the American Colonists by prohibition of their trading with other countries and by stringent navigation laws, so, in like manner, she imposed such high imports on woollen cloth exported from Ireland, and so restricted the trade, that Irish merchants found it impossible to continue the woollen factories with advantage. In the end about forty thousand Irish Protestants, once prosperous, were reduced to idleness and poverty. Owing to this cause in great part, Joyce, in his history of Ireland, states " that as many as 20,000 Presbyterains left Ireland for New England, and when they departed our shores they carried with them the commercial and industrial talent and one-fourth of the trading cash from our country."

From the above epitome of the history of Irish Presbyterians,it will be seen that it is no exaggeration to assert that in great part the success of the American Revolution depended on the ardent support of Ulster Nonconformists. It was the Presbyterian Church in America that taught the colonists to unite and assemble among themselves for common defence. They brought over from our shores the system of government that still rules the Presbyterian congregation, that of Presbyteries, Synods, and General Assemblies. These bodies met periodically, with elders and ministers as delegates, and discussed affairs pertaining to their different localities, and by correspondence, which they carried on at intervals, united the Presbyterians over large areas in a closer bond of brotherhood. When troubles crowded heavy and fast on the States, in the years leading up to the Revolution, Samuel Adams of Boston, introduced on similar lines the Committee of Correspondence over the States, and this led to the Union of the thirteen States which organised the colonies from Maine to Georgia in defence of Independence. To give some idea of the numerical strength of the Irish Presbyterians scattered over the entire States at the end of the war for Independence, we give some statistics taken from Bolton's History of Presbyterians in America. He thus tabulates them—

70 Communities in the		New England States.
35	,,	Pennsylvania.
100	,,	Virginia and Maryland.
50	,, ·	North Carolina.
70	,,	Georgia and South Carolina.

There were few Presbyterian settlements in the Dutch Colonies of New Jersey and New York. In Hanna's and Bolton's Histories of the Scottish-Irish in American Colonies we have constant references to emigrants in large numbers leaving the Bann Valley in the eighteenth century. The Bann Valley stretched from Coleraine to Kilrea, Garvagh and Aghadowey on the Derry side, and Ballymoney and Finvoy on the Antrim side. In the list of those constantly emigrating from this locality we find the same names as are to-day common over those areas, names such as John Bell, Abraham Holmes, John Wallace, James Reid, &c. In 1719 there were seventy families left the Route and Bann valley districts for Boston, and in 1722 one hundred families. Among these were the M'Keans from Ballymoney, who played a prominent part in the Revolution, and one of whom signed the Constitution, had been an officer in the war and was afterwards Governor in one of the New England States. Other names occurring among the list of passengers that sailed from Larne and Belfast in those times are John Stuart, John Morrison of Aghadowey, James Gregg, John Mitchel, James Anderson, Allen Anderson, Randal Alexander, M'Gregor, Steele, Taylor, Cochrane, Hamilton, Miller, Steenson, Newell, Young, Evans, Hunter, Johnson, Ross, Nelson, and Rev. James Woodside. It is worth noting, too, that they all sailed with their wives and families and kinsfolk.

Many of those Ulstermen have distinguished themselves in various walks of life in the States. Knox, an Ulsterman, was a general in the Revolution War, a personal friend of Washington's, and at one time, his aide-de-camp ; he afterwards was Secretary of War under the American Constitution during Washington's term as President. Charles Thompson, another distinguished Ulsterman, was born in Ireland in 1730, emigrated in youth to New Jersey, and married one Hannah Harrison, aunt to President Harrison. Thompson was a ripe scholar, and a fluent speaker, and was the Secretary to the Continental Congress during the entire war. He was one of those who signed the Declaration. He had in his custody the entire records of Congress from 1774 to 1789, when the Constitutional Government came into force. He died on the 16th August, 1824, at the ripe age of 94. Another, a distinguished surgeon, patriot and scholar—Benjamin Rush—was of Irish origin. His name figures amongst the signatures to the Declaration of Independence. To-day Presidents and Congressmen vie with each other in revering and perpetuating his memory. He was an ardent advocate of temperance in his generation. Hamilton, the first United States Chancellor of the Exchequer, and one of the most brilliant and versatile pillars of the Revolution and Republic, was of Ulster origin. Even Jefferson, so much a Galloman American, was on his mother's side of Irish descent, and General Montgomery, a gallant soldier in the Colonial wars, and a brave general under Washington, whose death was much lamented early in the Revolution, hailed from Donegal. In face of this bead-roll of fame Ulster, we think, has every right to be proud of the part she has enacted in the establishment of American freedom and democratic institutions.

Lecky, writing of those Ulster emigrants, says : "They went with hearts burning with indignation, and in the War of Independence they were almost to a man on the side of the insurgents. The famous Pennsylvania line were mostly Irish, and Montgomery, who became one of the earliest of the American commanders in the War of Independence, was a native of Donegal." Marmion, another writer of note, and one whose testimony is even more reliable than that of the great historian, inasmuch as he wrote of contemporary events, records that "Thousands of men, driven from their holdings, dissatisfied with the country, and expressing the deepest resentment against the Irish landlords, emigrated to America. Arriving there at a critical moment, and actuated by their wrongs, they joined the armies of Washington, then contending for Independence, and contributed by their numbers, as well as by their courage and conduct, to separate the United States from the British Crown." In another place Marmion says, speaking of the profusion of Irish names in the lists of the regiments from New Hampshire, Massachusetts, and New York, assembled at Boston in 1775, "To this newly-organized army of Independence, the Irish emigrants, who had been driven from their native homes by oppression from landlords, flocked in great numbers, rightly concluding that by the overthrow of the British forces in America, they were revenging themselves upon their late odious and relentless taskmakers, nor were there any in the American ranks more enthusiastic in the cause, brave in the highest degree, and abiding by the General until the cause of American Independence was firmly triumphant." Amongst the first arrivals to help to swell the American army to 20,000 strong at Cambridge, outside Boston, after the report of the battle of Bunker's Hill, and enrol himself as Colonel under the banner of Washington, was Daniel Morgan, the son of a County Derry man, the officer who, along with the infamous, through brave, Arnold, made victory sure for Gates at Saratoga, the hero of the Congress and the trusted friend of the General. Morgan did not come alone, he marched into line under the General, with 500 brave warriors, mostly Irish. These intrepid Irishmen were the sharpshooters who, in Boer fashion, popped off the tinselled officers of the enemy at the word of command. From Maryland, Virginia, and Pennsylvania, there came in, before the report of the first skirmishes of the Revolution had died away, numerous Irish troops eager for the fray. These contingents were led by William Thompson, an Ulsterman, and member of the original "Society of Friendly Sons of St. Patrick."

The statement has been made, but it is incorrect, that at the famed battle of Bunker's Hill the Irish were unrepresented. Such a charge is unfounded, as we may gather from one fact taken from the "Historical Collections" of New Hampshire, that in one regiment alone, raised in Bedford, there were seventy-two Irishmen who fought at Bunker's Hill—part of the men in the front rank, stationed at the rail fence, who twice drove back the redcoats with the bayonets fixed on their guns, and thus saved the main body from annihilation. There is another absolutely trustworthy source of history, the testimony of the records of the British House of Commons bearing on the part taken in the Revolution by Irishmen. One Joseph Galloway, a deserter from the rebel ranks, purchased by British gold, examined before a Committee of the House of Commons and asked, "What were the forces in the service of Congress chiefly composed of?" stated, "I can answer with precision. There were scarcely one-fourth native Americans (whites), about one-half were Irish, the other fourth English and Dutch." We have in this evidence, which was confirmed by other testimony given before the special committee, a confirmation of the historic exclamation of Lord Mountjoy, when news arrived in Parliament of the capture of Cornwallis: "You lost America by the Irish." Before this same Committee, Major General Robertson, on the testimony of General

Lee, a rebel leader, says that " half of the rebel army were from Ireland." Was it any exaggeration of the elder Pitt when he asserted that " Ireland was with America to a man." In Hansard (Vol. 19, p. 860) we read the following speech of Townsend, pleading the cause of Ireland : " My lords, consider in God's name, in time, consider what you owe to Ireland, to gallant and suffering Ireland. Suffer not your humiliating proposals and offerings to be laid at the feet of Congress, in whose front of battle these poor Irish emigrants perform the hardest service." Need we emphasise further the part taken by Ulstermen and other Irishmen in the cause of American freedom?

The reader will be curious to know did the great Washington ever recognize, by word or act, the fact that Irishmen were near him and around him from first to last in the Revolution. We will quote two passages taken from "The Irish in America " (Mr. Maguire), recounting how Irishmen in the States in 1790 presented an address to the then President. They tell him " how high are their hopes that they will enjoy equal rights of citizenship, and as a title for claiming these hopes, they remind him of the blood spilt under his own eyes in their exertions for the defence of their common country." Washington, prudent statesman as he was, thus wisely replies : " That all who conduct themselves as worthy members of the community are entitled to the protection of the civil government." " I hope," he adds, " ever to see America among the foremost nations in examples of justice and liberality. And I presume that your fellow-citizens will not forget the patriotic part which you took in the accomplishment of the Revolution, and the establishment of their government, or the important assistance they received from a nation in which the Catholic religion is professed." The biographer of Washington, his adopted son George Washington Parke Curtis, says, speaking of the soldiers who kept the flag flying in the war, up to the coming of the French, amongst whose ranks, moreover, were the French Irish Brigade, in the service of France, " Ireland has furnished in the ratio of a hundred to one of any nation whatever." "Then," he says, "honoured be the sons of Erin for their good service in the War of Independence. Let the shamrock be entwined with the laurels of the Revolution, and let the truth and justice, guiding the pen of history, inscribe on the tablets of America's remembrance eternal gratitude to Irishmen." Is it any wonder that, even to-day, these words of Curtis are bearing fruit in the land of liberty ; any wonder that Irishmen in the Republic are potent factors in ruling and guiding the destinies of the mightiest nation on earth, as they were the powerful elements, under their great general, in achieving its emancipation. If Ireland gave to the cause of America such a naval hero as Commodore Barry, the Father of the American Navy ; such soldiers as Brigadier John Sullivan, Knox and Morgan, Montgomery and Stack, when her cause needed brave and great men, need we wonder if Americans, down the generations since the Revolution, have honoured our name and race, and admitted them into their cabinets and councils, and raised monuments over the union to immortalize our Irish-American heroes and statesmen ? Ex-President Roosevelt, at a meeting of the Friendly Sons of St.Patrick, the oldest Irish Society in America, might well say : " I always feel at the banquets of the New England Society, that I am the President of the Friendly Sons of St. Patrick, whom I so often find here with me represent the victims who are dragged at the wheels of the Roman chariots. I am half Irish myself, as well as half Dutch. The Dutch are a conquered race, but the other half of me has avenged the Dutch."

The progress of affairs in America, it may be pointed out, had marked effects on the political situation in Ireland. The facts which history disclose to us leave no doubt on our minds that the liberal cause in Ireland, which, in the eighteenth century was the cause of Dissenters and Catholics, rose and fell with the success or failure of our American friends in the Revolution. There were no Volunteers in Ireland until a British army, 9,000 strong, had been captured at Saratoga;

until an army, 20,000 in numbers, had been cooped up and
hemmed in by the rebel forces on the heights of Valley Forge,
above Philadelphia; until the French King and nation had
formed an alliance for offensive and defensive purposes
against England during the war with America; and until Spain
and France had mutually agreed to curb the power of Britain
on the seas. Then it was that the Volunteers sprang, eagle-
like, into prominence, ostensibly, no doubt, to protect their
Irish coasts and Irish homesteads from French and American
freebooters and naval heroes, like Paul Jones. But these
Volunteers had no legal sanction in the land; they were toler-
ated because England had no regular force in Ireland worthy
of the name. At the end of the American war, in 1782, we
are told that there were only 5,000 British forces to garrison
the nation of Ireland. Where did the Volunteer movement
originate? In Belfast, the port from which, for a century,
our northern kith and kin in tens of thousands had been
emigrating with feelings of hate engendered by the oppression
of tithes and taxes and by penal laws and suppression of their
linen industries. Was not this the same port to which, month
b: month, vessels were returning from the American Colonies
bringing back news of the progress of the war in the States to
their anxious and liberty-loving friends in Ulster? In proof
of the contention that the Volunteer movement was an initial
revolution on Irish soil, in union with the bloody revolution
being waged against the then sworn enemy of liberty and
democracy on American soil, I may be excused for giving
the following extract from Dr. Reid's History of the Presbyterian Church in Ireland (Vol. III., pp. 344 and 345). "The
perilous condition of Ireland soon convinced the British statesmen that a system of procrastination in alleviating the Presbyterians from the odious Test Act and other disabilities
would be inexpedient. During the long recess of Parliament,
from August, 1778, to October, 1779, the Volunteers rapidly
increased, and when it reassembled they amounted to 42,000
men. Discontent had become more intense, as the trade of

the country had been nearly ruined by the American War, and the people began to make political demands in a tone which inspired the government with the most serious apprehensions. . . . . . On the 12th October, 1779, the very first day of the next session of parliament, Sir Edward Newham moved for leave to bring in a bill for the relief of the Dissenters. The Bill soon gained the assent of the Irish Commons. There was much delay after this Bill was sent over to England for confirmation, and much dissatisfaction was brewing in Ireland over the procrastination. At length, on the 11th of March, 1780, it was returned unaltered, and thus with the Royal consent passed into law. Government, however, received little credit for a measure which had been so long denied, and which was now so ungraciously conceded ; and the Presbyterians felt that they were indebted for this piece of tardy justice, not so much to the enlightened wisdom of fraternal rulers, as to the brilliant array of their own armed advocates." On that memorable day, two years later, when the Volunteers had increased their power and numbers in the land, one hundred and forty corps of armed men met in Convention in Dungannon Parish Church (15th February, 1782) and boldly asked for the same rights for their Catholic countrymen as they themselves gained from a grudging ministry, and asserted their right to Irish Independence, free from English control except the kingly signature and headship.

The Volunteers did not disband at Dungannon. It was signified to them that Grattan, the leader of the popular party in the Irish Commons, would, on the 16th April, bring in a bill to establish the Independence of the Irish Parliament, and on the 17th one hundred thousand armed Volunteers paraded the streets of Dublin and met in Convention to deliberate on " the Claims of the Country." Dr. Reid adds that the " Irish Parliament, which was little other than a Court to enact the will of a narrow-minded aristocracy, quailed before the threatened danger, and the Lord Lieutenant in despair sent in his resignation to the British minister." In a letter, dated 1782, April 18th, the despairing Duke of Portland, noted above, wrote Mr. Fox " that if liberal measures are delayed, you may recall your representative, and renounce all claim to this country." Was it not in 1782 that hostilities ceased in America, and that Franklin and Jay began to negotiate the Treaty of Peace in Paris, which George's minister reluctantly signed on behalf of his master in September, 1783 ? From these undoubted facts of history a natural conclusion is that our Irish, and especially our Ulster forefathers had contributed a leading share in the consummation of the Revolution in America, and sounded, moreover, the death knell of personal government in Britain, and brought about the speedy relaxation of the drastic penal laws which had been in force for two centuries in Ireland.

General Montgomery, already referred to, who fell early in the Revolution in an endeavour to capture Quebec, was, as we have said, a Donegal man. His death was a great blow to the cause of America. He was, says the historian Shaffner, " one of the bravest and most accomplished generals that ever led an army to the field." But he was not more illustrious for his skill and courage as an officer, than estimable for his private virtues. All enmity to him on the part of the British ceased with his life, and respect for his private character prevailed over all other considerations. His body was taken up from the snow-clad streets on the heights of Quebec the next day after he was slain, and honourably interred by the enemy. Montgomery, says the chronicler, " was a gentleman of good family in Ireland, who having married and purchased an estate in New York considered himself as an American, although he had served with distinction in the Colonial Wars, under the British flag." Congress directed a monument to be erected to his memory, with an inscription expressive of their deep veneration for his character, and the many signal and important services he rendered their cause, so that by it should be transmitted to future ages an example of patriotism, boldness of enterprise, indomitable perseverance and contempt for danger and death. A monument of white marble, with emblematic devices, was accordingly erected to his memory in front of St. Paul's Church, in New York.

We may fitly conclude these remarks about the Irishmen of the Revolution by the following quotation from *Munsey's Magazine* of April, 1906 :—" When the war of Independence began there were Irish in the firing line everywhere. They had a personal, as well as a colonial grievance against Great Britain, and here was a chance at last to even old scores. A writer of these times describes them as ' a hardy, brave, hotheaded race, excitable in temper, unrestrainable in passion, invincible in prejudice. They were impatient of restraint, and rebellious against anything that in their eyes bore the semblance of injustice. They were the readiest of the ready on the battlefield of the Revolution.' In those critical days, when thousands were dilly-dallying the Irish were hot for action. It was John Sullivan who struck the first blow, four months before the historic fight at Lexington, by capturing military stores at Portsmouth. The O'Sullivan family, of which he was a member, furnished three governors for the young Republic. Their mother in her old age used to say that she had often worked in the fields carrying the Governor of Massachusetts, while the Governors of Vermont and New Hampshire tugged at her skirts. The father of the Sullivans, Major Philip O'Sullivan, born in Co. Kerry, in his old age used to quote an old Latin rhyme which runs thus, ' Was Adam all men's sire and Eve their mother, then how can one be nobler than another ? Enobled are we not by sire or dame, till life and conduct give us noble fame.' The first British warship captured at sea in the Revolution was by an O'Brien. The first American General to fall in the war was Richard Montgomery, whose virtues compelled Lord North to lament his loss. It is a remarkable fact that the only three monuments in front of the oldest church in New York, St. Paul's, on Lower Broadway, are in memory of three famous Irishmen, viz., Richard Montgomery, Dr. Wm. MacNevin, and Thomas Addis

Emmet. Three of the signers of the Declaration of Independence were Irish born: Matthew Thornton, James Smith and George Taylor. Five others were at least of Irish descent: Edward Rutledge, Thomas Lynch, Charles Carroll, Thomas MacKean and George Reid. The Secretary of the Assembly, who read the Declaration on the first day of the Republic, was Charles Thompson, Irish born and son of an evicted tenant. Washington, to show his gratitude to the Irish who fought for liberty under him, often honoured the Friendly Sons of St. Patrick by dining with them in Philadelphia at their re-unions. It is to be noted here that this Society was the first to raise funds for the war to the amount of half-a-million dollars." It would be invidious to single out other individuals who distinguished themselves in the war, but historians have given prominent places in their narratives of the war to Count Dillon, Anthony Wayne, Generals Morgan, Sullivan, and Fitzgerald.

Miscellaneous Essays,

AND

Some Personal Impressions of Present-Day America.

[The following essays and personal sketches which I have ventured to publish together as a kind of second part, and in some sense, a companion picture to the studies of the Revolution, were written some years ago, partly as a result of my reading of American history, and partly as the outcome of actual experience in the States. The reader need not, therefore, be surprised if the impersonal "we" of the historian occasionally slips into the more personal and intimate "I" of the narrator of events seen at first-hand. The essays may not form an organised and connected whole ; but they reflect, I believe, as far as they go, a fairly faithful picture of the America of to-day, and carry out the main object I had in view, of showing how the old democratic ideals of the Republic, so lustrously evident at the time of its triumphant birth out of the Revolution War, are still, in the main, the predominant influence of the National life, and that America, sordidly commercial as she is, and corrupt in parts, is yet the guiding star of democracy, and constitutionally the best model for the people that has yet appeared among the nations.—J. O'B.]

AMERICAN PROGRESS DURING LAST CENTURY.

THE OLD COACHING DAYS.

AMERICA has made wonderful progress during the last hundred years. When Washington, in the beginning of the War for Independence, was appointed Commander-in-Chief of the Confederate army, he practically had no army or navy to command. The United States were then but thirteen in number, and were cut off by Florida from access to the Gulf of Mexico. Florida, New Orleans and the territory west of the Mississippi belonged to Spain, and only about twenty-five years later passed by purchase and conquest into the possession of the Federal States. Maine was the most northern of the states, and there was no union territory beyond the Alleghany mountains. The average breadth of the States did not exceed two hundred and fifty miles. The entire northern country beyond the St. Lawrence, including the Great Lakes, extending south and westwards from Lake Michigan as far as St. Louis, and embracing towards the Pacific all the territory of the present State of Washington, belonged to England. This vast and almost unexplored country was in the occupation of the scattered Indian tribes, and slightly garrisoned by a few English forts around Vincennes, Kaskaskia, Chicago, and the Ohio and Missouri rivers. The population of these thirteen States did not exceed four millions, of whom about one-fifth were slaves. Now the United States has a population of eighty millions. At the time of the signing of the Declaration of Independence the United States only embraced 827,844 square miles. In the year 1803, during the presidency of Thomas Jefferson, the territory known as the Louisiana Purchase was bought for fifteen million dollars from Napoleon, who, at that time, was in possession of Spain. He sold it because of his need for money to carry on the European war, and his anxiety to shut out the English from any hopes of future possession in the event of his failure to subdue them. He had also the further motive of putting the Americans in a position to rival the English in North America, and prevent them from acquiring further territory in the States.

Louisiana added 1,172,931 square miles to the original territory. At present the entire area of the United States is over three million square miles, and includes fifty-two States and territories and districts, all represented at Congress, all claiming the President of the Republic as their supreme governor and law giver ; all subject to the American Constitution, as drawn up in the years succeeding the independence of the States ; each subject to and acknowledging the

" star-spangled " banner; and each claiming as a right, protection from the central executive against invasion or injustice from any quarter. At the time when Washington ruled Congress, in the old government building in Philadelphia, which was then the largest city in the Union, the only cities in the Union were Philadelphia, New York, Boston, and Baltimore, of which the aggregate population was a little over 70,000; whilst of the entire colonists not more than three per cent. lived in towns. Taking population as an index of commercial, industrial, and manufacturing advancement, America has made marvellous progress. Almost thirty-four per cent. of the eighty million inhabitants to-day live in cities, whilst New York's population of 23,000 has advanced to four millions in about one hundred years. Philadelphia's thirty-two thousand is now one million three hundred thousand; and Chicago, St. Louis, Washington, Pittsburgh, and scores of other large cities of to-day were either prairie wastes or little villages in the last decade of the eighteenth century. In the beginning of the last century, and in fact, until about 1830, the population of America was very much hemmed in by the Alleghany mountains. The few commercial centres then existing developed numerically, socially, and industrially, but progress was slower in country districts until the steamboat supplanted the flat-bottom craft and sailing vessels on the rivers and coast line. The population was thicker along the rivers and inland, as shipping on rivers, &c., was the chief means for transit of produce from the country to the coast and cities lying east along the Altantic and gulf seaboard.

About 1825 a great impetus was given to western emigration and colonization by the opening of the Erie Canal. It connected the great northern lakes with the Hudson river, and ran across the country from Buffalo to Albany, a distance of three hundred and sixty-three miles. Lake Erie being six hundred feet above the level of the Hudson, the graduation rendered navigation easy on the eastward route. By many

P

the canal was looked upon as a great waste of public money, and the country people called it Clinton's Ditch. It was constructed by the State of New York, in which territory it solely lay, and took eight years for its completion. A steamboat was launched on the Hudson as early as 1807. The first steamboat was designed by Robert Fulton, and the trial trip up the Hudson from New York to Albany, a distance of one hundred and fifty miles, was performed at the rate of five miles an hour. The people assembled in great numbers along the route to see the wonderful invention, which most people expected would prove a failure. She was called in derision "Fulton's Folly." It was about the year 1811, before the steamboat supplanted the flat-bottoms on the Erie Canal, and the Ohio and Mississippi rivers. The development of the west gradually began from the introduction of the steamboat. Timber,cattle, corn and other produce were brought to eastern markets more quickly and cheaply ; passengers in great numbers passed up and down the rivers and canal, and reclaimed tracts of land sold at low rates by the government ; cities sprung up rapidly. The people no longer lived solely along the banks of rivers ; they branched out inland and westwards. Soon the experiment of steam locomotion that proved so successful on water was applied to land transport, and railways were invented, rude and crude, no doubt. That was about the year 1828. The rails at first were made of wood, iron sheeting being afterwards added as a covering, and the idea of the up-to-date metal rails was only gradually evolved. Wonderful has been the development of the railway in the last century. In 1830 only a few miles had been laid from Boston ; now the United States has over one hundred and eighty thousand miles of permanent way, extending north and south, east and west, from Atlantic to Pacific. Through mountain and valley, forest and prairie land, trains daily fly at enormous speed, carrying the produce of the west to the east, and carrying westward the manufactured goods of the east. This railway development in the east is well nigh perfect, but yet much railway building is in contemplation in middle and western territories to-day, which will be a source of wealth to the states in general, and a means of colonising and increasing the value of the land in those thinly-populated territories across the country. Electricity, to-day, has practically revolutionized the world, and no limit can be placed on its possibilities in the future. Steam power worked miracles in its day. It abolished the old stage coach, which rarely exceeded forty miles a day in summer, and little over half that distance in winter. It brought about the disuse of the dangerous ferry boats, and the post rider who carried the light and often half empty mails bags of eighty years ago. The quick despatch of mail by train was a marvel, and the wonder of the age prior to our time, but electricity has caused and is destined to cause greater wonders. It has by the telegraph and telephone connected towns and cities and peoples thousands of miles apart. There are fewer secrets between people at different ends of the earth to-day than were between the early colonists on different sides of the Hudson or Ohio one hundred years ago. The transatlantic cable of half a century ago was the marvel of the age ; to-day messages can be despatched without wires or cables, and received and despatched even in the middle of the ocean. To America we owe most of the inventions in connection with electricity, and as this power of nature was first invented and put to use in the United States, so, too, it has been more utilized and perfected in its native home than anywhere else in the world. Every city and town and village has its electric trams. It has universally supplanted oil and gas as a means of giving light. But the most marvellous result that electricity has produced, and is destined to produce in still greater perfection is to be found in the quick and cheap transit of rich and poor from one place to another in our crowded cities. The poor man for a few cents can, like the rich man, leave his work at eventide and pass—not as formerly, to his congested home in the crowded slums—but to the suburbs, where, thanks to electricity, he can live with wife and family in an atmosphere of pure air, cleanliness, and comfort unknown before. In this respect electricity has solved problems that in the days of our fathers baffled the ingenuity of the philanthropist. It would be impossible to exaggerate the importance of steam and electricity as factors in the foundation of the commercial greatness of the United States, when one considers the rivers and lakes covered with steamships of all classes and all sizes, laden with thousands of tons of merchandise and innumerable passengers ; when one views the railways, stations, the streets, the docks, the quays, everywhere bustling with activity, with their trains passing and re-passing interminably ; when one visits the innumerable post offices with their hundreds and hundreds employed all hours of the day and night in carrying letters, sorting and despatching, and where the electric wires are ever busy sending messages over the world. What a change from the days of Washington ! The old float boat on the river, and the sailing vessel on the ocean ; the old stage coach, working its painful way through woods, across rough hills, and through ravines and mountain gorges, and passing the lakes and rivers on ferry boats. In those early days of the Union two stage coaches with twelve horses were sufficient to accommodate all the people and carry all the goods passing between Boston and New York. The journey was a long and tedious undertaking. It was a more difficult task than a journey of thousands of miles would be to-day. To Boston a hundred years ago, was as tedious a journey from New York as San Francisco or Liverpool is to-day. And in addition to the travelling being slow you ran risks from wind and weather, from freebooters and highwaymen. Now you travel with speed undreamt of by our forefathers and with the comfort and luxury enjoyed in a first-class hotel. In the old days the mail coach only travelled three times per week in summer, and twice in winter, and for the most part was carried on horseback. A couple of saddle-bags were sufficient to accommodate the post passing to or from any of the points of commercial importance. In country districts an old man on horseback jogged along with the post knitting, singing, and reading the letters as he passed to kill time. There was then little intercourse among the colonists, and there was much foolish prejudice locally. There was little national patriotism. Patriotism was more of state importance than national. Men's interests were confined to home rather than foreign affairs. Things happening a few miles apart were often unheard of for days and weeks. Quicker methods of locomotion, the telegraph and telephone, have changed all this and so broadened the view, expanded the minds, and increased the knowledge of the people and the nation. It was but natural with such limited means of acquiring information that prejudices, jealousies and rivalry, that local self-importance and pride should exist, and in a more intense degree then than in modern times. The wonder now is how the national patriotic spirit so spread and moved the people scattered over the thirteen states, that they cast aside all selfish, local, and narrow considerations, and united as one man under Washington to

" Burst in twain the tyrant's chain,"

and fight and die as patriots for freedom and fatherland.

Briefly told, the genesis of American prosperity is this : Emigration was stimulated and vast numbers emigrated westwards. The land became more valuable, and transportation of food and manufacturing eastward and westward became cheaper. These agencies also united the colonies and colonists in the eastern and western and midland districts. In the early days of the Union trade with foreign countries was of little importance. The mineral resources of the country were undeveloped. The gold fields of California, the copper mines of Arizona, the silver mines in the central states, and the other wonderful mineral treasures of iron and coal and petroleum were little known. You had no iron and steel factories around Pittsburgh ; you had few commercial or manufacturing industries in New York or Philadelphia ; little gold in circulation ; and all the credit of the nation lay in her progressive population, and her undeveloped resources. What a contrast do we find to-day ! We find a nation that assumed the right of self-government, entering upon her mission almost a bankrupt before the nations of the world, without capital at home or credit abroad ; to-day one-third of the world's products come from her factories, made on American soil by American firms, by the co-operation of American capital and labour and skill. To-day the output of manufactured goods in the United States is greater than the combined products of England, Germany and France ; whilst one-fourth of the four hundred billions which constitute the world's wealth belong to America, and the money market of the world is regulated by the Wall Street Stock Exchange. The consumption of produce in America is enormous. She is able to consume ninety-seven per cent. of her output, and yet she has in one year exported about four hundred million dollars worth to foreign markets. Her revenue for one recent year from the Post Office amounted to one hundred and thirty-four million dollars, a marvellous advance on fifty years ago, when the Post Office revenue only realized eight million dollars. Another fact worthy of notice in connection with American capital is that only fourteen per cent. of the invested capital in factories comes from Trusts, whilst almost eighty-six per cent. is the capital of private individuals.

THE CATHOLIC RELIGION IN THE STATES.

TOLERANCE OF EARLY OATHOLIO SETTLERS.— HEROISM OF OATHOLIO MISSIONARIES.

THE Catholic religion in America has made great progress during the past hundred years. Prior to the Declaration of Independence there was no church government or organisation amongst the scattered Catholic colonists. The religious wants of the colony were looked after by a few missionary priests sent as pioneers by the Foreign Missionary Societies, and subject directly—as foreign missions are—to the Propaganda, which Congregation directly provides for the care of souls in pagan and new-formed colonies. Few, if any, secular priests were amongst the first preachers of the Catholic faith in the new country. The American Missions were chiefly directed by, and recruited from, the learned and pious and energetic sons of St. Ignatius of Loyola. It was about the year 1789, the year that Washington was made President of the new-formed American Republic, that Pius VI. created the first Catholic diocese in Maryland, the most Catholic State in the Union, and first colonized by exiled English Catholics, under that most eminent Catholic Lord Baltimore, about the year 1634, in the reign of Charles I. Maryland might be termed the cradle of Catholicity in the United States. It was in this state that religious liberty first obtained a home. " Its only home," says Bancroft, " in the wide world was the humble village that bore the name of St. Mary's, where about two hundred Catholic exiles, led by Leonard Calvert, brother of Lord Baltimore, landed on the northern bank of the Potomac river, founded Baltimore, and colonized the present State of Maryland." This territory, be it remarked, was handed over by the English reigning sovereign to Baltimore and his exiled friends without any reservation or right of superintendence by the English monarch, Lord Baltimore obtaining possession of the colony by an express patent, free and untrammelled for all time from English interference. Not alone was it the first settlement to obtain self-government, but it was the first to equalize in the eyes of the law all shades of Christian faith. The exact words by which this state of Maryland led the way for the sister states to extend civil and religious liberty to all colonial settlers have an interest of their own. They are as follows :—" Whereas the enforcing of the conscience in matters of religion hath frequently fallen out to be of dangerous consequence, in those Commonwealths where it has been practised, and for the more quiet and peaceable government of this province, and the better to preserve mutual love and amity among the inhabitants, no person within this province, professing to believe in Jesus Christ, shall be anywise troubled, molested, or discountenanced for his or her religion or in the free exercise thereof." How broad-minded and liberty-inspiring was this enactment, emanating from a proscribed colony of exiled Catholics, compared with the intolerance of the Huguenots, English Puritans, and High Church party in the states adjoining during those first years. Sir Walter Raleigh and Lord Delaware founded the religious and civil constitution of their respective states on exclusively Protestant and English Episcopalian lines. In some of the states only Protestants had civil and citizen rights. In other territories enforced obedience by military authority compelled all to attend Protestant service. There were occasionally amongst those fanatics such broad-minded enthusiasts as William Penn, Roger Williams and Anne Hutcheson, a band of liberty-loving anti-episcopal Puritans who migrated first to Holland from England and finally settled in America, and made Massachusetts their state centre. But from the following quotation one can discern how far behind the age those liberty-loving

reformers were, compared with their despised Catholic countrymen in Maryland. We do not include Penn nor Williams
as endorsing the following views of the Massachusetts state,
but they are views which were endorsed in Virginia and other
districts. " The rock on which the state rested was religion.
A common faith had gathered and still bound the people
together. They were exclusive, for they had come to the
outside of the world for the purpose of living by themselves.
Fugitives from persecution, they shrank from contradiction,
as from the approach of evil. And why should they open their
asylum to the oppressors ? Religious union was made the
bulwark of the exiles against expected attacks from the hierarchy of England. Their religion was their life, they welcomed
none but its adherents. They would not tolerate the scoffer,
the dissenter, the infidel, the Quakers, or the Papists. Infidels
and witches shared the same fate, and when contumacious
death sometimes was the penalty for such heretics." These
men, who loved liberty so much, and who braved the perils
of the ocean, and left home and country rather than submit
to coercion in religion, strangely became in their new home
and in a foreign land more exclusive than their English masters
from whom they fled. Had they remembered the saying of a
great preacher of liberty, they would have moulded their
constitution on Maryland, knowing that " the thrust of a
sword cannot kill a thought, nor the axe of the executioner
slaughter a principle." Had these great early pilgrims and
Puritan reformers, who fled from prelacy and monarchy—led
no doubt by the watchword of Luther—extended a tolerance
towards others similar to what they claimed for themselves,
their names to-day would shine out more brightly in the
pages of American history. They might now, alongside their
persecuted Catholic countrymen in Maryland, be pointed to
as the pioneers of real civil and religious liberty in the United
States. But it is to be feared they interpreted in too narrow
a sense the words of Luther, viz., " The gospel is every man's
right, and it is not to be endured that any should be kept

therefrom. But the Evangel is an open doctrine. It is bound to no place, and moves along freely, under heaven, like the star which ran in the sky to show the wizards from the east where Christ was born. Do not dispute with the prince of peace. Let the community choose their own pastor, aid and support him out of their own estates. If the prince will not suffer this let the pastor flee into another land and let those go with him who will as Christ teaches." These apparent digressions and quotations closely bear upon the subject of the progress of Catholicity in the States, prior to the union. They show us how little religious toleration there was for Catholics among the first European settlers from the different Protestant nations. They point out to us how the Dissenters from Holland and England and France who loved civil liberty, and hated persecution for conscience sake, could not tolerate any who thought differently from themselves in matters of religion. This narrow prejudice continued in many of the states up to the beginning of the war, and long after all the states united under the banner of civil liberty borne by the confederated states. It is true that many notable and eloquent preachers of religious as well as civil liberty lectured the states on their duties to their fellow-citizen of every denomination and religious persuasion. Some states did like New York, which, after the example of Maryland, in its first great state paper proclaimed that " no person professing faith in Jesus Christ shall at any time be disquieted or questioned for any difference of opinion." Virginia, in the year 1776, procured the passage of a bill legalizing all forms of worship. Rhode Island, led by the liberty-loving Roger Williams, came into line with Maryland and New York, and most of the states equalized all forms of worship soon after the war for Independence was fought and won. Massachusetts, however, lingered on in its exclusive sectionalism after most of the states had proclaimed freedom of conscience and worship for all. Such names as those of Roger Williams, William Penn and Lord Baltimore bear favourable comparison with those of Sir Walter Raleigh,

Locke, Lords Delaware and Shaftesbury. The former preached and practised equal rights for all free-born citizens on American soil. Their creed was a democratic creed of government of the people, for the people, with complete freedom of conscience for all who believed in God through Christ. The last named preachers and politicians would fain have enacted laws to coerce the consciences and the intellects of the governed, and subject them to the arbitrary will of the English sovereign and his Parliament and prelates. The doctrine of the Massachusetts state, that no Jesuit should enter the colony under pain of death, found pliant patrons in such English governors as Shaftesbury and Locke. Men like William Penn, the exiled English Quaker, paved the way for the great Charter of Religious liberty for all creeds in America. " We must," he says, " give the liberty we ask. We cannot be false to our principles ; God and nature have made us free." Another name that earlier, and as effectually as that of Penn, had stamped its impress on the age and moulded the minds of the masses to think of liberty, to act as free men, and to long for the inevitable dawn of emancipation for the country, was that of Roger Williams. " At a time," says Bancroft, " when Germany was in the battlefield for all Europe, in the implacable wars of religion, when even Holland was bleeding with anger of vengeful factions, when France was still to go through her fearful struggle with bigotry, when England was gasping under the despotism of intolerance, almost half a century before William Penn became an American proprietor, and two years before Descartes founded modern philosophy on the methods of free reflection, Roger Williams asserted the great doctrine of intellectual liberty. It became his glory to found a state (Rhode Island) on that principle, and to stamp himself upon its rising institutions in characters so deep, that the impress has remained to the present day, and can never be erased without the total destruction of his work. He was the first person in modern Christendom to assert, in its plenitude, the doctrine of liberty of conscience, the equality of opinions before the law, and in its defence he was the harbinger of Milton, the precursor and superior of Jeremy Taylor."

The work of Catholic missionaries, prior to the year 1789, was chiefly directed towards the Christianizing of the North American Red Indians, along the banks of the Hudson, St. Lawrence, Ottawa, Ohio and Mississippi Rivers. The Fathers who devoted their utmost zeal to, and often lost their lives in their holy work, belonged to the Jesuit order. Some missions were established by Franciscans and Dominicans, but the French Jesuits, under the protection of the French flag, formed more missions, converted more to the faith, discovered more territories, and made more useful diagnoses of topological and geographical phenomena than all the other explorers and missionaries combined. " The Jesuits," says Lord Macauley, "had good as well as evil strongly intermixed in their character, and the intermixture was the secret of their giant power. That power could never have belonged to mere hypocrites. It could never have belonged to rigid moralists. It was to be attained only by men sincerely enthusiastic in the pursuit of a great end." No one, of course, expects the whole truth from Lord Macauley, but even he, the reader sees, admits sincerity in the Jesuits. The end that inspired the Jesuits and all Catholic preachers and teachers was naturally the establishment of the Catholic faith. Charles Macay, in his History of the United States, writes thus of the Jesuit Fathers : "Never was perseverance more indomitable, or fortitude more heroic, than theirs. Never did lives more ascetic or self-denying, or a more cheerful endurance of tortures and of death, adorn the roll of Catholic or Christian saints and martyrs. Exposed to every hardship and privation, cut off in a horrid wilderness from all intercourse with their civilized brethren, they endured their lot without a murmur. Some perished under the tomahawk of the savage, others were burned and tortured at the stake, or wandering alone in the trackless forest, experienced the lingering agonies of starvation. But neither peril nor death could damp their devotedness. If one fell in the breach another was ready to fill his place, and to carry on the conflict and capture the fort of paganism for the Christian faith. Their work was not alone to Christianize the savage, but also to civilize him." The names of Fathers Brebeuf and Daniel, as well as Allouez and Marquette, will live in the history of French Canadian and North American discoveries. These missionary Fathers were the first explorers of the lakes and rivers extending west, and north, and south, along the St. Lawrence from Quebec. Most of the Christianizing and civilizing impressions made on the savage tribes along the Lakes Huron, Erie and Michigan, the Ohio and Mississippi rivers, can be traced to the gentle, kind and Christian manner with which these holy Fathers approached and treated with the different tribes. It was the Jesuits who first planted the standard of the Cross among the wigwams of the northern regions, and it was a Jesuit Father who first wielded the crozier of the Apostles in the eastern states. John Carroll was an Irish Jesuit, and the first Bishop consecrated for North America. He was made Bishop of Baltimore in the first year of the United States Federal Government. His see being the oldest in the Union, is honoured, like our own Armagh, with a Cardinal Primate in the person of Cardinal Patrick Gibbons. Bishop Carroll at first stood alone, and was the only prelate in the United States. His successor to-day has, surrounding him in the great Republic, thirteen Archbishops, seventy-two Bishops, and several Apostolic Vicars. Bishop Carroll commenced his apostolic labours surrounded by about thirty priests ; to-day the Cardinal Primate has around him and assisting him 13,267 priests, of which number 3,330 belong to the various religious orders of the Church. In the year 1790 there were about 40,000 Catholics in the entire states out of a population of four million souls. At the middle of the last century the Catholic population had increased to 1,700,000, whilst now there are over fourteen million Catholics, almost one-fifth of the entire population. The above facts and figures speak eloquently of the spread of the Catholic religion in the States.

One naturally asks the cause of Catholic expansion and progress during the hundred years that have rolled by. It would seem to us that the chief cause for this marvellous increase is to be found in the amended acts of the Constitution. Article No. I., which was declared in force in 1791, says, " Congress shall make no law respecting an establishment of religion or prohibiting the free exercise thereof." The spread of Catholicism was inevitable in a country where all free born citizens enjoy perfect liberty in choosing and practising their religion. To this freedom of worship without legal hindrance or prejudice, we may add, as a cause of Catholic expansion, the higher birth rate of Catholic families compared with other denominations. We may also take into account the increased Catholic emigration of recent times, and many conversions to the old faith. Catholics may well feel a legitimate pride in moralizing on these facts. We see that when our holy religion has a " fair field and no favour " it is a healthy plant of rapid growth. That vitality which it owes to its Divine Founder, and which under the most grievous restraints will preserve it, makes it, when not handicapped or confined, flourish with abounding energy. There is no doubt that taking the human race as we find it, with its propensities towards evil, its tendencies towards materialism, its hankering after worldly things ; taking also into account the powerful influence that wealth and honours and preferments exercise on the views and lives and actions of the masses—considering all these circumstances and many others that act upon the social, political and religious ideas and aspirations of the people, the Catholic religion in America, as elsewhere, has powerful forces arrayed against it. The Church has no golden bait to draw volunteers to her banner—no prize but the pure and unalloyed Apostolic doctrine that she preaches and exhorts, by honest efforts, her children and admirers to practise. She has neither wealth nor power to offer in return. She in no way minimises the difficulties that beset the practice of Catholic teaching. Hers is an honest and unchangeable code

of morals and doctrine, immovable as the rock of Peter.
Hers is the narrow gateway that warns those who wish to
enter against strange novelties in faith and morals—agreeable,
it may be, to frail human nature—but new, and just because
new, therefore opposed to the unchangeable Apostolic truth.

The obstacles that Catholic progress had and has to contend against in America are many. There are, in the first
instance, not enough priests to follow the scattered flocks
out west. The expenses of building new schools, churches,
and parochial residences are enormous, and a severe tax on
the resources of the Catholic people. The opposition that
religion has to meet from the want of all religion in the state
schools, throws the responsibility on Catholics of building
and maintaining, from private and voluntary contributions,
schools to educate, in secular and religious knowledge, the
youth belonging to the faith. At present the Catholics in the
different states have built and equipped, and supplied with
an efficient teaching staff, no fewer than 4,000 schools, in
which a million pupils are instructed in sound secular and
Catholic doctrine. This number is still far short of what the
necessity of the Catholic case demands. In building schools
and churches the Catholic faithful are nobly aided by remarkably generous contributions from wealthy American millionaires. We need only mention, as an instance, the names of
Mr. Maloney, an Irish American, whose Catholic generosity
is known almost wherever Catholicity exists, and Reverend
Mother Catherine Dresel,foundress of the Sisters of the Blessed
Sacrament, who has devoted her immense fortune of forty
million dollars to the cause of Catholic charity. The generosity
of the Catholic faithful of America is unbounded. The liberality of the Irish Catholic is known to the whole world. The
Irish in America are the bone and sinew of Catholic congregations throughout the length and breadth of the continent.
Go where you will, north, south, east and west, you will find
the Irish Catholic layman and priest. If you look to the
eastern states you will find every diocese invariably with its

Irish-American Bishop and priests. Amongst the Bishops you find such names as Farley, Ireland, Gibbons, Quigley, Ryan, M'Fall, M'Donnell, Foley, etc. Among the priests, likewise, everywhere you find Irish or Irish-Americans ministering to the wants of the faithful. Whilst lately travelling through the states we invariably, when passing through the cities, visited some of the parochial residences, and in no case did we meet any but Irish-born priests. In New York, such names as Crolly, Donnelly, and Kirwin were common ; in St. Louis, were met Dempseys and Joyces ; in Chicago, Judge and Cox ; and in Niagara, Nolan. In New York, an establishment of the Dominican order which was visited contained fourteen or sixteen Fathers, all of whom, except one, a Belgian, were Irish Americans. During a sojourn in St. Louis we took special note of the remarkable spread of Catholicity. We saw a city which had no church or Catholic priest one hundred years ago, now with hundreds of priests and nuns and teaching brothers, with its splendid colleges and schools and monasteries, its Archbishop and its cathedral, and sixty-five Catholic churches. We saw there churches dedicated to Irish saints, and in the church of St. Patrick, off Broadway, an Irishman was Rector in charge. We visited the cemetery of Calvary, some miles outside the city, on the west bank of the Mississippi, and on the northern suburbs of the city, on a commanding elevation, beside Forest Park and near O'Fallon Park. This cemetery is entirely set apart for Catholic purposes and contains five hundred acres. It is beautifully laid out with main entrance, winding, circular, and cross walks, decked with flowers and evergreens on every side ; to the left a delightful lake surrounded with myrtle and laurel and evergreen, overhanging concrete walks. The monuments are of an expensive class and in good state of preservation. In the cemetery Irish names predominate, in fact one would fancy oneself passing through an Irish burial place. In the Calvary corner, where stands a massive red granite cross with a life-size image of our Saviour carved upon it, some thirty or forty monuments are erected to priests who died in the city during the past few years. Most of the names on the monuments disclose an Irish origin, and out of the entire number of priests interred, not more than ten per cent. lived to be older than forty or forty-three years. It struck us as very remarkable that those priests should die so young, whilst all around them lay the bones of men who had passed the three score and ten; men, no doubt, useful in their time, men who perhaps left behind them mourning widows well provided for, and a family well advanced by honest toil. Such men as these last spent their lives for the few, and their lives were long: the priests, who worked for the many, who ministered to the poor, the orphan, and the widow, who relieved distress wherever they met it, who soothed the sorrowful, preached penance to the sinner, aided the dying, prayed for the dead, rejoiced with the young and the happy, and grieved with those who needed consolation—the priests, the ministers of God and His ambassadors to men, were cut off in the prime of life and vigour, they, whose every word and act and desire was to be " all things to all men, that they should bring all to Christ ; " they who had a kind and charitable word for the sinful and wayward ; who were gentle and forgiving toward the Magdalenes, whose only wish was to find out the lost sheep, and carry them back to the fold as suppliant penitents. Why, oh angel of death, did you pass over the countless sheep and strike down their shepherd ? Why did you leave the child and summon to judgment the father, so loving, so kind, and so necessary to watch and guard his spiritual children ? Can we divine a reason ? Yes, those Levites in the vineyard of the Lord lived a long life in their few short years. The race was hard, the prize was a rich one; they gained their crown. They fell at the goal of duty, fighting for and defending their flock. Do not those countless monuments of Catholic piety and Catholic generosity, and true practical faith tell their tale ; those churches raised by the untiring labour of those young martyr priests, those schools and convents and monasteries and presbyteries erected by their untiring energy and zeal—do they not tell their tale of the tombs of the dead priests as we pass by ? Does the early demise of those self-sacrificing missionaries not point to the fact that they were martyrs to the call of duty ? Is there not as much related in the single announcement : " Died at the age of 40 years. A good priest and a faithful pastor " as would fill volumes ? It is the history of a good pastor laying down his life for his flock. It is the story of the heroic commander dying in the front of his army, leading on the charge against the enemy. In paying the above tribute to the self-sacrificing lives of the priests of St. Louis we embrace in our commendation and appreciation the entire priesthood of America since the union. The Bishops and priests of America founded a church in a desert. They found, on landing on the western shores to raise aloft the standard of holy church, that the heavens above were their canopy and the rough hewn stone their altar. Theirs were the hands that raised all of those countless piles of Catholic buildings, to-day the boast of America, and the glory and the pride of the Catholic world. Freely did they spend their lives in the noble cause of building up the faith in this free and fertile land. Well did they work for their Master, and like Him might it not truly be said that they " gave up their lives for the brethren." All honour and glory to those pioneers of Catholicity in the western states. All honour to the Irish saggart whose footprints can be traced from ocean to ocean through every state, and whose noble sacrifice in the holy cause of church must ever be remembered with gratitude and pride, not alone by Irish Catholics, but by all Christendom !

There is an idea abroad that the American priest is less bound by canonical discipline, more given to sociality and worldly customs, than the priesthood in other countries. There is an idea that he is first a man of the world, and next a minister of the Gospel. There is nothing real in these conjectures. The American pastor is natural in the sense that all free citizens are natural ; there is nothing artificial about him. He is a subject of a free nation where every man is the equal of his fellows. He is proud of his country, and proud of his privileges of citizenship in the grandest nation on earth. He cannot understand why socially and as a citizen and brother he may not freely mix with worldly society as a gentleman ; still remaining the true priest and faithful pastor. He holds to the doctrine that when he donned the clerical garb, and put on the priestly dignity, he did not divest himself of the rights of manhood and freedom to act and think as a free agent on a free soil. Whilst going so far he does not claim, nor desire to assume the right to claim exemption from the rules and discipline and obedience to ecclesiastical supervision and control. There is a free, offhand, go-ahead manner about our clerical friends out west that is as natural to them as his sanctimonious visage is to the Quaker or the Puritan. It is a mannerism common to his nation : it is peculiar to this progressive and free-born race. The American priest has all the distinguishing traits of his fellow-citizens, without their vices or their vulgarisms. Some people say, and not without a semblance of truth, that the freedom from restraint in acting, thinking, and living ; the privileges born of the constitution and nurtured for a century by a proud, free and progressive race, must affect and carry along in the current of democratic and in some sense of unlimited liberty, the church and the pastor, and so loosen the bark of Peter from her moorings. But no, it is an erroneous idea to suppose that any laxity of discipline, or a leakage in faith or morals can ever occur in the plan of the church or the lives of the pastors. The American priest is trained in colleges as noted for rigid discipline as any ecclesiastical seminaries in Christendom. The superiors, who are stern upholders of clerical decorum and strict obedience to rule, enforce discipline, and penalize disobedience to rule. Whilst due liberty is allowed for all lawful and healthy relaxation among the young clerics, abuses are severely and often summarily punished. The Bishops of America, who rule the dioceses and inspect the discipline of the priests and seminarists, are a most exacting and edifying body of men. The American hierarchy are wonderfully energetic. They pass around among their priests, and inspect the workings of the missions very frequently. In America the building up and expanding of the mission has been the anxious concern of the Bishops during the century just closed. In this part of their duty they are assisted by a Vicar-General and a committee who discuss and direct all projected building operations. All plans and specifications &c., are submitted to their council, and operations commence only when the building society approves of the plans. Out in the midland and western dioceses the advance of Catholicity is not as great as the progress of colonization demands. New ecclesiastical edifices, schools, churches, and parochial residences are constantly rising up in town and country. The young and energetic and laudably ambitious priests are encouraged and applauded by their ecclesiastical superiors for their energy and zeal in raising funds, and building churches in lately formed missions; their pluck, perseverance and success in such work is generally rewarded by promotion in due time according to merits. In the older dioceses, such as New York, Philadelphia, Boston, and Baltimore, the supply of locally-educated priests is sufficient for the wants of their respective dioceses. In the new formed missions the system of borrowing priests from neighbouring Bishops is the principal means of supply. At present, on account of the enormous influx of Italian workmen into the states, the demand for native Italian priests is very considerable. Formerly, more than at present, the wish of every American Bishop was for Irish priests. Now, however, the Italian, the French, or the German missionary is more sought after to cope with the native Catholics of their own nationality, who are amenable to the advice of a pastor who speaks their own language. The great problem now for pastors of souls is how best to keep the faith alive in the Italian emigrants landing on American soil. The Italians are a people susceptible of much good and much evil. As a rule they are less reliable and less truthful than those who come from more northern shores—Poles, Swedes, Slavs and Germans. The Italians are an idealistic and spiritually and devotionally-inclined people. They are more impressionable than their northern brothers. The Italian, when a practical Catholic, is a most edifying member of holy church, and a useful member of society; if opposed or indifferent to religion he is a disgrace to Christianity, a bad citizen, and capable of any crime. The conserving of a lively and practical Catholic faith among Italians in the States is, therefore, anxious work for the priests and of much concern to society at large.

LIFE IN AMERICA.

AMERICAN MANNERS.—CRIMINALS WHO ASSUME IRISH NAMES.

An emigrant from Ireland, landing on the shores of America, finds himself in a position of disadvantage when placed in comparison with emigrants from other European nations For the most part our people find themselves unfit for any occupation but labour. They spend their youth at home as labourers either in city or country, most of them being the sons and daughters of farmers. They have no trades; they are unskilled and untrained. Technical education was a thing unheard of up to a few years ago in their native land. Not so with the German, the English, or the many other peoples that continually pour into the states to swell the population. The latter come prepared by a sound education and training to enter the lists as skilled artisans. Their course is clear; the openings for such a respectable class of immigrants are

numerous.   In an expanding nation that is constantly pushing
out its borders and developing its resources, the trained and
tried tradesman is a welcome addition.   The Irish immigrant
may, no doubt, by sobriety, honesty, industry and native
ability advance himself step by step, but no matter how well
he may have been brought up, how comfortable his home may
have been, how hard so ever it may be to his native pride and
his inherent self-respect, if he is without friend or patronage
on the Columbian shores he must begin at the bottom rung of
the ladder.   He must toss to one side his shining cuffs and
well-starched collars ; he must belt his loins, tuck up his
shirt sleeves, and dearly earn his bread by the sweat of his
brow and the strength of his sinewy arms.   I have met young
men from home who were brought up in most comfortable
surroundings, and who knew not how to earn a silver dollar
except by manual toil.   If at home they would be marching
around with kid gloves and silver-mounted walking stick,
smoking their cigars like young gentlemen ; here they are
working side by side in the stores, at the docks, or on the
railways, with men to whom they would not have spoken
when in Ireland.   Every man landing on the free shores of
America is the equal of his fellow-man.   It is a country in
which worth makes the man ; rank and title count as nothing
in the eyes of the law ; such distinctions have no place in the
Constitution.   Every man can reckon on a fair field to
develop his talent and native resources, and advance his
status, but the competition is keen, the competitors are many,
and well equipped for the contest.   The employer of labour
in the United States is a cold, calculating individual ; he is a
practical man of business.   He regards mankind primarily as
money-making machines.   "How much work can this man
perform ? how much per cent. profit will I have from his
labour ? " these are the questions he puts to himself.   If he
cannot see a clear profit in you, like an ordinary investor of
capital, he has no further use for your service.   Young men
who are not ashamed to work have a chance, but they will

not get preferment unless by merit. Sobriety, honesty, and industry are the passwords to promotion. There is no room in the struggle for place and position for the laggard or the drunkard. Looking at the struggle people have to make in America to work their way in the battle of life, the thought naturally occurs to one that if their pride and vanity would only permit them to toil with the same energy at home, without caring for the opinions of those around them, they could succeed equally as well in Ireland. And that this is so is the opinion of most people who speak candidly on the subject of emigration.

Irish people in America should consider well the locality and occupation that best fits in with their early training and experience. " The shoemaker should stick to his last." If a man has been reared on a farm he should go west to the rich lands on the other side of the Mississippi and Missouri. With a little capital he can, even in these days, purchase sufficient land to enable him to settle down to farm, and in the course of a few years, if industrious, he will find himself prosperous and gradually amassing wealth. If a man has a trade he should, of course, seek employment in the prosperous towns and cities of the states. The man with talent, self-respect, pluck and determination is always sure to rise. Wealth, honours, and promotion reward the possessor of these qualifications, and fame follows in their wake with unerring certainty. The millionaires in America to-day invariably began life as poor boys, with the proverbial half-crown in their pocket. Roosevelt came of humble origin, and earned his first wealth out west rearing horses and cattle. Parker, at one time democratic candidate for president, supported himself while at school, and still loves his farm. The candidates for vice-presidents on both sides in 1904 (when these observations were written) began very poor, one a brakesman on the railway, and the other an errand boy. Both to-day are very rich, Davies being a millionaire. There are many Irish millionaires to-day in America, who sailed away fifty years ago in poverty.

Their fortunes were, in many instances, the result of accidents and good fortune combined with native talent and ambition. Integrity and self-respect are the qualities most to be desired in our emigrants to the free shore of America. But to all who may have an unsettled mind as to whether they should stop at home or sail for the land of the Stars and Stripes, I would say, "stay at home, help by your industry and skill to develop the resources of your native land. There is work for all in Ireland, and why should we, after all, rear sons and daughters in our poverty-stricken country that they may sweat and toil with head and hand to make the land of Uncle Sam, as it is, the greatest land on earth ? "

Americans are becoming very fastidious about their toilet, their food, their manners ; they are fast bidding to lead the world in all that goes to make up polite society, good taste and style in dress, cooking, &c. The Americans have the dollars, and these they do not spare in their endeavours to emulate our aristocracy and leaders of society. Times are changed since Dickens described the Americans as a nation of tobacco chewers, who squirted the dirty, oily juice around like rain, threw their legs over chairs, and upon tables and fenders in a most distressing fashion. The American hotel menu is equal to anything you will meet with in our European resorts. The cooking and attendance in American cafes are perfect. From no waiters anywhere will you receive such polite attention as from the American "niggers," who are in great part the chefs and butlers in the restaurants. The Americans as a nation are faultlessly neat in their general style of dress. With the ladies neatness is a habit, and in town and country the men are invariably well "put on." The men carry themselves with a manly bearing. They do not wear any unnecessary appendages. As a rule the American shaves clean ; some in military fashion wear moustaches, but rarely will you meet with gentlemen sporting side whiskers, or the goat-like tufts under the chin that used to be so common. The ladies dress handsomely. Like the men they are practical, and have no superfluous trimmings to their every day attire. Like their European sisters they are fond of dress and run after variety and novelty. But they rarely allow their tastes to run away with their good sense. You will not often see American ladies dressed in the brilliant colours of the French or the eccentric modes of London fashionable society.

The American loves comfort and good cheer. His home and surroundings where possible are in keeping with his ideas of happiness and economy. The large and costly mansions of the great are few in America compared with the wealth of the citizens. It is only in late years that there has been any boom in the erection of those stately mansions, rich in ornamentation, classic in style and design, with lawns and ponds, and parks and terraces. The feudal ideas of high walls enclosing deer and game, with fortified castles, steeple and tower, with strong iron gate, barred and bolted, have not caught on much in democratic America. In the home training of their sons and daughters American fathers and mothers direct the minds of their young towards the practical ; they keep before them business ideas. They train them to act a manly part in the social, commercial, and national life of their country. Except the thriftless sons of the very wealthy, the rising generation in America are efficiently prepared morally, intellectually, and physically to enter successfully on the battle of life. In general address, polish and social etiquette, the American character is and always must remain distinct from that of European nations. They may improve their native American manners, but eradicate the distinctive Americanism of their race, or assimilate so with other countries as to become swallowed up in them, they cannot. Americans are too proud of their country, too independent by nature and surroundings, too democratic, to follow in the lead of other nationalities. European nations have their manners and fashions emanating from and radiating around the nobility and the court. Fashion in Europe runs in old grooves ; it is only the colours and style or cut that changes. There is a feudal conservatism which, for good or ill, acts and reacts in European society. The Americans are an unconventional, plain, blunt, practical race, from the president of the Republic to the street car conductor. Their judges wear no ermine ; their counsellors don no gowns or wigs ; their public officials, senators, governors, have no unessential adornments to hamper their office. In America there is little of the tinsel of officialdom. Work makes the man among Americans. Lincoln is not less honoured because he spent his youthful days hewing logs, nor is Garfield less a martyred hero because he was an itinerant preacher and schoolmaster, as was also the great M'Kinley. Americans are courteous and never vulgar ; they are unaffected, though brusque in manner. They are not trained to cringe or fawn on the great in pedigree or wealth. There is no courtly hollowness, or any drawing-room affectation about the American character. The spirit of free democracy, of self-reliance, of business habit, of self-possession, makes the American people distinct from the nationalities from which the nation has been augmented. Other nationalities are soon assimilated by the American, and in time make one with it. Out of the nationalities of Europe has arisen a distinct nationality with notes and characteristics peculiarly its own. Love of America, love of liberty and independence and self-reliance are the characteristics of all true Americans.

Before leaving the consideration of life in present-day America, I cannot, as an Irishman, refrain from referring to a matter which intimately concerns the good name of the old land, and that is the now very prevalent habit among criminals of all nationalities in America of assuming Irish names. The United Irish Societies in the United States have appointed a committee to investigate the cause of this, and if possible provide a remedy. The custom has become notorious. There are people of the criminal class, without one drop of Irish blood in their veins, posing as " Sons of Erin," and thus degrading the fair name of Ireland in the eyes of the Republic.

From a late investigation of the Irish Societies, it has been found that in New York city, in the years 1904 and 1905, the names of Irish origin coming before Criminal Courts of Appeal and the General Sessions ranked only fifth in number, although in the list were many from other nationalities with assumed Irish names. Amongst the 3,246 of supposed American origin 348 Italians, 344 Russians, 310 Germans, 192 Irish and 122 English. We find from the result of the investigations of this committee, with Major Crawley in the chair, that among the Italians such names as Patrick Flynn and Michael Hennessy occurred. I remember looking through the criminal lists on view in one of the sections of the Washington public department records, at the St. Louis Exhibition, and I was so surprised at the frequent occurrence of Irish names among the criminals that I asked the keeper of the books were they all really Irish. " Ah, no," he said, " the Italians, and French, and Germans assume names of other nationalities to hide their own. These emigrants are never so depraved in crime that they have not a spark of patriotism, and besides they think they will be less liable to detection by taking Irish names, as Irishmen have no nationality when they come out here." It is to be hoped that these forgeries of Irish names by criminals will be put a stop to in America, and I think it is not impossible a similar committee could find work to do in a similar cause in Great Britain itself. I fancy that all who are known under Irish names at Scotland Yard or the Liverpool Bridewell are not genuine Irish.

DEMOCRATS AND REPUBLICANS.—
TWO CONVENTION PICTURES.
(Written in 1904.)

THE DEMOCRATS IN SESSION.

Now that the Democratic party of America have held their
Convention and selected their candidates for the offices of
President and Vice-President, we may with advantage " take
stock " of the influence of this political party, deliberating
on Democracy in the states. It is fresh in the memory of
those interested in United States politics how jubilant the
friends and well-wishers of the Republican Party were at the
harmonious proceedings and result of their Chicago Convention. The Republican delegates saw nothing in their opponents
but disruption and decay. They believed them a party in
name, without a leader to follow, a platform on which to stand,
or a programme for the future. They (the Republicans) had
but one name before them for President; the Democrats
seemingly had many names from which to choose, men of
differing factions and platforms. The difficulties that the
one thousand Democratic delegates, who assembled at Convention Hall in St. Louis, on July the 6th, had to contend with
were many and serious, but the main business of this, as of
other Conventions, was the choice of a man to carry the standard of democracy and of a platform upon which he and the
democracy of the nation could stand. Since the presidency of
James Buchanan, who sat in the chair of state prior to
Abraham Lincoln, and just before the Civil War, there was
but one Democratic president, Grover Cleveland, who was
elected twice for the highest honour in his country's gift.
Cleveland is still a power in Democratic politics, an active force

in the party, and by many he was spoken of as a possible candidate for re-nomination at the Convention. The majority of delegates, however, thought him an impossible nominee, whilst expressing due admiration for his brilliant powers of mind and loyal adhesion to Democracy. Who then should be acceptable to the majority of state delegates ? Bryan carried the party behind him in his extreme Democratic views on silver and tariff. It was chiefly in the silver coinage standard that he lost ground. At the same time it was felt that there was some truth in the statement of his opponents that his extreme " populism " would land the nation into radicalism and riot. There is no doubt that Bryan polled more votes than ever his party polled on previous occasions ; still the delegates at St. Louis were instructed to vote for a different leader, and a sounder ticket. Bryan's name, therefore, was also impossible. It was evident at Convention that Bryan was aware of the fact, that he had many personal friends, but few political followers among the delegates. Bryan was prominent at the Convention and Bryan and Bryanism had to be reckoned with.

As a public orator Mr. Bryan has few superiors. He has a commanding appearance, is strong and big of frame as well as in intellect, having broad shoulders and a deep chest containing powerful lungs. He has a pleasing countenance, a voice that commands attention and reaches to every ear no matter how big the gathering or how spacious the hall. He is unique as a popular speaker : satire and sentiment, logic and facts and figures come to him with equal ease, and can be varied by him with wonderful effect on his audience. His powers of enduring fatigue are enormous. He is the delight of his friends, the scourge of his opponents, and the spoiled idol of the masses of the people. Like all strong characters who are in earnest and enthusiastic about their own cause he may be beaten back, overpowered, nay, routed by superior force, but, like a tactful general, he approaches the enemy again if necessary by circuitous routes and with all the successful resources that he knows how to command. He may be forced to yield, but he yields his vantage ground step by step, and if the cheering, brawling throng that ever follows in his wake did not on that occasion allow a peaceful retreat, his greatest maligners, during the memorable fight of four days which this Goliath of a past Democratic creed made for his old ideals, could not accuse him of any want of eloquence, argument and force in his persistent and dogged opposition to superior forces. The delegates had received, almost to a man, their mandate to vote down Bryanism, as carried on the Bryan banner since 1896, and twice unsuccessfully put to the test in the elections of '96 and 1900. Amongst the one thousand delegates at St. Louis, Bryan and his silver standard could only rely on twelve votes from his own state of Nebraska, and a few from a number of states in the middle west, whose prospects from their sliver mines stood to improve with the recognition, by the states, of a silver as well as a gold money standard. The majority of delegates came, not so much to convince, to argue, and reason, as to vote. With no uncertainty in their minds they knocked aside the silver plank from the platform of Democracy and rendered Bryan an impossible leader. The work of Convention so far was merely negative. They were able to agree about the fate of Bryan and his programme. But they feared—some say from dread of Bryan's opposition—to accept, as a body, the gold standard. We shall see later what effects this omission in their plank had on their future deliberations. It is well for the success of Democracy that Bryan's power in the party should be at an end. It is well for America as a nation that it should be so ; it is a blessing in disguise for Bryan himself. He is a comparatively young man. His future has many possibilities, but the Convention of his countrymen and his party have made it plain that his hopes need not be centred on the Presidential Chair of the Republic. Bryanism and radicalism, and indeed rowdyism, were too closely allied for his party to rule a nation, and hold evil-doers in check. The term "populist" sounds well to the vulgar ear, but a nation's rulers, a nation's legislators, whilst favouring the side most representing their own policy, must, with a firm hand, dispense the nation's laws and dispense justice equally towards all in the community. Rulers should be able to restrain the lynchers, the rowdy, and protect the entire community by the strong arm of legislation and executive administration. The existence of certain extreme elements in the mass of Bryan's supporters made it, in our opinion, impossible that he should pursue a broad and impartial governmental policy.

Why Bryan's " silver plank " was so brusquely disposed of at the Convention is easily explained. When Mr. Bryan was nominated eight years ago, the " silverites "proclaimed that the depression in trade and the low prices were caused by scarcity of circulating medium. They contended that gold was " cornered " for the use of the " big bugs," and that prosperity would only return when the people had the privilege of taking fifty cents worth of silver to the mint, and having it stamped " one dollar " and made legal tender. This device of Bryan's, enabling debtors to repudiate half their debts by the cheap dollar, created a panic in trade, and foreigners called home their gold. With Bryan's defeat in '96, prosperity and trade revived. When Bryan sought re-election in 1900 on the same ticket, circumstances had much changed in trade and commerce, and in the circulation of gold. In four years the circulation of gold had increased from four hundred and ninety seven millions to eight hundred and eleven millions. To-day the circulation of gold per head of the population is thirty-one dollars ; eight years ago it was only twenty-one dollars. There are 1,111,392,949 dollars gold, and 433,595,888 dollars paper in circulation in the states at present, about double the amount of currency in 1896. The great output of gold in late years in Alaska, Klondyke, and South Africa has so increased the quantity of the yellow metal over the world that many silver nations are enabled to establish gold as the standard (as, for instance, Russia, Japan, and India), whilst many countries are restricting the coinage of silver. Events, therefore, and natural laws had been more potent than politicians in settling the monetary standard for America and other nations. The monetary question having, therefore, been brushed aside by a vote of the delegates, and a platform arranged, after long and weary hours of debate and deliberation, the serious and important consideration of a candidate came next before the Convention. Many minor aspirants besides the two old standard bearers were mentioned, but the almost unanimous choice of the nation's representatives was fixed on Judge Parker of New York.

Where now does Democracy stand, and what are its prospects of success? It seems to us that this once powerful party has now staked its future success not so much on affirmation as negation. Their programme is a renunciation of past leaders, and, in part, of past platforms. The Chairman of the Convention stated in a few words where the party stands. " We wish," he said, " our government to be reconstructed on the democratic republican basis, on which the fathers of the republic intended it to rest—a government of the people, for the people, and by the people, instead of a government of the classes by the classes, and for the classes. We desire to see our public affairs progressing along the lines mapped out and contended for by our great Democratic presidents—Thomas Jefferson, James Munroe, Madison and Jackson. It is our policy to insist on reduction of exorbitant taxation, so that extravagance in appropriations shall cease, that economy shall prevail in all the transactions of the government, that all the departments shall be thoroughly investigated from top to bottom by Congressional Committees, that all evil doers shall be driven from public service and properly punished, that the trusts shall be proceeded against by indictment as ordinary criminals, that the Constitution accompanies the American flag into our new possessions. Our party never was a free trade party, but we favour reduction of exorbitant tariff rates to a reasonable basis. Why should our farmer pay one third more for his plough from an American workshop than a farmer at the end of the earth pays for the same articles manufactured in American firms ? We contend in matters of taxation that highest tax should be imposed on luxuries, lower on comforts, and least of any on necessaries. The above is a summary of our plank and position from which our party will not be driven or coaxed or bullied."

The official platform, as expounded by the spokesman of the Convention, representative John Sharp Williams, went over all the ground. It was too finely spun out. It lacked in what ex-President Cleveland suggested for their platform— " Shortness, strength and boldness." The words " retrenchment and reform " would have been a better war-cry to rally a distracted and disunited party. The watchword of the party could have been well compressed in the formula : " Down with militarism ; down with autocracy." They might have stood on the solid Democratic doctrine of "A friend to the people, a foe to lawless monopoly, and an upholder of the Constitution of our country." The enemies of Democracy see nothing in this platform that commands any serious consideration. Some of them sarcastically call it " the view with alarm and denounce with emphasis ' platform.' " Another critic of Democratic policy asserts that the Republican party stand on a splendid record, whilst the opposition stands on " debasement and demagogery." They have no constructive policy, they advocate reaction and destruction which would overrun our industries and check our national progress. Again, " They are consummate in the paltry science of courting popular favour ; they falsely infer that they have the capacity to govern, and they will be the last to discover their errors." The eloquent words of Governor Black in his nomination speech at Chicago Convention will best voice the opinions of Republicans about their opponents. He says, "they were like scattered bands without guns or ammunition. If they had them they would use them against each other. The only evidence of battle was the discord among generals and privates of their party. They feel that they must destroy their own comrades before fighting the enemy." In passing judgment on these remarks of Mr. Black, one must take into account many circumstances. Politics and policies and party programmes are not like first principles, unchangeable. Current events, natural causes and certain tendencies in the legislation and tactics of the opposition that point towards extremes and hence towards injustice and inequality often direct the policies and point to the platform that a party on the defensive must adopt. Sometimes states and individual leaders and their followers are so riveted to their ideas that the warring among friends becomes a necessary preliminary to any common " plank." This party feud may be fierce and bitter, long and distracting. It requires an amount of common sense and forbearance, compromise and party loyalty, to bring about the desired effect. It is all very well to enthuse the masses, to rally them to the creed of Jefferson, and the doctrine of Munroe, but we, as sensible men, must in this age of common sense take in circumstances of time and place, and the progress and advancement of civilization, education and enlightenment, the colonization and expansion in new states, and many other influences of the age, that act as factors of change in the policies of parties and governments. The craze for expansion that wisely induced the government of Jefferson to purchase Louisiania, and so double the empire's territory, is no longer a political creed with the Democratic party. The tariff legislation and the money standard " plank " have been so long discussed and legislated upon by Republican and Democratic governments since Harrison, and M'Kinley, and Cleveland's time, that the electors of the nation can gauge accurately what the times and circumstances of the age demand. If, then, there was at St. Louis much party disputation, much discarding of dogmatic generals, and much compromise in past and present creeds, before a future course could be mapped out and defined, there were many excuses for contention and much need for such a course to ensure united future action. The eloquent words of Mr.

Lyttleton of Brooklyn, who nominated Judge Parker for President, at St. Louis, bear us out. "No man here," he said, " can have his exact way. No leader can take us along the narrow ledge of his unquestioned logic ; no section should swerve us from the course that leads to union and fellowship ; no man is greater than his party ; and no party is greater than its principles. There is no principle that does not rest upon conditions, and there are no conditions that may not change. There is no platform that can last for ever. The world is moving along and ever working out mighty changes. A political party is an agent for interpreting events with intelligence, and it must advance with the progress of the age, or it will be deserted. A spirit of compromise is a necessity to secure a united platform." The spirit of compromise prevailed at St. Louis. This fact was conclusively proved, not alone in the adoption of a common platform, but in the nomination of a standard bearer. Another circumstance in connection with the union of forces on common issue was that there were no party defections ; as far as external signs demonstrate, the Democratic machinery is once more in perfect working order, and in a suitable condition to engineer the party campaign during the coming November elections.

Judge Parker, the standard-bearer in whose hands the destinies of his party are placed, is chief judge of the Court of Appeals for New York State. He is a man who has mixed little in politics. All that is known about his political creed is that he always voted the Democratic ticket. His share in political strife was more of a local than a national character. His rapid promotion from an humble origin to the highest judical position entailed constant and persevering application. His retiring disposition led him to pursuits more congenial to his nature than political warfare. Reared on a farm, educated in a local school in his native state, he worked his way from the farm to the law, supporting himself by teaching. His application to business was notable, and his success as a pleader won for him fame and affluence. His country habits of farming still cling to him. He owns his father's farm, and another estate on which he lives at Esopus, on the banks of the Hudson, in Ulster county. Here he spends the summer months studying, reading over the cases awaiting decisions by his Court, farming, raising sheep, cattle and hogs as a speciality. He is fond of a good horse and is a splendid rider. He is up at six every morning, and during the summer takes a swim at half past-six in the Hudson river. In. outward appearance Judge Parker is tall, erect and robust. He is fifty-three years of age. His hair is auburn, he has a pleasing countenance and quiet manner, is fond of humour, and an agreeable, though reserved companion. He speaks fluently with a pleasant accent. He is a favourite with his brothers on the bench and patient with advocates. He is a man of dispatch, first at the post of duty and last to leave the chair. He consults with the bench, and never assumes the office of legal dictator. He found his department in the Court of Appeals almost swamped by arrears of work; now it is thoroughly reformed, and cases are dispatched in rotation with an order and precision hitherto unknown. Until two years ago little was known or heard about Parker outside his own state. Since he came into prominence in an important legal judgment up country, his friends and admirers have boomed him as the most suitable man for Democratic President. The honour conferred on him at St. Louis was thrust upon him. He never sought the distinction and on a former occasion he refused political honours. Since his name came to be on every tongue his lips have been closed and no one can say how he views the clamour and the storm of enthusiasm that his name has evoked in Democratic circles. All that his friends can say for him is that he was the first Judge in his native state, an honest man, and a sound Democrat—a man that loved justice and hated evil doers, whether he finds them in the ordinary life or the political arena. He holds fast to principles, and he has the capacity to expound and defend his creeds and opinions. One of his nominators said to the delegates, " he is a man who should appeal by his fitness to the regular Democrats and to the independent voters." He is the very antithesis of Roosevelt. He has sound Democratic principles, tried executive ability, great personal popularity, wide learning in the law, profound respect for justice and the constitution, a clean record, and a capacity and intellect for dealing in a large way with large problems. He has been called the "Sphinx of Esopus" on account of his absolute refusal to speak on political subjects, or to be drawn out on the affairs and prospects of the St. Louis Convention. He spoke, however, in no uncertain tone in his famous telegram addressed to Mr. Sheenan at Convention, in reply to his announcement of nomination for Presidency. His action was bold, manly, and straightforward. It fell like a cannon shot among friend and foe alike, and for a time created a panic, and almost paralysed the entire assembly. His telegram was : " I regard the gold standard as firmly and irremovably established and shall act accordingly if the action of the Convention to-day be ratified by the people. As the platform is silent on the subject, my view should be made known to Convention, and if it is proved to be unsatisfactory to the majority, I request you to decline nomination for me at once, so that another may be nominated before adjournment." Some one had blundered, for it had been said that Parker's policy would be the policy which found expression in the platform of his party. No ! Parker gave no mandate to any delegate to express his views. He saw that a compromise of silence on silver was to be forced on Convention by Bryan. Parker saw also that Bryan would be in some sense a dictator to the standard-bearer of his party ; hence by one bold stroke he struck down the silverites so that he would control the reins of his party, in case they endorsed his views about gold. After some consultation and deliberation the following reply was dictated to Parker and ratified by Convention : "The platform adopted by this Convention is silent on the question of monetary standard, because it is not regarded by us as a possible issue in this campaign, and only campaign issues are mentioned in platform, therefore, there is nothing in views expressed by you in the telegram just received which would preclude a man entertaining them from accepting nomination on platform." A party that resisted the eloquence and personality of Bryan ; a party that submerged personal, minor, and local interests ; a party that stood the strain of Parker's historic and unprecedented telegram ; and, after five long and trying days' hard work and serious deliberations, left the Convention Hall united on all the issues of Convention, and firmly resolved to carry out the programme of their party, deserves to succeed in its resolve.

THE REPUBLICAN CONVENTION.

LET us now take a look at the other side of the picture as disclosed by the deliberations at the great Republic Convention in Chicago in the same year, at which I had the interesting experience of personally assisting. The Convention was held in the spacious Coliseum of Chicago, a theatre-shaped circular building, said to have seating capacity for 15,000 people. The entire building was packed from ceiling to floor ; platform, passages, and even the eleven exit doors were thronged. The numbers present, each session of Convention, fell little short of 20,000. It was a wonderful assembly. Right in front, around the platform, sat over a thousand delegates, representing the different states and territories that are federated in the United States Republic—representatives from Florida on the south-east, and Maine on the north-east ; delegates from every state from New York to Washington ; from the Hawaii Islands in the Pacific, to the latest recruits in the Philippine Islands and Porta Rico. The delegates chosen to voice the opinions of their states sat together under their respective banners. Each state is represented in proportion to the number of electors and the relative importance and extent of its territory. The state with the lowest representation was Hawaii Islands, from which six delegates were sent to voice the opinions of a population of 150,000. New York state, with its population of over seven millions was, of course, numerically ahead of every other state in the Union. The Convention each day opened with a prayer or invocation by a minister of one or other of the religious denominations represented. As all forms of religious belief are equal in the eyes of the nation, a minister of a different denomination is chosen for each opening service. The prayer on the second day was announced by Father Cox of the Holy Name Cathedral. The Convention in session was an historic scene not likely soon to fade from the memory of those present. It was not the oratory of the speakers that made the occasion a memorable one ; business men do not make the most attractive speeches. Still, the speaking was by no means below the ordinary standard, and two of the speakers reached a really high level of excellence. Nor was it the immense assembly itself, unique as it undoubtedly was, considering its cosmopolitan character—a delegation one thousand strong, coming together from places thousands of miles apart, sent as chosen representatives from fifty-two states and territories and districts, with an aggregate population of eighty millions. They, in their official capacity, voiced the views and carried the votes of the great Republican party from every town and hamlet and ranch and island in the federation. The millionaire sat side by side with the common citizen ; the dark man mixed freely with the white ; the lady in jewels and lace sat as an equal on the same bench with the lady in business or the housemaid. But not these circumstances alone made the occasion so memorable. No, it was not the absence of rank or distinction ; it was not the note of equality, that spirit of freedom, that atmosphere of liberty that each American citizen enjoys and takes pride in possessing. Neither was it that absence of kingly pomp and courtly etiquette and titled pride that renders national assemblages in America so practical and so natural. Above and beyond all these things there was one other that gave the Convention a unique significance and that was the end that the Congress had in view, and the means adopted to reach that end. The end in view was to nominate a candidate who should rule a nation, who should hold the reins of government in his hands, who should be the guiding star of the people, their captain, their chief for four long years. It was to choose a man who should evenly and wisely and justly carry the scales of government ; one who should rule all classes and sections with equal sway ; who should reconcile opposing interests and be a father to the nation ; a guide, philosopher, and a friend to every creed and class, to every race and caste, a friend to the poor as well as to the rich, one in whom an expanding and swiftly progressing nation might see reflected the ancient fathers of their Constitution. Not alone was the end in view a momentous one for any assembly or any nation ; the means used to attain that end were also singular—even unique. The proceedings took place on a public stage before the watchful gaze of 20,000 faces, a nation without waiting on the wires for every word of the deliberations. Every word spoken was spoken to the four winds of heaven, and every nation by its representatives in the Press was witness of the scenes enacted. The destinies of a nation were in the balance ; an anxious people entrusted to a trusted delegation and a national Convention the records of their past administration, and asked a new charter and a new mandate for the future. In a word the Coliseum in Chicago was the public arena for a great contest in political ideas ; the whole American nation was the audience and the entire world interested spectators. It was this democratic character and the vast scope of the event that to me seemed to be the source of the charm and novelty of the surroundings to a stranger. It was the absence of all time-worn convention, and the buoyant and ardent spirit of patriotism, born of love of liberty and love of country, that impressed and inspired one so much. To the outside public the deliberations of a great national Convention might, superficially viewed, seem a very perfunctory business; but the delegates and their leaders had an arduous and difficult task. The outside public only read the result of their private conferences in the resolutions at the public meetings ; they have the reasons presented and the programme explained and the " platform " of the party placed before them by the orators selected from amongst the delegates. They are not witnesses of the many hours private deliberation in committee ; they know not the opposing opinions and different interests that come up for discussion before matters are ripe for public debate. Each state has its different views about national affairs ; each locality has different interests to be considered, and those in delegation must voice the opinions, and discuss their interests in connection with the interests of the nation as a whole, before anything like unanimity is obtained. But once a " platform " for the party is decided on it is presented by an orator deputed for the occasion. The programme was ably and eloquently placed before the Convention on this occasion by a talented lawyer who holds a high position in the Cabinet of the Republic. His statement of the past achievements of the party and their present and future political creed was a classic oration and received, as it deserved, the applause of the nation. It will be freely used as a text for many an orator before the Presidential election in November.

The chairman of Convention was no less a personage than the popular Speaker of the House of Representatives, Joe Cannon, familiarly known to his countrymen as " Uncle Joe." The duty of chairman of Convention is a delicate and difficult one. The success of Convention much depends on the suitability of the selection of chairman. A popular chairman is a necessity to command the attention and respect of the audience. A strong determined one is indispensable to enforce order and obedience. A tactful chairman with strength of will and sound judgment is always a success with an American audience. Mr. Cannon was a most successful selection for the high position. The chairman's duty is to make a speech outlining the work of the Convention, and the past and present policy of his party. Mr. Cannon's speech was unique in its homely originality. He compared the Democratic party to a loud cackling hen that has laid a small egg, and again to a shallow river hurriedly rattling over a rough surface, while his own party he likened to the deep river smoothly rolling towards the sea, strong in its course and deep in its volume. His oratory was natural and familiar, his similitudes taken from country life and his delivery enlightened by a simple directness that enlisted the good will of his audience. The chairman, by the way, carries a kind of mallet, by striking with which he procures order. Another function of the chairman of Convention which Uncle Joe performed most dramatically, and to the delight of his auditors, is the handing each speaker to the front of the platform, and introducing him by a felicitous little speech or a familiar slap on the back. Passing from the chairman of the Convention to the delegates one was forcibly struck by the mediocrity of the orations delivered on the occasion. The occasion and surroundings were such as to stimulate an orator to eloquence. One can well imagine the inspiring influence that such a memorable concourse of delegates and spectators would have been to arouse the patriotism and burning and lofty eloquence of the orators of other days. On such an occasion, with such a mighty audience, and with such a noble cause—the nomination of the successor of Washington and Abraham Lincoln—one might have expected a Webster or a Clay, a Henry, or even a M'Kinley to have risen among the throng of speakers. Surely, with almost a thousand delegates, representative men from their own states, men who filled the highest positions that their brother citizens and friends could elect them to occupy—men who were governors of states, mayors of large and prosperous cities, representatives and senators to the capital of their country—one might have expected occasionally to have been enchanted by flights of real oratory. If such were the hopes and expectations of many in the thronged hall, they were doomed to disappointment. Many of the delegates, indeed, inspired by an out-of-date sentimentality, rang the changes on the courage and daring, the sufferings and trials, that " the nation's martyred sires " endured in defence of the liberties " they now enjoy, and the land they love." Such oratory was generally the enthusiastic outpouring of young recruits in their novitiate as public speakers, or the pseudo-eloquence of an old political war-horse repeating paragraphs from speeches delivered half a century ago. From first to last, however, there was no orator of the magnetic kind able, by his burning words and the force of his eloquence, to draw with him, as by a magic wand, the ear and mind, and soul of the vast meeting. One there was, and one alone, who seemed able to reach the heights of true oratory, that was Mr. Black, the delegate who nominated Roosevelt for President. His oration, as read in the press, is powerfully cogent, well arranged, beautifully thought out and artistically worded. A few sentences may be quoted as an example of his style and an exposition of Republican policy. "The man," he said, " has been already singled out to bear the standard and to lead the way. No higher badge was ever yet conferred. But great as the honour is, the circumstances that surround it make that honour more profound. You have come from every state and territory in this vast domain. The country and the town have vied with each other in sending their contribution to this vast throng. Every highway in the land is leading here, and crowded with the members of that great party which sees in this splendid city the symbol of its rise and power. Within this unexampled multitude is a representative of every rank and condition of free men, every creed and occupation. But to-day a common purpose and desire have engaged us all, and from every nook and corner of the country rises but a single choice, to fill the most exalted position in the world. He is no stranger waiting in the shade to be called suddenly into public light. The American people have seen him for many years, and always where the fight was thickest and the greatest need was felt. He has been alike conspicuous in the pursuits of peace, and in the arduous stress of war. No man now living will forget the spring of '98, when the American mind was so inflamed, and the American patriotism so aroused, when, among all the eager citizens surging to the front as soldiers, the man whom this Convention has already in its heart, was among the first to hear the call and answer to his name." Again he says : " He is no slender flower, swaying in the wind, but that heroic fibre which is best nurtured by the mountains and the snow. He believes that in shaping the destinies of this mighty nation, hope is a higher impulse than regret. He believes that preparation for future events is a more important duty than an inventory of past regrets." Again, " This is a time when great figures must be kept in front. If the pressure is great, the material to resist it must be granite and iron." " Events sometimes select the strongest man, as lightning goes down the highest rod. And so it is with those events which for many months with unerring sight have led to a single name which I am chosen only to pronounce. Gentlemen, I nominate for president of the United States the highest living type of the youth, the vigour and the promise of a great country and a great age, Theodore Roosevelt of New York."

The orator's peroration was a signal for a scene of the wildest enthusiasm. The immense audience, in which youth and old age, white and black, rich and poor, indiscriminately mixed, rose to its feet and sent forth a deafening cheer. The bands began to play the national airs. Hats were wafted high above the head, bannerettes and flags were hoisted from platform and gallery ; the eagles, borne as state emblems by the Alaskan delegates, were poised high on poles above the surging, cheering and applauding throng. The " Stars and Stripes " fluttered from every bench in the spacious hall. On a banner, carried on a high pole, was exhibited before the audience a picture of Roosevelt. This banner, as it waved and flaunted, and rose and fell, became the focus for every eye and the signal for the enthusiastic mass to renew and renew again their cheers and plaudits. For fully twenty minutes the bands never ceased playing, and the audience never wearied applauding. It was only after repeated calls from the chairman, and a continued hammering on the table with the mallet which " Uncle Joe " carried in his hand, that order at last was secured. Such a scene of enthusiasm has rarely been witnessed at any previous Convention. Certainly never in the history of Republican National Conventions was there so much unanimity. Many Convention-going citizens remember scenes on similar occasions that ended in heated words and often hand to hand fights, among the opposing factions. The work that the Convention of 1904 performed in three short days was often formerly the work of two or three weeks. How are we to account for such expedition and such cordial co-operation and unanimity ? There were more states represented on this occasion than were ever incorporated in the Union previously. There were, besides, more contentious questions than ever before called for consideration. How, then, account for such phenomenal harmony ? Such unanimity, such enthusiasm, such unfeigned jubilation, and such determination to go forth to enforce the mandate of the Convention were not nor could not be the result of mere chance. No ! this satisfactory harmony was the resultant of much forethought, much party deliberation, and much compromise. There was no towering mind or magnetic personality amongst the political acrobats who performed before this packed array of delegates and spectators. It is true that the name of Roosevelt commanded the applause of the assembly. His record as a patriot and a statesman when favourably portrayed by the Convention's orators commanded their respect and enthused the listeners. But this, of course, would have occurred should circumstances have pointed to any other prominent Republican as the nominee of the party. No doubt the peculiar and tragic circumstances that placed Roosevelt in the Presidential chair

on the demise of his lamented predecessor, and the fidelity with
which he kept the solemn vow he made at the bier of his dead
chief to carry out the policy of the deceased statesman, acted
on the minds and feelings of the delegates and brought about
unanimity on this particular issue. Many may have seen in
the nominee of Convention a robust, go-ahead, strong and fearless man who typified in his person the American citizen
of the twentieth century. His sterling qualities of
head and heart, frankness, honesty and straightforwardness
may have influenced in some degree the unanimity of the
nomination. Still, the more you analysed all this harmony
and enthusiasm, the more you were convinced that some unseen influence was at work to unite in so solid a manner the
sentiments and votes of the nominators from the States. A
description of the petroleum pump which one often sees in
America will suggest a possible solution. In the centre of a
corn field you see erected a large pump. It has a long iron
handle supported by a simple frame work. Suddenly this
handle begins to oscillate, a rod works up and down, and brings
up petroleum from the well beneath. The pump works away,
though whence comes the requisite motor energy you cannot
see. From the pump a steel wire runs secretly among the
corn and weeds. This wire is connected with a little hut
containing an engine that keeps moving it. Many wires run
into this hut. The curious machine actuates them all, and
every wire, though hidden from view, leads to a pump. Some
of the pumps are near the hut, and some far off among the
hills and woods, but all are worked by the engine in the hut.
A man sits in the hut and controls the machine that works the
wires. Sometimes a wire becomes disarranged and ceases to
turn the pump, but the engine works away and pulls the other
connected wires as before. Like unto this is the Republican
machinery, pumping the oil of harmony. You have huts
located in New York and Washington. These machines are
worked by the millionaires and trusts. The governors of states,
the senators in Congress, and the statesmen of the nation, as

well as the orators at Convention, and the legal advisers of the party are connected like the pumps with the machinery in New York and Washington, in Wall Street and the White House. The belief is prevalent amongst the mass of the electors throughout the length and breadth of the states, that the "platform" of the Republican party was in readiness months previous to the Convention. The legal orator, Mr. Elihu Root, was cognisant of the position he was to occupy. He was the pump that produced the greatest results. Behind Mr. Root, and behind the entire Convention were the wires of a powerful organization.

The Republican party is the party in power. They call themselves the conservative party, the upholders of law and order, and the real successors of Washington and Lincoln ; they are backed up by the most powerful among the millionaires in the country. The danger to be feared and averted for the future in this mighty land is the monopoly of wealth and power by the rich " kings " who rule the stocks and markets of America, and in fact, of the world The greed for gold and the grasping after it by every means, fair and unfair, is a growing evil. There is too much concentration of capital. When wealth and power become focussed in the few, the interests of the many become imperilled. Americans once purchased freedom by sacrificing their lives in defence of liberty. They threw off the tyrannical yoke of their English rulers and in later years they procured freedom for the black race that toiled on plantations to enrich their masters. The remedy for the evil lies with the electors. The people hold the nation's destinies in their hands. The great American Constitution has liberty written on every page. The nation's fathers, who framed their charter, gave it as a legacy to a free people to preserve. It rests, then, with the people to decide what political party, which section of the nation is the best custodian of their rights and liberties. A just government of the people and for the people must be balanced like scales on a beam. At present the fulcrum is to the one side, and it rests then with the electors to organize a powerful opposition, who shall restore equilibrium. To resist the baneful influences and counteract the dangers ahead there must be an opposition with a solid programme. This party must receive its solidity from its " platform " and the principles it propounds. It must enlist men of probity and genius to announce its claims to the support of the electors. It should have written across its standard the motto—" Liberty and Justice."

There are dangers to be avoided by the party in opposition ; dangers that often attend the side of popular agitation. As a rule eloquence and oratory are more soul-stirring in opposition than in the mouth of power. Again, where liberty is the watchword of the nation, and the spirit of equality and independence the inheritance of the individual as well as of the masses, to control the crowd when under the influence of eloquent pleading in their defence becomes a difficult task. Hence riot and insubordination often result from the passionate enunciation of the Democratic " platform," and the adversaries of Democracy find in the turbulence of the masses a text to defend their past government of the nation. The Democrats then must be alive to the dangers of radicalism and riot in their midst. They must take their stand on the just administration of the laws for all. They should preach a crusade against trusts and combines, and advocate an honest executive purged from bribery, corruption and jobbery.

It may not be out of place here to say a word on the terms Republican and Democrat, which at first sight seem somewhat misleading. The Democrats claim to be as truly patriotic and as firm defenders of the Constitution as the Republicans. Both parties are firm upholders of the Independence of the United Federated States. They only differ in their aims and objects and the application of the laws and intrepretation of the Constitution. They differ as to the ways and means that may best suit the wants of their nation and the amelioration of their race. The terms that would best differentiate the two parties are "Conservative Republicans" and "Democratic Republicans." These terms, however, might not please the parties. The Republicans claim to be conservative inasmuch as they uphold the original Constitution, and strictly conserve the rights and prerogatives of the legislature. But they claim to be democratic in as far as they are a party of progress and reform who formulate their platform to suit the wants of the age, and the advance of the times, steadily keeping in view the extension of their nation in territory, in trade, in commerce, in cultivation, in population and in civilization. The Democrats would hardly quarrel with the term "Democratic Republicans," nor would they yield to their opponents in loyalty to the rights and prerogatives of their self-governing nation, and if such loyalty is conservatism, they in so far are conservative. They are Democrats because they claim to voice the politics of the democrary. They claim that under their banner is marshalled in solid phalanx, the poor man, the working man, and the middleman, whilst in the opposite party you will find the large capitalists, the stock merchants and the magnates who boss the commerce and trade of the nation. Early in the last century the terms Federalist and Republican were synonomous as applied to political parties, whilst the term "Republican Democrats" stood for the opposition. The Republican party was founded by Alexander Hamilton and the Democrats by Thomas Jefferson over one hundred years ago, but the original aims of these parties differed very much of course from their present policies.

ROOSEVELT.

A BIOGRAPHICAL AND PERSONAL SKETCH.
(Written in 1904.)

THE history of America, since the summer of 1775, when, at
Boston, the first stand was made for freedom, has been the
history of heroes and heroic deeds. Washington stands out
in bold relief as the father and founder of the Republic; Lincoln
the second hero in order of merit, looms high above his age
in the middle of the nineteenth century; and Ulysses Grant,
the greatest general of his time and the commander of the
Union forces, and successor to the martyred Lincoln as President, ranks in history as the third great defender and nation-
builder in the estimation of his countrymen. Minor lights
you have, coming down the calendar of honoured names in
the nation, men such as Jefferson and Jackson, Munroe and
Patrick Henry, Adams and Hamilton, and Franklin ; names
that will not soon fade from the pages of American history.
Future historians will place in the roll of honour of these last
the name of Theodore Roosevelt. Roosevelt, as President of
the nation, was not a mere figurehead in the government of the
Republic. When he was called to the helm of state, on the
lamented death of M'Kinley, he was comparatively a young
man. He saw the light of day over half a century ago in the
city of New York. As a youth he " trekked " out west along
with a few daring and venturesome companions. In North
Washington he purchased a grazing ranch, and here for many
years he managed most successfully a large farm, on which
he trained horses and raised cattle and sheep. During those
years his fame locally, as a dashing, daring horseman was
proverbial. The wild, reckless life that western squatters lead

helped much in moulding the character of young Roosevelt.
It gave to his exterior bearing a manly, dashing, and robust
expression. The direct and offhand manner in which even
in his official capacity, he transacts business, was formed in
those early years, when he mixed with rough and burly
companions—dare-devil spirits like himself. A few years
later, when still a young man,we find him serving his novitiate
as a politician, and acting a manly part in local and national
affairs, no doubt, as yet, lacking in political knowledge. The
wave of patriotism that swept over the States during the
Spanish war caught the young enthusiast and forced him to
the front. It was during this war that our hero was brought
into prominence, and that his name was made famous over
the continents of America and Europe. The rough riders
from the backwoods organized and led by him in the war
rendered his name famous, and stamped him as a fearless
commander. It was the privilege of the writer to be present
in the Coliseum of Chicago in the summer of 1904 when the
Republican delegates assembled in presence of almost twenty
thousand auditors to announce a platform for the election
to be held in the following November, and to nominate the
President. The unanimous voice of the delegation was in
favour of the squatter from the west—the captain of rough
riders. Speaker after speaker eulogized the candidate.
Delegates from Alaska vied with delegates from Maine in
sounding the praises of Roosevelt. He was the hero of that
mighty throng. Roosevelt's magnetic personality has been
a powerful factor in his great success. Mr. Payne, a republican
leader and life-long opponent, writing in 1904 to the Press
after twenty years of strenuous opposition to him says:
" Roosevelt is frank and straightforward, and one of the
ablest statesmen this country has ever produced. I opposed
him many years ago. He was then a boy fresh from College. He had no knowledge of politics or of the duties of a
politician or statesman. He is no coward ; he has physical
and moral courage, and since he came to Washington he
has developed in a wonderful manner."

Roosevelt stands for the *beau ideal* of the Republican party. He is more feared than loved by Wall Street magnates. Those millionaires who rule the nation and who control the finance of the country dared not oppose him because he was the favourite son of the States. Yet they knew in their heart of hearts that he was sworn enemy to trusts and monopolies. He held and still holds the sway in the hearts of the rank and file of the voters of the country. He never turned his back on his rough rider companions. He stood up for the dark brother from the south, as well as the Red Indians from the north-west. He is familiarly known to the vulgar throng by the homely name of "Teddy," an appellation which savours of a certain kind of popularity that no politician despises at election times. The defects of public men can best be gleaned from what their opponents say of them. The following are some of the personal attacks made against Roosevelt by the Democrats. They say that the deeds reported of him were more the exaggerations of Pressmen than actual performances in the Spanish campaign. In fact they deny his moral and physical valour, and say that his words were always stronger than his acts as a statesman. They say that the leader of a vast nation should be cool in temperament instead of being impetuous and rash. His nick-names about his opponents cannot be defended as prudent utterances. He calls the Democrats "office-mongering scoundrels." It was said of him that he was rash in action, and no one knew his next move or where he would land the nation. The friends of Roosevelt did not lessen their respect for him, bur rather loved him the more the fiercer the opposition became. His honesty and frankness were qualities that endeared him to his admirers. His energy and indomitable perseverance and love for work were proverbial. His motto seems to have been "try, try, try again." Opportunity and achievement with him were synonomous terms. The versatility of his genius and accomplishments is marvellous. His love of sports and manly exercises is well-known to the world at large, and unexpected

as it is in a man who has been so formed by temperament and
surroundings for an active and strenuous life, he is noted
above the ordinary for oratory and literary attainments.
He is the author of several books which are widely read and
highly appreciated among litterateurs. His book on the
Spanish-American war is looked upon as a standard text-
book of history. One example from this book will illustrate his direct,vivid and forcible style. It is his account of
the destruction of the Spanish fleet in Manila Bay by Admiral
Dewey. " I saw a prize fight once where one man hit the other
under the chin as quick as lightning and the fight was over in
nine seconds. The man who was hit fell before he saw his
opponent raise an arm. Dewey must have made the same
sort of fight in the ports at Manila." As a debater and public
speaker his style is forcible and direct ; some would be inclined
to remark that he was too impetuous and hot-tempered, and
that he was inclined to be carried away by the impulse of the
moment and the enthusiasm of the crowd. The same remarks
might be applied in a greater or lesser degree to all public
speakers when they are speaking in party defence. But it is
not from the platform so much as the presidential chair that
we should gauge Roosevelt's oratory. It is rather in his calm,
studied and statesmanlike utterances, in his inaugural and
farewell presidential addresses, that one should seek for his
qualities as an orator. For as cogent, terse and wise
addresses those phillipics delivered to the Congress of the
nation in Washington will favourably compare with the best
orations of statesmen of ancient or modern times. They have
been compared with much truth with the occasional public
utterances of William of Germany—a type of ruler, by the
way, that Roosevelt is said to rival in more ways than oratory.

Some of the public utterances of the late President have
been much admired for their patriotism, wisdom and philosophy. Here are at random some extracts from his orations :
" Every great nation owes to the men whose lives have formed
part of its greatness not merely the material effect of what

they did, not merely the laws they placed upon the statute book, or the victories they won over armed foes, but also the immense, but indefinable moral influence produced by their words and deeds upon national character." About politics he says : " Practical politics must not be construed to mean dirty politics. On the contrary, in the long run, the politics of fraud and treachery and foulness are impractical politics, and the most practical of all politicians is the politician who is clean and decent and upright." "Something," he says, " can be done by good laws—more by honest demonstration of the laws—but most of all by frowning resolutely on the preachers of vague discontent. In our political and social life alike, if we wish to succeed we must base our conduct on the decalogue and the golden rule."

It was my privilege in the month of June of this year to meet the subject of this sketch at his official residence in Washington and grasp his hand and receive his cordial greeting. I prized very much the honour of meeting the President of the mightiest of nations, and one who next to the Supreme Pontiff, holds the highest office on earth. The honour was made all the more acceptable and memorable from the simple nature of the ceremony, devoid, as it was, of all the pomp usually attendant on interviews with mighty potentates. I here recount the interview as noted down at the time : " On June the 14th I sauntered out from my hotel in search of scenes of interest in the beautiful and historic capital of the nation. After a few minutes walk I found myself in the company of a most efficient official in the public buildings in proximity to the White House, the official residence of the President. He, an old veteran of the civil war, and pensioned officer, as well as paid servant of present government—a Kerryman, besides—became my guide and historian for the occasion. His information to me was most valuable, and his directions about introductions to President of incalculable service to one unaccustomed to such honours. He directed me to Colonel Crozier, Secretary at White House. To this important servant of the President I soon presented my card, and in him I found a most courteous and obliging gentleman. It was Tuesday ; the Secretary came to me, and with regret said that to-day being cabinet day no one except members of the cabinet could see the President, ' but come to-morrow at noon,' he said, ' and I shall arrange an interview.' I thanked him and departed. At 12 o'clock on the following day I was ushered into the Blue Room contiguous to the office of the President, in company with others waiting for the same purpose. Punctual to arrangement the President emerged from his office and commenced to converse with two interviewers announced before me. I was all expectancy, and I must admit somewhat nervous. But all nervousness and reserve were soon set at rest on the approach of this plain and natural and unconventional gentleman. The frank open manner in which he reached out and took my hand in his strong grasp put me quite at my ease, whilst the homely manner in which he addressed me surprised me and assured me that I was in the presence of a natural unaffected man. ' Glad to know you,' were the brief and simple words with which he opened our little chat. He inquired familiarly about my country, my sojourn in Washington, &c., closing the necessarily short interview with another strong grasp of the hand, and an unaffected and sincere ' I am delighted to make your acquaintance.' " The impression of such an interview must naturally vary with the expectations of the individual. If one expected much formality, much display, and the courtly etiquette with which kings and princes surround their persons to add importance and dignity to their titled names, one would naturally be disappointed. The President steps alone and in a most simple manner from his active work in his office to the reception room hard by. In outward appearance Mr. Roosevelt is like the ordinary business or commercial man that one meets in our busy towns and cities. In height he is about five feet nine inches. He has square shoulders, on which a strong round head sits erect on a firm neck. His brown hair is beginning to be mixed with grey. The eyes are a good index of the fiery temperament; the nose is prominent more from its solidity than its elevation. The eyebrows, like the eyes, show the temperament of the man, and give the impression that the owner is inclined to nervousness, if not to rashness. The forehead is square, rather than high, which gives to the facial appearance a strong and manly character. To sum up these hurried impressions one would say that there was fire in his eyes, determination in his mouth, firmness in his chin, intelligence in his forehead and an indefinable expression of genius in his strong countenance. In general appearance he possesses little that at first would attract or yet repel one who was a stranger. You feel he is such a one as you would rather have for your friend than enemy; that he is capable of strong passions and equally strong action; that his power also for loving and hating is intense. The erect and manly bearing at once points out the soldier and the man of deeds. Had Roosevelt taken the army as his profession instead of the forum and the Senate he is such a one as you would expect to rise to the highest rank in the service of his country. You would always expect to find him in the front of the firing line where the fight was fiercest and the danger greatest. There is apparently about his character little of the cool, watchful plotter and intriguer. However, it is not so sure that he has not latterly found the truth of the old adage " experience teaches." He came as an untrained western herdsman to political life, and from a reckless captain of rough rider volunteers, rash and devil-daring, he became successful senator; and finally it was his lot to succeed to the highest position in the States. Pluck and perseverance alone never could have done so much. Surely greatness and genius must be stamped on his every act to mark him out for the first man among the statesmen of his time and President of the nation.

In private life Roosevelt is a kind husband and father. His servants are very much attached to him. He still keeps an old Irish Catholic nurse who was in his father's service

when " Teddy," as she names him, was a child. This present
summer he sent her on a holiday to Rome to which city her
faith has drawn her for the third time. This ruler of a nation
feels no weariness at meeting the rough companions of other
days (when farming out west or rough riding in the war), for
his former acquaintances there is always a pleasant word and
a grip of his strong rough hand.

THE ST. LOUIS EXHIBITION.

Everyone visiting the world's fair at St. Louis was impressed after his own fashion. The following sketch from
notes taken at the time is from an Irish standpoint. To form
even an imperfect idea of that exhibition required weeks of
inspection and close study. The site was an immense park
located in the suburbs of the city, railed in by a high wooden
enclosure several miles long. Electric cars carried the tourists
to the " Fair " at a speed equal to our own fast running
trains. How stood poor old Ireland beside the other
exhibitors of the world? Well, she could not be expected to
rival America, England, Germany or France, having behind
them wealth and the patronage of powerful governments ; but
when we consider the many difficulties our friends had to face,
we must say the promoters of the Irish section were doing a
good work for Ireland. What we in Ireland should make the
most of when we exhibit side by side with foreign nations
is not so much the actual products manufactured in Ireland,
as the possibilities of our country's productive powers, and the
resources which we have demanding development. If we can
show the foreigner that our resources are worthy of encouragement and patronage, and that with kind co-operation, assisted
by scientific and technical training, we might develop into a

prosperous commercial nation, then we have gained our true object as exhibitors. We need not expect to rival the Parisian who leads the world in the matter of silks, furs and fineries of all descriptions, but we can exhibit to advantage in the line of patterns of linen, in embroidery, in lace, and in the weaving industries. Are not the Irish muslin, lace, poplin and linen famed the world over ? We cannot compete in cutlery, jewellery, guns, watches and machinery with the English or Germans ; but we may lay claim to rival these wealthy nations in our models and designs in shipbuilding. Have we not launched from our firms the largest and the fastest and most perfect vessels on the ocean ? We can show a favourable record in our past and present achievements in carving, engraving and embellishing in wood, stone and metal. Our carving in oak and our manufacture of instruments of music, especially the Irish harp, cannot be surpassed. We have a past record to be proud of in our woollen industries; our blankets and our tweeds, our weaving and dyeing made us famous in past generations. There is reason to hope that these industries amongst us are again reviving. Let us hope that our Navan and Blarney tweeds, our Limerick and Carrickmacross lace, will increase and prosper as the years roll on. There is no better means of advertising our wares than such an exhibition as the World's Fair. We were told of one American gentleman, in the dry goods business, ordering sixty-four thousand dollars of Navan tweed, on seeing a web of this famed cloth in the Irish exhibits at St. Louis. This single example shows the utility of bringing before the world our products and resources, and serves to indicate how splendid a medium such exhibits are to focus the eyes of the foreigner on Ireland's manufacturing possibilities. I was much interested in the mineral section of the Irish exhibits, the varied selection of square setts, marble slabs, and granite and sand and limestone, neatly dressed, of every conceivable colour, and quarried from a hundred different quarries throughout the different counties of Ireland. America is deficient in durable paving

setts, the American paving stone being a soft and unsuitable
sandstone, rare and costly of production. In some instances
paving setts could be shipped across the ocean as cheaply as
the Americans could quarry, dress, and forward them to the
centres demanding supplies. Amongst the Irish quarries represented we noted a few northern ones. There were granite
and limestone from Ballintoy, Ballycastle, Cushendall, Knock-
nacarry, Whitehall, Carnmoney, Whitewell, Cave Hill ; and
also selections from Moy, Carrickabreda, Castlewellan,
Annacloy and Newry in Co. Down. You had blue granite
setts from Downpatrick and variegated granite from Slieve
Donard. In fact from Donegal to Cork and from Cork to
Dublin and the Wicklow mountains Irish granite seems to be
plentiful, and was well represented at St. Louis. From Co.
Dublin there were fourteen marble slabs of every variety and
colour, which presented a pleasing and attractive appearance.
The great scarcity of granite stone suitable for street paving
purposes is noticeable in the towns and cities as one passes
through the different states. Of course the eastern cities are
more up-to-date and better provided with suitable material
than the midland and western districts, yet unless in the main
streets and thoroughfares, the cross streets and suburban
avenues are far behind our Irish towns and cities, and in many
locálities they are rough and uneven with ruts. Some of the
cities and towns have nearly all the streets laid out in mathe-
matical order, and with as much regularity as the Parisian
Boulevards, and though the foundation is laid in granite,
the covering is concreted or macadamized and this at great
expense to the corporations. This chiefly applies to cities
like Washington, and rising tourist resorts like Niagara,
where no trouble or expense is spared to beautify and please
and attract. But go to Cincinnati ; the streets are more
disagreeable owing to defective bottoming and paving material
than Limerick was a few years ago. Chicago, with all its
industry and wealth, is simply deplorable. In many localities
of that city I have passed in an American carriage over miles

of the streets and avenues, and I do not exaggerate in saying that owing to the entire absence of stone or granite or wooden bottoming they were positively dangerous to life and limb. In St. Louis the condition of the streets is also extremely defective, and in numerous avenues the city fathers find red bricks the only alternative to the decayed and dangerous wood paving originally employed in constructing the streets. There is a wide field in most of the states for a durable paving stone similar to our Irish granite, and considering the cheapness of labour at home, and the opportunities of transit on the ocean, and the reduced tariff owing to shipping competition, it seems strange that we could not forward our dressed granite at as reasonable a price as American competitors. We certainly could forward an article a hundred per cent. superior to any to be found in the central or eastern states. Before passing from this subject of the mineral resources on show in the Irish branch of the Fair we must not omit to mention that there are two mining companies in County Antrim represented by samples of that rare and valuable substance known as " Macadam clay." These industries are worked, one at Toome by James Grant, Esq., J.P., and the other at Whitehead by Mr. Cooper. Amongst the other Irish exhibits of which we can only mention a few we were much impressed with the excellent collection of fishing requisites in evidence. For deep sea purposes and ocean trawling, nets and tackling of the most perfect material were conspicuous, and for inland river and lake uses rare and varied samples could also be inspected. But our friends of the rod had the rarest variety on show. Those devoted to the harmless pastime of angling on rivers and ponds could not desire or imagine a more interesting sight than the rods and gaffs and hand-nets, flies and tackle of all conceivable design. The promoters of our Irish exhibits could not have chosen a more suitable industry in which to excel, and they surpassed all rivals at the Fair in this branch of manufacture. Our convents and our leading warehouses in

Belfast, Dublin and Cork, as well as our spinning and weaving factories, deserve praise from lovers of Ireland for the manner in which they co-operated with the organizers to bring before the world the excellent products made in Ireland of lace and linen and embroidery and hosiery. It is a pity, however, that more of our rising and progressive weaving factories did not take the opportunity of advertising through the World's Fair, and at the same time doing a patriotic work for their native land. Those who take an interest in the products made in Ireland for Catholic church purposes could not fail to be pleased with the splendid selection of chalices, ciboriums, pixes, monstrances, copes, lace embroidered albs, and vestments for altar use of every shade and pattern, as well as lamps and candelabra of rare and chaste designs.

I may here mention that a notable deficiency in the manner of pushing Irish manufactures in the States is the neglect of advertising. I one day entered a shop in Chicago to purchase some snuff and was disagreeably surprised to find that the only " ground product " of the Raleigh weed they had in stock was manufactured and labelled in Scotland. This is not as it should be. In the book publishing and binding department at St. Louis the selection is Irish of the Irish, and the turnout in printing and binding by the Dublin firms represented is most creditable. Irish peat and Irish blackthorn sticks and Irish harps, all peculiarly Irish productions, are much admired by the foreigner. The antiquities of Ireland, the mementoes of the days of Ireland's greatness, the paintings and relics of many of Ireland's historic and illustrious sons, have a fitting place among the exhibits from our country. In vocal and instrumental music we hold, thanks to the talent representing us at the Fair, a proud place amongst the best ; whilst Irish genius and Irish wit and humour on the stage of the concert hall were the admiration of all. We consider it due to the responsible conveners of the Exposition to record our indebtedness for allocating so prominent a site for the Irish section. As you entered towards the chief entrance in

front of the immense hotel and restaurant constructed in the
grounds for the convenience of visitors, you obtained a splendid
view of the Round Tower, which reared itself in the
centre of the Irish grounds, whilst an ancient church of Ireland and a Blarney Castle, each very lifelike, met
the gaze of all. Within the Irish enclosure there was accom-
modation for thousands of spectators. The band-stand raised
in the centre of the outer square within the arena was neatly
fitted up ; whilst to the right could be seen a unique model of
an ancient Irish Cross, ten feet high, with its numerous curved
and circular and winding raised sculptural embellishments.
As a sample of Irish art it is worthy of the admiration of all.
The M'Kinley cottage to the left of the main entrance as one
entered was a most perfect model of a one-storey thatched
Irish farm homestead as such Irish homes existed one hundred
years ago. The ladies and gentlemen in charge of the exhibits
were well selected, and in true Irish fashion performed the
work assigned them with ability and right good will. An
Irish American from Dublin and New York, Mr. Lee, had
charge of the decorative part of the exhibition, and his artistic
Irish painting and decoration of the stalls and sign-boards was
very beautiful.

THE RED MAN.

During my visit to the St. Louis Exposition it was my good fortune to see many strange sights, and to acquire many new ideas ; but of all the wonderful experiences I had, I think my visit to the Indian Congress and Wild West Show takes first p'ace. Often in my youthful days I had read of the Indians in novel and history, and many a tale I had listened to with terror about the wild red man of the wood.. I was well aware from tales of the old Colonials and histories of the wild west, how fierce the Indian tribes were in times of war ; how much to be dreaded in times of peace, and how they hated the paleface and never lost an opportunity of revenge on those who wronged their race, and robbed them of their property and country. With memories of these tales lingering in my mind I need not say how pleased I was to have an opportunity of seeing the wild men of the woods to the number of seven hundred and fifty (warriors and squaws and their families) —an opportunity to see them dance and hear them talk and sing ; to view them as they flew with lightning speed on their swift steeds, dressed in their native dress of skins and blankets and feathers, with the totem or emblem of their clan painted on their bodies, or embroidered with beads on their garments. Not alone were the rank and file of the red race well represented at this Indian Congress—managed by Colonel Cummings, an American citizen and adopted chief by the tribes—but fifty-one famous Indian chiefs of different tribes came with their followers to the exhibition, at the summons of Colonel Cummings, and under the patronage of the United States Government. I saw these native warriors and chiefs passing by on parade, and I heard an orator of the tribes address an audience in his native language. He was a typical Indian chief, athletic and over six feet in height, with broad, square shoulders, coarse, heavy red features, with a forehead flat and low and receding. The glamour of romance still clings about the red race. Bishop Brindle says : " The North American Indian is the noblest type of a heathen man on earth. He recognises a Great Spirit ; he believes in immortality; he has a quick intellect. He is a clear thinker ; he is brave and fearless ; and, until betrayed, he is true to his plighted faith. He has a passionate love for his children, and counts it a joy to die for his clan. Our most terrible wars have been with the noblest types of the Indians, and with men who had been the white man's friend." Miles declares in his " Personal Recollections " that he has no sympathy with the view that would debar the Indian from citizenship, and he denies the truth of the statement attributed to Sherman, that " the only good Indian was a dead Indian." He says that " American Indians are excellent as diplomatists, statesmen, warriors and friends. Do not then in ignorance teach your children to hate and fear and despise the American Indian. He will soon be but a memory ; his character deserves recognition, and his virtues and noble deeds can be with advantage held up for the admiration of coming ages."

It is trite history that before the coming of the Europeans to America the Indians had free control of the entire continent. They roamed at will over the forest-bound continent, tracking the wild deer, and hunting the buffalo whose flesh was their staple food, and whose hide was their chief garment. It was their proud boast to call the mighty American continent their native land and their country. On the mountains and in the woods, on the rivers and lakes they sported and played. They knew every trail and pass and their canoes glided over every river and lake from ocean to ocean, and from the gulf to the most northern lakes. Sad and pitiful has been the fate of this once powerful race, as link by link it lost its moorings, and at last, owing to colonizing influences, was driven beyond the boundaries of civilization into the wilderness " before the face " of the white man. The general belief is that the North American Indians of to-day are only a remnant of a once very numerous and powerful race. Many of the old tribes have either lost their individuality and amalgamated with neighbouring tribes, or have been annihilated in tribal, international, and colonial wars. The entire race of Indians in North America might be classed under three great families, these families or branches being sub-divided into tribes and clans. The first would be that of the Indians who inhabited the southern part of·North America, to the east of the Mississippi, " the father of waters," and who were called Muskoki Indians, and embraced the Chicasaws, the Choctaws, the Creeks and the Seminoles. The second branch would be that of the Iroquois family, to whom belonged the Mohawks, Oneidas, Onondagas and Seneca tribes. They inhabited the Mohawk valley, stretching west from Albany on the Hudson river. This race was the bravest and most powerful of all the American Indians, and fought the fiercest fight and held out the longest against the French and English colonizers until finally subdued about 1700 by Frontenac, a French general. The third family of North American Indians known to the early colonists inhabited the remaining territory east of the Mississippi, and were called Algonquins. The Indians, physically, are a powerful race. Intellectually they are superior to most uneducated and uncivilized savage races. There is a remarkable similarity amongst the individuals of the race. They are in size, and strength, and power of endurance superior to most civilized races. Their lives, as those of their fathers for centuries, are passed in the fresh bracing air of the prairies, woods and mountains. The best sportsman, the surest marksman with the bow and arrow, the boldest and most daring warrior, the man who has killed most of his enemies, is always a favourite with his clan, and generally becomes a chief. Hence swiftness of foot, daring and skill on horseback, and in all kinds of outdoor sport and manly exercise is prided in and practised by the

T

males of the tribes. In colour the skin of the Indian is of a copperish red hue. The hair is dark. The male, like the female, is beardless, and both wear the hair at full length down their backs. In facial appearance they are by no means repulsive, like the African negroes. They resemble much the New Zealand Maori in physical and mental organization, differing only in the colour of the skin. The Indians are very tenacious of racial customs, and very hard to bring under the influence of modern civilization. They are a sensitive, proud, and truthful people, faithful to their friends, and cruel towards those who deceive them. They may be broken, but so stubborn are they about amalgamating with foreigners or receiving foreign ideas that it is difficult to bend them. Some of the sayings of the ancient wise among them are as sacred to the tribes as the Commandments are with Christians. "The vices the Indians borrowed from the paleface are the only debts he will not pay." "The paleface taught the Indians to swear, and gave them plenty of cause to do so." "The Indian scalps his enemy; the paleface skins his friends." "If the Indian could lie like the paleface he would rule the earth." "What the Indian hates he kills, what the paleface loves he spoils." "If the paleface had a conscience, the Indian would have a country." "The paleface writes treaties in the sand with the point of his sword." These and many similar sayings might be quoted to show how futile it was in past days of war and deceit towards the native tribes to reconcile them with the white races, or induce them to become friendly with those whom they held at such discount. Not alone was it the highest claim to eminence in the clan to be brave in battle, but it was held in like degree a note of dignity, and a point of honour, to endure without emotion the severest pain and torture. Campbell's Outalissi is the type of the race.

"As monumental bronze, unchanged in look,
A soul that pity touched, but never shook;
Trained from his tree-rocked cradle to the bier
The fierce extremes of good and ill to brook:
Impassive, fearing but the shame of fear,
A stoic of the woods, a man without a tear."

The domestic and home life of the Indian was of the simplest and rudest description. It was on the banks of some smiling river, or beside a lake or fountain that the clan, with their elected chief, pitched their tents, and built their wigwams with the bark of trees. In some instances as many families as twenty or thirty, related on the maternal side, lived in one long continuous wigwam. The chief generally lived apart in a dwelling larger and constructed with more care and cost. The female portion of the family performed all the drudgery and did every kind of work. They laboured the land, wove the blankets, cooked the food, dressed the skins used for clothing and bedding, and cared for the entire household. The braves or warriors looked upon the women as inferior to them and treated them accordingly. The first duty of a male Indian was to be a sportsman and a warrior. The weapons which he carried in battle were the war-club, the bow and arrow, and the tomahawk. A sharp-edged stone served for the blade of his tomahawk, and bone or flint were the points of his arrow. In times of peace the braves devoted their time to hunting the game of the mountain and prairie, and fishing the rivers and lakes. He made his own canoes from the bark of trees and skins. These shallow boats were their constant companions on journeys. They used them to carry their furs and blankets and wares to market. They were so constructed that two men could easily carry them from river to river. The famous snowshoe, four feet long, with curved toe and heel, was made by the men and used to great advantage in travelling, sometimes helping them to accomplish as many as forty miles a day. Besides constructing the canoes and making the snowshoes, the men busied themselves in times of peace in manufacturing implements of warfare, and decorating their person with paint and feathers. Their amusements were the war-dance and song, athletic games, the narration of deeds of daring, and listening to the oratory of the chiefs. Much of their time was spend in gazing listlessly in a vacant stupor on the forests, and on the clouds that rolled aloft above their heads. This vacant, thoughtless life, indulged in during long periods, imprinted an habitual gravity and melancholy on their minds and character. Wonder and fear caused the untrained and undeveloped mind of the Indians to divine a cause for the phenomena that they saw around them. They heard the thunder roar, and saw the lightning flash, heard the wind rush and rage around their wigwams, and often uproot the mighty oak of the mountain forests. Fear was the first instinct aroused by this unseen power, so dreadful in its anger. They named it the Great Spirit or Maniton. It commanded the winds and the thunder and clouds. In his mighty hand the destinies of the living and the fate of the dead alike rested. He must be appeased. Thus reasoning they were led to offer sacrifice to the Deity. Their sacrifices were often of human remains. They were very superstitious and had some confused idea about guardian spirits that cared for every man. Their idea of heaven was that of the " happy hunting ground." They looked upon the next life in Paradise as similar to the present, only joyful and painless, a life in which hunting and sporting would be their constant pastime. Hence when a person died they placed beside him in the grave his implements of warfare and sport, and supplied him with a sufficient quantity of food for the long journey he was supposed to be entering upon. Often a member of the clan voluntarily gave up his life to accompany his dead chief or sachem on the journey. Mothers gaily dressed their dead infants and placed toys and food beside them, tearfully following them in their flight towards the " happy hunting ground." This belief in immortality was most consoling to the Indians. It made them less fearful of death. It comforted them in their trials and dangers. It caused them, however, to care little for the aged. They believed that life in old age was not worth living, and so they removed their aged kinsfolk far from their native village, and left them in the forests to pine and die. With death the wished-for " happy hunting ground " was entered, and here all the pleasures and sports on earth would revive. In this happy paradise there would be plenty of game, a delightful country, and every conceivable enjoyment. This belief in a great unknown spirit who ruled every being, and was present in every place, together with the belief in a resurrection of the body and immortality, led some antiquarians to surmise that the Indians, at an early date, came from the east, and were of Jewish origin ; whilst some concluded from the sacrificial mounds and pyramids that are to be found in North and South America that the aborigines of the entire continent were of the same race as the Egyptians, Hindoos, and Chinese. The colour of the skin and similarity in other points led to the conjecture that they were related in origin to the inhabitants of the Indian Archipelago. There is a belief existing, and theories are advanced, to prove that the Northern Indians, like the Goths and Vandals in Europe, are not the original tribes that built the pyramids, but a more powerful though less gifted race which swept out the southern and central American Indians from their fertile valleys, and either annihilated them, or forced them to take refuge in Mexico. One thing is certain, that the American Indians were a numerous race, scattered over the entire continent. That they were highly religious is evident from temples and altars built over the localities they inhabited, that they were united under a code of laws and government, is shown from the immense fortifications and mounds, underground works, raised forts, and secret passages, to be met in thousands from Mexico to Michigan, and east from Missouri to the Alleghany mountains, which could not have been constructed unless by tribes and clans well organized. Amongst all these tribes spread over the continent a physical similarity may be traced. This similarity is noticeable in their religious manners and customs, as well as in the monuments extant, which facts certainly entitle us to draw the conclusion that all the tribes and branches belonged originally to one great family, which family was the aboriginal parent race of the Red Indians of North and South America. The government of the Indians among themselves, and prior to their subjugation by the United States, was most democratic. The tribe selected its own chief by vote; heredity rarely influenced the election. The bravest, most popular warrior generally was elected. The chief was assisted by a sachem, or wise man, who acted as counsellor and judge; but the word of the chief was supreme, and the sachem's position was, in many cases, a merely nominal one. The tribes were composed of many clans, who mostly lived in separate villages, and for the most part spent their lives in community, having everything in common. This condition of things is now entirely changed. The reservation system of allotment and parcelling out farms to individuals, together with the encouragement to thrift and trade and commerce, and the educating process in native Indian schools, built for the Indian youth, have all helped to obliterate the old landmarks, and to encourage civilized manners and customs amongst them. It might be said with truth that the Indian Congress and "wild west" exhibition at St. Louis is the last great gathering of the tribes and clans. So that in future the Red Indian, except in name and colour, will be a thing of the past. I have witnessed their performances at the arena in the ground of the Congress in St. Louis. Their proficiency as horsemen, in the circuit in front of the grand stand, was most surprising. It was truly a splendid sight to view these powerfully-built men, decked out in all the paraphernalia of their race and clans, seated on the swiftest and most sure-footed steeds I ever saw, standing at attention in the most perfect order and discipline, under the command of their adopted chief, Colonel Cummings. They were spread out in lines in the grounds in hundreds, decked in plumes and feathers of every shade and colour. The famous Navajo blankets of every colour and pattern gave to those warriors and braves a pleasing and variegated appearance. I might add that those blankets, woven by the Navajo Indians of New Mexico, surpass any cloth ever woven in civilized countries, both in beauty of design and excellence of workmanship, as well as in durability. Each horseman was painted and tatooed with the totem of his tribe ; each sat erect and proud on his favourite charger, and when the word was given for showing their feats of horseman- ship and deeds of prowess the scene was a most impressive one. They went through sham battles with precision and under the strictest obedience to the voice of their leader. They used their firearms with marvellous accuracy and lightning speed. now alighting from their horse going at full speed and in a second mounting again ; now standing erect on the horse's back and facing the foe in the charge again ; hanging on by one foot to the saddle and firing their musket safely from the side. Seeing them we could not wonder that the Indians were so feared and dreaded by the colonists. Had they been civilized and trained as we now see them under Colonel Cummings, they would not have been so easily relegated to the woods and mountain passes.

I have been a wondering witness of the perfection in military drill displayed by about fifty young Indians, educated and trained in the Indian Polytechnic schools. A more per- fect, more muscular, or more disciplined band it has never been my privilege to admire. While they gave a practice of the college games before the spectators in the grounds one could not help marvelling at the splendid physique, the manly bearing and wonderful agility of these civilized college Indians. Their display was perfect, and though a most fatiguing per- formance—it is a game similar to Irish hurling—never seemed to exhaust their energies. In drill those same young men, after going through with rifles and bayonets a display of military skill that one should say exhausted all the scientific inventions and artful manoeuvres of the commanding officer— they, under orders, attacked a fortification, without ladder or hook scaled a breach twelve feet high in a few seconds, rushed the trenches and set fire to the enemy's camp. They performed this feat of valour in perfect order and according to the most scientific principles of warfare. The native North American Indians are capable of much loyalty and devotion to their

chosen and trusted leaders. Warriors of their own race have
ever been adored by the tribes and clans, and even the white
man, when he won their affections and gained their confidence,
has been followed, obeyed, and adopted into their tribes.
Colonel Cummings, president and manager of the Indian Congress and United States agent and diplomat to the natives,
by his tact, his kindness, as well as by his strictly upright and
truthful dealing with these typical haughty, sensitive, and
pardonably-superstitious braves, has won their allegiance and
goodwill. In the year 1902 he was adopted into the great
Sioux nation, as the son of Red Cloud the high chief, and received the name of Chief Lakota, or Chief of the Indians.
The occasion was made memorable by a solemn ratification by
the Sioux nation, and feasts and dances and sacred ceremonies
were the outward expressions of their goodwill. They presented him with a scalp shirt made of finely tanned buckskin,
and ornamented with beads, royal ermine, and one hundred
and eighteen scalps, a priceless gift from the tribes. He was
also presented with a beautiful buffalo robe with the totem
or emblem of the chieftainship painted on the fleshy side.
This mark of goodwill to the white race and loyal obedience
to their Indian white chief sounds the death-knell of the
uncivilized Indian, and the day is fast dawning when it will
be said " the Red Man was." The end of the buffalo was
typical of the fate of the savage red man, and soon like the
buffalo, or like the Irish wolf-dog, will they become a tradition
and a name. There is just another instance on record where a
white man gained a similar influence and received a like honour
at the hands of the Indians. That is the case of Sir William
Johnston, nephew of Sir Peter Warren, an Irishman, who,
about one hundred and fifty years ago was adopted by the
clans and tribes, and used the entire race against the French,
in the English and French wars for supremacy, in the beginning
of the eighteenth century. Johnston in a similar fashion to
Cummings, in the year 1765, called together the chiefs and
sachems of all the North American tribes at Fort Niagara,

and caused them to ratify their allegiance to his cause against the French colonists.

In those days the Indian was more savage, more persecuted, and less tractable to win over. The white man then hunted them from their lands, and never made a treaty with them but to break it. That Johnston was capable of subduing their proud, revengeful, and sensitive nature, and bringing them round to trust him and love him, argues for his Irish genius and natural tact ; at the same time it proves that the Indian then as now was not incorrigible if treated with honesty and kindness. Johnston set about winning them over from the day he settled in their midst. His physical and mental qualities alike fitted him for the task. Like Cummings he was tall and manly in bearing. His temper was well under control. He was of mild and melancholy countenance, like the Indian. He was gifted, like all Irishmen, with wonderful powers of eloquence—a gift the Indians very much admired. He adopted their language, their dress, and their customs. He lived amongst them and learned their loves and hates, their secret joys and sorrows, and became the adored hero of the race. Having the ability to ingratiate himself into their confidence, he had equally the tact and genius to turn their allegiance to account in the cause of his country. A short dialogue between Johnston and King Hendrick, a famous sachem of the Mohawks, will best illustrate the Indian character and Sir William's tactful treatment. One day the King, on seeing a richly-embroidered coat in Johnston's castle, determined on a cunning device to get possession of it. "Brother," said he one morning, on entering the castle of Johnston, "me dream last night." "Indeed," says Sir William, "what did my red brother dream ? " "Me dreamed that coat be mine." "It is yours," frankly replied Johnston. Some time later Sir William visited the wily and brave old sachem and calmly observed to Hendrick : "Brother, I had a dream last night." "What did my white brother dream ? " rejoined the sachem. "I dreamed that all this tract of land

was mine," pointing to a district 20 miles square. Hendrick
looked very grave, but added, " Brother, the land is yours,
but you must not dream again." A little later Johnston led
out the Indians and militia against the French. On this
occasion the old king was by Johnston's side, and made the
following remark about the English regiment, which was small:
" If they are to fight they are too few ; if they are to be killed
they are too many ; keep them together and you can't break
them, take them one by one and they are easily snapped."
The Indians name the members of the family after the old clan
fashion, familiar in Ireland and other nations centuries ago,
before the surname and Christian name came into use amongst
us. When a child is born it is named according to its birth,
Coon oo ga, or " first-born boy ; " Ha ga ga, or " second-born
boy ; " Hamonka, or " third-born boy ; " Na ghu ghoon a ga,
or " fifth-born boy," etc. ; and the girls in a similar manner,
according to the language of their clan, Hu-nung ka, or " first-
born daughter," Wee hung ka, or " second-born daughter,"
and so on. This sameness of naming is relieved of monotony
and confusion by adding to each name the father's or mother's
name. These names they retain until, on the occasion of
some feast by a relative or warrior, they have nick-names given
them by the host. I can still find in some parts of the North of
Ireland a resemblance to this Indian custom. For example,
in Rathlin Island, where there are sixteen families more or less
related, called M'Curdy, each boy is named after the father
and often has a nick-name added, Joseph Michael Jack, *i.e*,
" Joseph, son of Michael, son of Jack." Then you have John
Rua, John Oge, John Pharaig, Michael dun Randal. I think
you will find a similar system of naming and distinguishing the
families in Ballyscullion between Toome and Portglenone,
where for two or three miles along the banks of the Bann
most of the families are named Scullion, and I am informed
that in old Tyrconnel, in Donegal, the O'Donnells are distinguished to-day very much after the old clan system.

The chiefs, when elected by their clans, change the name

by which they were previously known to some descriptive appellation, either of their own choosing or selected by the vote of the clan. Chief Red Cloud, for example, received his title owing to the appearance himself and his braves presented in their warlike raids on the colonists who " trekked " out west, sweeping down upon the unsuspecting emigrants, and encircling them with their war-whoops, clad in flowing red blankets, and with red war paint like a prairie on fire. Chief "Shot in the Eye" received his name owing to the loss of an eye sustained in a battle against the Americans in 1876, at Montana, where General Custer and his entire regiment were annihilated. Chief Hard Heart was so called on account of his cruel and unmerciful treatment of his enemies in battle. In this manner the chiefs receive the titles by which they are known amongst the tribes and clans. Many and bloody and fierce have been the wars waged by the Indians against the American Government during the past hundred years. It has been reckoned that the United States Government have sent their armies at least forty times to oppose the Indians on the borders and drive them further west to the reservations allocated to their use. In these wars from five to twenty thousand men and officers have been more or less constantly engaged up to as late as the year 1891. The number of white soldiers slain in battle by them has been computed at over nineteen thousand ; this number does not include the isolated cases of massacre and murder among the defenceless colonists, which would increase the death roll by some thousands. The actual number lost in these battles and raids in the Indian armies cannot accurately be computed, as the Indians, like all uncivilized people, conceal their losses and carry their dead off in secret. The Indians slain in battle during the past hundred years cannot be less than forty thousand. We must remember that the American Indians are not naturally the warlike and aggressive people that partial historians picture them. They often had much reason to complain of the robbery and treachery, lying and fraud, that the colonists and gover ment perpetrated on them. Often we find them driven from their lands to make room for the colonists, who prized their lands and purchased them from the government. The States never gave the Indians a title to their lands, and they only allowed them to hold by their territories until colonists came to purchase. The Indians generally had to be content with the bargain the States agent offered them, and when ordered to some poor barren reservation they had no alternative except a hopeless opposition and a destructive war with better equipped foes. In Southern Washington, in the district of Walla-walla, where they converted the land into a smiling productive region for farming and sheep and stock, chief Joseph and his tribe were driven by force across a thousand miles of country before General Myles and his American army, and confined to a poor reservation in a northern territory. This chief and his tribe are said to have made as memorable a retreat as Napoleon from Moscow, or Xenephon with his ten thousand. To-day most of the Indian tribes live in reservations. Some of them have settled down to farming and stock raising. Many of the tribes on the wild and barren mountain ranges have little desire or inclination for useful industry; they prefer to live, as their fathers, by shooting, and fishing, and rudely raising Indian corn. But since the government have curtailed the allowances originally granted by charter to the tribes, when they gave up their ancient territories, and have aided them by education, and encouraged them to conform to modern customs of self-reliance and self-support, many are becoming expert in farming and other commercial pursuits. I understand that the old " medicine women " still survive among some of the Indian tribes. According to the accounts I have received I think they very much resemble the fast disappearing class of old women in Ulster who used charms, and incantations, and spells to cure the sprain, the colic, varicose veins, and the innumerable other ills supposed to be amenable to treatment of that kind. I may be wrong, but I think even to-day, in the far back country districts, our old charmers are still using their incantations in the cause of suffering humanity. The method of the Indian enchantress is best explained by giving, in detail, a typical instance of the treatment of an Indian child, ill with pneumonia. An account is extant of how an old woman placed a sick child on a buffalo robe spread upon the floor of her wigwam, with its body bare from the waist upwards. A pot of herbs was placed on the fire hard by, at which the old dame stood. Around the room sat the musicians and members of the clan, while the gleam of the fitful light cast weird shadows, rendered more uncanny still by the skins and antlers hanging around the tent, the rattling and tingling of many chains, of turtle bones, and badger's claws, and the tin fringes of the various robes. The old lady doctor ascertained where all the sore spots were, whilst the pipes and drums played to drive away the evil spirits. Then she began to pray and chant, at the same time painting her face and the face and body of the child in brilliant vermilion colours. Then she took a small wooden bowl and drew within it from edge to edge two lines in the same vermilion in the form of a cross. Into the bowl she poured water. During this time the herbs in the pot had been simmering. Over the brew of herbs she uttered a strange incantation, and then gave a dose of the concoction to the sick child. Next she took from her medicine knapsack a curious stone and heated it in the fire, and, whilst the piping and drumming proceeded, she, in a minor key, chanted and after touching the water in the bowl and the hot stone, she applied her finger to the sores on the child's chest. This operation she repeated and continued for two hours. The strange thing is that often a perfect cure resulted from such treatment.

The Indians have no written language, and there are almost as many dialects amongst them as there are clans. It has been reckoned that some two hundred and eighty-nine languages, more or less different, are spoken by the North American Indians, and in some instances these languages differ as widely as the different languages of Europeans. However, their language can be reduced to a few families and classed under uniform and general heads. There is first the language known as the Algonquin, which was mostly spoken in the Northern States by such tribes as the Pokanokets, Narragansetts, and Pequods, and by the tribes located in Virginia, along the Delaware and Ohio rivers. The Wyandot was the language of the Hurons, and of the Iroquois, who dwelt on the Southern banks of the St. Lawrence, and the central district of the state of New York. This language was the parent language of the Mohawks, Oneidas, Onondagas, Cayugas and Senecas. The third branch, who dwelt in North Carolina, and in and around the Alleghany mountains, viz., the Tuscaroras, the Uchees, and the Natches spoke a language of their own. The fourth group of tribes spoke the Mobilian language and embraced the Choctaws, Chikasaws, Creeks, and Yamassees. The great Sioux tribes in the west spoke the Sioux language. Historical events, wars, and dates and records were handed down in tradition by the orators and sachems and wise men of the tribes, whilst mounds and monuments and statues and carved slabs and painted tablets, as well as beads and shells, aided the memory and helped to recall past events in the history of their race.

LaVergne, TN USA
23 November 2010

205998LV00004B/41/P